AN IRISH VOICE

T0159470

AN IRISH VOICE

Gerry Adams

ROBERTS RINEHART PUBLISHERS

Published by Roberts Rinehart Publishers
An Imprint of the Rowman & Littlefield Publishing Group
4720 Boston Way
Lanham, MD 20706

Distributed by National Book Network

ISBN 1-56833-202-5
Library of Congress Card Number 97-67695

Book design: Ann W. Douden
Cover photographs © Jonathan Becker
Typesetting: Red Barn Publishing, Skeagh, Skibbereen, Co. Cork, Ireland

☉™ The paper used in this publication meets the minimum requirements of
American National Standard for Information Sciences—Permanence of
Paper for Printed Library Materials, ANSI/NISO Z39.48–1992.
Manufactured in the United States of America.

CONTENTS

Foreword

I QUICKLY LEARNT when I came to America in 1979 that the free speech that journalists and politicians enjoy here cannot be taken for granted elsewhere in the world. This came home forcefully to me when I first met Gerry Adams in Belfast in 1983, when I interviewed him for an Irish newspaper in San Francisco which I then edited.

Adams at the time was a member of the British Parliament, yet the ban on him going to London had only been lifted after his election victory and it was to be subsequently re-imposed. Imagine a US senator being banned from going to Washington, DC and you get some sense of the internal exile that the British government sought back then to enforce on Adams.

In the Irish Republic the situation was not much better. Adams was not allowed on the airwaves, either television or radio, because of a law forbidding interviews with Sinn Féin members. Meanwhile, newspaper interviews were infrequent because of a self-censorship mentality that permeated much of the media.

That censorship in the media had tragic consequences for many years, as the lack of sustained information and analysis about the North meant that there was little or no understanding of the developing situation there, particularly after the IRA hunger strikes, when the demonizing of Adams and his followers was almost total.

He, of course, was also not allowed into the United States, and in the era of Reagan/Thatcher cooperation the likelihood of an American audience ever getting to hear or see him seemed hopelessly remote. The view propagated about him by the British back then was as a fanatical terrorist who would stop at nothing to achieve his bloody aims.

But the Gerry Adams I interviewed on that occasion in 1983 hardly lived up to the British stereotype of a humorless fanatic. He had a very nice line in self-deprecatory wit, and unlike many politicians was neither pompous nor self-important. He was also curious in the interview, asking many questions about America – indeed, turning the tables at one point and quizzing me for some twenty minutes on the Irish-American dimension.

I stated in my introduction to that 1983 interview, "One could

1

ask the question, does he take himself as seriously as everyone else does?" Having got to know him much better since, I know the answer to that question now is no, he doesn't, and it is perhaps his most appealing quality – the ability to know and understand that the real priorities of life are family, friendship and the *craic*, as well as the all-consuming politics. It is a lesson many politicians everywhere could absorb.

In the years that followed I, like many others, tracked his career. Despite the worldwide censorship, his voice was becoming increasingly well known. I read *The Politics of Irish Freedom* on a flight back from Ireland in 1986 (later published in the US by Roberts Rinehart as *Free Ireland: Towards a Lasting Peace*.) What was startling to me was the amount of fresh analysis and perspective the book contained on the Northern Irish situation. It was my first inkling that the overwhelming view that Sinn Féin had little to offer in terms of new thinking was well wide of the mark.

The stereotypes about the Republican movement were so deeply ingrained in Ireland, Britain and America, however, that Adams rarely got to take his message to a wider audience. Northern Ireland was akin to a fly stuck in amber for most of the American media. Nothing ever seemed to change there, and the diet of violence begetting violence seemed endlessly repetitive.

But the ice-caps were melting, and the Hume/Adams peace initiative, widely derided in the Irish media when it was launched, was the new beginning. I am proud to say that it was recognized as such in Irish America almost before anywhere else.

It was also clear that the new situation in Ireland needed an American response. I was fortunate enough to play a role in shaping that response by realizing early on that the then Democratic challenger for president, Bill Clinton, offered a new and exciting opportunity for America to get involved.

My involvement in helping secure American support for the new process brought me into frequent contact with Adams, whom I had not met since 1983. As part of the new outreach it was Adam himself who brought up the idea of doing a column for the *Irish Voice*.

I immediately agreed. After all, if I was hell bent on showing how a fresh American approach could help with the peace process, it was also a fine idea to allow one of the architects of that process, Gerry Adams, to have a voice in the US.

Thus was born the Gerry Adams column. For balance, we also took columns from Unionist voices, most notably the leader of the Ulster Democratic Party, Gary McMichael, who is also a fine writer and original thinker.

We expected criticism, and there was some, but overall our American readers understood the principles involved in allowing free speech to a man long denied it on these shores. Many of the letters were from surprising sources, people who disagreed with Adams and what he stood for, but agreeing with the great American principle of defending his right to say it.

Adams was still banned on the airwaves and in much of the Irish and British media so the *Irish Voice* column was, I think, an important link. I like to think that he exploited that opportunity, that many of the great developments to come were first signaled in the pages of the *Voice*.

Throughout the halcyon days of the US visa, the first trip to America, the historic ceasefire, the visit of President Clinton to Northern Ireland, through the shattering news of the breakdown of the ceasefire, the renewed efforts to keep it together and now, the success so far of the new peace initiative, Adams has kept our regular readers informed – and many others from the White House on down who follow his column.

There is one column I believe that particularly stands out, where Adams described how he and John Hume went to meet the IRA after the first ceasefire broke down. It was a time of great trauma and apprehension for everyone, after the sky-high hopes and expectations of the first cessation had been cruelly dashed, essentially by the refusal of the John Major government to act honorably.

In that column Adams gives us a rare insight into what would happen next. I found that column immensely reassuring in the sense that it signposted that, despite the enormous setback of the ceasefire breakdown, the IRA leaders they met were still open to pursuing a peace rather than a war strategy if the conditions that had been laid down were met. I knew then that all was not lost, despite all the press speculation to the contrary.

There are times in the columns when Adams the public man lets his private side peek through. Debbie McGoldrick, who edits his column, does a remarkable job of getting to the human side of him, often calling him to cajole him to include those kind of lifestyle bits that make him more than just the famous face who leads Sinn Féin.

I have sometimes used the column as an occasion to call him. I remember his concern after the Manchester bombings, which seemed to ruin all chances of a new peace process, his satisfaction when, against all odds, he won a visa to the United States, his anger when Private Lee Clegg was released from jail after serving a derisory two years of a life sentence for shooting a young Catholic girl.

I believe these columns will serve as part of an important historical record some day, as a diary in progress from the principal architect of the Irish peace process which has given the world such hope that conflict resolution, wherever it happens, can make our planet a better place to live.

A Jewish friend came to my office in Manhattan soon after the second IRA cessation and told me that it was a very important day for him. "My friend, we are all watching you Irish," he said. "If you can sort out your troubles, it gives us all hope."

I know that Gerry Adams, by pursuing the peace process against all odds, has nurtured that hope and saved many lives. I am glad too that American readers of the *Irish Voice* and now readers of this book of his columns will understand more of what motivates this outstanding Irishman of our times.

Niall O'Dowd
August 12, 1997

Introduction

THIS BOOK IS an edited version of articles I wrote for the Irish-American paper, *The Irish Voice*. The editing involved is minimal and only to allow the pieces to fit more comfortably into this genre. The originals were written over a period from early 1993 up to 1997. By virtue of the times that were in it they cover the beginnings of the Irish peace process of 1994, the IRA cessation of that year; its lengthy crumbling collapse, the ending of the IRA cessation; and the efforts to build a new process.

Reading over them I was reminded of developments and nondevelopments and other events which I had forgotten in the twists and turns of the situation over this period. I was also reminded of my visits to the USA. According to Richard McAuley, Sinn Féin public relations officer, who accompanied me on most of the visits, I have been there nine times. Our trips are recorded in the visa waivers which are noted at length in our passports. As former political prisoners he and I were denied visas, until President Clinton famously granted waivers. I found some of the language used by the bureaucrats who actually issued the waivers quite hilarious.

One of Richard's reads:
1. Not to solicit or accept funds.
2. Not to attend or participate in any functions for which admission is charged if the charge for admission exceeds the actual costs of the function.
3. Not to attend, or otherwise participate in, any function at which there is to be fundraising.
4. Only exception to the foregoing restrictions is that R.G. McAuley may be present at functions where Gerry Adams engages in fundraising, and may assist in that fundraising activity during the time that Adams is physically present at the function.

I have to confess that before I went to the USA I had a stereotyped view of the place and its people which I have now revised. All of my trips were frenzied frenetic roller coaster rides so I can claim no special in-depth knowledge. But I did get a unique insight; and from my first forty-eight-hour touchdown to the longer

5

visitations I have developed an intrigued curiosity about the place and especially about the Irish in America, who are everywhere. One of the first things I learned is how small Ireland is. Our island could be gobbled up in the corner of any one of the larger states, and our population of five million would be swallowed whole in most of the bigger cities across the US.

And yet, from this small island, the Diaspora stretches right across that huge land mass. One of the personal elements of my visits which remains with me yet – indeed, it was a privilege – was being able to meet so many Irish people or so many people from the island of Ireland – the rich Irish, the poor Irish, the political activists as well as the apolitical. They were the Famine Irish, or those who went in the wake of the Black and Tan War, the Treaty or the Civil War; or those who went in the '30s, '40s and '50s because they couldn't afford to live in Ireland, or the illegals of recent years.

It would be wrong to exaggerate the power of Irish America. At the same time, it is important to note that the Irish in America are the most diligent voters, and that their influence permeates all levels of government, so much so that a number of US Presidents have been of Irish descent. It is also a matter of historical fact that the Irish Republican constituency in Irish America has stayed faithful over the centuries to the cause of freedom and justice in Ireland.

The people who traveled with me could be forgiven for believing that everyone in the US was of Irish extraction. This is not only because of the warmth of the welcome we received at the public engagements, but perhaps more so because of the number of people who also approached us wherever we were. In hotels, in the street, on planes and in airport lounges, on our way in and out of newspaper offices and other buildings.

"Hello. I'm from Louth."

"Whataboutya. How's things in Belfast?"

"*Fáilte romhat. Corcaigh abú!*"

"Were you ever in Nenagh…or Ballymun…or Ring…or Galbally?"

So it went on.

It was also an education to move from city to city, and to see how the Irish from one particular region or regions had settled there. Thus it was in Springfield, Massachusetts, that the people of the Dingle peninsula had settled. Indeed, the last family off the Great

Blasket Island live there. That for me was very sad: to be greeted in Gaeilge by Kerry people so far from home. Even though there was undoubtedly here in middle-America more prosperity, I still had a sense of people who longed for home.

In Philadelphia, Tyrone was gathered. Mayo was somewhere else. An old man described to me how this happened.

"Did you ever see a flock of birds?" he asked. "They're flying together in a huge mass, and then one of them flutters down, and another follows, and another, until they've all landed. That's how the Irish came to live in particular areas."

The pain, the awful homesickness of those who were plucked from Ireland and placed in the strangeness of an *oileán úr* (new world) must have been soul destroying for many.

On Ellis Island I also got a sense of how frightened some immigrants must have been. The first generations must have suffered great home sickness. No matter about the reason for their exile, the longing for home must have been heartbreaking, especially if they suffered difficulties in their new life. To be a displaced person without a sense of roots is desolation itself.

Of course, for the second or third generations – the American Irish as opposed to the Irish Americans – the pain would have lessened. But the need to belong, to reclaim one's roots, obviously remained. Why else would some forty-four million Americans take the trouble to claim their Irish extraction?

Theoretically, emigration today is not as final as it used to be. The American wake that once preceded the departure of exiles who would never return is no longer. The relative cheapness and the speed of air travel allows the exiles to return.

A friend of mine once said to me that many people who emigrated in the '50s return, decades later, to Ireland on visits, and are disillusioned. This is because, my friend said, they find that many of the material benefits that once were American – color TVs, wall-to-wall carpets, decent homes – are now commonplace in Ireland. Maybe this is nonsense. My friend had other theories about the Irish in America. The dream of coming home is more important, he felt, than actually returning.

That is not true of today's exiles. They commute across the Atlantic. Or some of them do. I met a man from Kiltyclogher who lives in Boston. This man told how he had come home for a few weeks, had gone away again, and then back home again. Betwixt and between. Between two worlds. *Idir eatarthu.*

Senator Chris Dodd tells a funny story about this dilemma. It's about two Irishmen drinking in a bar in Galway.

"Wouldn't it be great," one of them was saying to the other, "to be drinking in the Bronx dreaming about drinking in Galway?"

I have relations in Canada. My favorite aunt out there told me of how her generation of Irish became assimilated into Canadian society in the 1950s. They "became" Canadians. Until recently, that is, when increasingly they felt the need to rediscover their roots. Some of this was assisted by their children who really were Canadian but who were curious about their parents' homeland, about their roots.

The recent controversy over Grosse Isle brought a lot of this to the surface right across Canada when the Canadian Irish found common cause. Grosse Isle is an island where the famine ships – the fever ships – discharged their sick and dying Irish cargoes into the contamination camps. Thousand of us died there. A plan to convert the island into a national park was thwarted when a spontaneous wave of protest roused the Irish throughout Canada.

I found an interesting sequel to this in Montreal. Six thousand Irish died in that city. They were the ones who escaped Grosse Isle but not the fever of the famine ships. Their orphaned children were adopted by French-speaking people throughout Quebec who allowed them to keep their Irish names. This act of decency was indeed, in my view, one of solidarity by people who recognized the need for self-identity and a sense of place.

In my limited travels elsewhere, everywhere, I have met the Irish. I remember years ago reading *Rotha Mór an tSaoil* or, in its English version, *The Hard Road to Klondyke*. This tells the tale of a Donegal man Mící Mac Gabhann and his travels.

At one point he tells of being lost in a blizzard in the Yukon. He sees a light ahead of him. He shouts out in Irish at the light, and receives in return, a greeting in Irish also. At the time of reading this I thought he was spoofing. Now I'm not so sure...

The first time I went to the White House as I walked up to the door a voice from the press corps which was assembled on the lawn called out "*Failte romhat go an Teach Bán.*" Another time, as we were being ferried from meeting to meeting on Capitol Hill, there was an untypical and welcome break between sessions. Our guide ushered us into a huge palatial room for a wee rest. I flung myself into a chair. There was something stuck behind it, cutting into my back. I pulled the chair away from the wall. The offending item was a hurling stick – one of those plastic-y ones, not ash, but a *camán* nonetheless. How it got there, or why, remains a mystery. No one knew. All I can say is that the sight of such a familiar part of Ireland, and the feel of it, was reassuring so far from home and during such an important mission.

In the White House afterwards, for a meeting, I seated myself gingerly for fear of another hurling stick behind my chair. There wasn't, but there were plenty of Irish surnames about the place. After the meeting Ciaran Staunton drew attention to the photographs of large cows which adorned the walls of our meeting room.

"Them's Herefords," he exclaimed with a tear in his voice. "I haven't seen once since I left Mayo."

He gazed misty-eyed beyond the Herefords and the White House, beyond America towards Clew Bay.

"Herefords?" Mairéad Keane asked. "In Mayo?"

"Bullocks," I thought.

It's funny, the things that remind you of home, that make you homesick, that let you know you're an exile. That night at a hugely successful gathering of the Washington Irish, a Belfast accent asked me if St. Paul's GAC had won the County Antrim final. They had. For the first time in fifty-four years. My questioner was delighted.

All these things connect us to what we are. And these connections today find an acoustic throughout the USA in Irish music and dance, in literature, in corporate America and in politics – whether in a local borough or in the White House itself. No longer are we told No Irish Need Apply.

Now the struggle for peace, for democracy, for freedom, unity and justice in Ireland can be actively enhanced and advanced by Irish people in the USA using their influence to move governments and especially the British government to do the right thing in Ireland. That certainly is the potential of this moment as I pen these lines at the end of July 1997 and the beginning of a new IRA cessation.

We have a long way to go before there is a lasting peace in Ireland. This book chronicles the failure of one phase of the peace process. From these mistakes maybe it is possible for us to learn how to consolidate and to build upon the possibilities of a new one. I hope so.

For those who made this book possible – Niall O'Dowd and Debbie McGoldrick, Jack Van Zandt and Mary Hegarty, Steve MacDonogh, Mairéad Keane and Richard McAuley – my warmest thanks.

For Colette my love and gratitude. For the rest of you, good luck. I will leave the last words of this introduction to Martin McGuinness and one of his poems, "Postcard."

Have you ever seen
A Manhattan sunset
From the window of
An Aer Lingus jet?

On the 26th September 1995
Jamesie and I did.

Gloriously crimson
it was

Blackening
Awesome
Skyscrapers

Slipping
Towards
Montana

Far Away

From
Bloody
Foreland.

Le gach dea mhéin
Gerry Adams
Belfast, July 30, 1997

My Family's Brush With Death

An attack on Gerry Adams' wife and son was one of hundreds on Nationalists throughout the North of Ireland after Loyalists intensified their armed campaign following a 1988 arms shipment from South Africa by British Army agent Brian Nelson.

COLETTE ADAMS IS a sound woman. In 1971, as our friends kept watch for British Army patrols in the adjoining streets, she and I stood in the room behind the altar in St. John's Chapel on the Falls Road. After the evening Mass congregation had left, Father Des Wilson married us.

It was a simple ceremony, witnessed only by a few friends. My Da in Long Kesh lamented his enforced absence when he heard that his oldest son was wed. Colette's mother and her sisters, along with my mother, God rest her, turned up with her close friend, Mrs. Shannon. They all greeted us as we emerged from the side door of St. John's. Colette's father Jimmy, God rest him also, was too emotional to attend. He stayed away and cried sentimentally to himself.

Fr. Des refused to accept the traditional payment from our best man, who retired with it and the bridesmaid to the Rock Bar. There were no wedding photographers, no reception, few presents. Years later our friends were to surprise us with all of these at a surprise anniversary party, but at the time we were happy to cadge a lift from our friends Tony and Alex, who were on their way to Dublin.

At Dundalk we stopped, and while Fats Domino *Blueberry Hill*-ed from the pub juke box, we drank a toast to ourselves – Colette, Tony, Alex and me – and then off to Dublin for a few stolen days.

It was the month of internment. Dublin as well as Belfast was gripped by the excitement of it all, and one evening Colette and I stood anonymously on the fringe of a large crowd outside the GPO on O'Connell Street and listened to the pledges of Dublin politicians. We set off back to Belfast as the meeting finished. From the rhetoric to the reality in a few short hours.

A week later, at five o'clock one morning, the British Army raided Colette's family home for her. Her father and mother feigned surprise at the news of their daughter's marriage and of their new son-in-law. Colette wasn't there, of course. She had no house of her own then, but our friends had opened up their homes to us and we lived the precariously nerve-wracking existence of life on the run, hunted, like scores more, by the soldiers of another country in our own city.

Two years later, I was in Long Kesh. One night I was called from the cage to be informed by the screw that Colette had given birth to our son. That was September of 1973. It was to be four years before Gearóid and I and Colette walked together or shared a meal or a bed or watched the snow or went to a movie. Even in 1976, our reunion was temporary, but we were, and are, like hundreds of others. We are not exceptional and life on the run is now a way of life for political dissidents and their families in Ireland.

Colette has endured all of this and reared our son into a fine young man. They live not far from where Colette and I grew up. The area is still heavily patrolled by British Army patrols. There is a barracks at the bottom of the street. Last week, despite all this "security," Colette and Gearóid were the intended victims of a grenade attack.

Fortunately, reinforced glass deflected the device which was lobbed at a front bedroom window. Colette was in the room at the time, in bed watching a late night film. It was about twelve midnight. Gearóid was in another room studying for exams. I wasn't there, but I heard the blast and minutes later a friend told me what had happened.

By the time I arrived at the scene, the British Army and RUC were there in strength. Colette was bringing tea to the elderly neighbors and Gearóid was telling a burly RUC man that his mother did not want the RUC in her home. The front of the house was pockmarked by shrapnel, the path and garden covered in glass. The fragmentation grenade had bounced off the window, rolled off the porch roof and exploded in the garden, wrecking the porch and its surroundings in the process.

I cannot walk through West Belfast without being stopped or confronted by British forces. Those who tried to kill Colette and Gearóid were not so inconvenienced. They escaped without hindrance.

The grenade used was one of a batch imported into Ireland from South Africa by a man called Brian Nelson. Nelson was a British Army agent, and his bosses placed him in the Ulster Defence Association (UDA), a Loyalist organization, using him in his role of UDA director of intelligence to target dissidents, including civil rights lawyer Pat Finucane. Nelson is now serving a prison sentence. He was arrested as a result of the Stevens Inquiry into collusion, and he received a derisory sentence after striking a deal that involved a cover up of his activities.

As part of the deal, Nelson pleaded guilty to relatively minor charges, and ten serious charges, including two of murder, against him were dropped. In return, there was a cover up of many details of his day-to-day activities as a British agent, and particularly his arms-buying trip to South Africa, which, it was revealed, was sanctioned by British Intelligence. The arms deal involving British Intelligence placed weapons in the hands of all the main Loyalist groups. They have used them with ferocity since then. Patrick Mayhew, the British Minister in charge of the North, was the British attorney general at the time of Nelson's trial. It was he who sanctioned the deal with Nelson.

The re-armed death squads have used their new weapons in the recent attacks here on bookmakers' shops, in the attack on the Milltown Cemetery funerals, and in scores of other killings. The attack on Colette and Gearóid was the latest product of this collusion.

They were lucky. So am I, not least because I was blessed with such a family. And we are blessed in our friends.

The People of West Belfast Won't Be Tamed

President Mary Robinson's visit of June 1993 to the College of Further Education in West Belfast and her meeting there with public representatives, including Gerry Adams, generated considerable controversy.

ACRES OF NEWSPRINT and hours of broadcasting time have been consumed in the debate which marked Mary Robinson's recent visit to West Belfast. The controversy has been blamed by some on the media, and yes, I suppose they bear some of the responsibility, especially the British media whose treatment of the West Belfast visit was in marked contrast to the coverage they normally give to the activities of the President of Ireland.

For example, they failed to mention the recent Presidential visit to the English Queen, Elizabeth. Meetings between the heads of states are normally worthy of some media notice, unless of course one of the heads of state is an Irish one.

By contrast, Robinson's West Belfast visit was headlined. As the archetypal Nationalist wee "Sammy McClarnon" might say, "It just goes to show you." Wee Sammy knows what he's talking about.

But the media wasn't entirely to blame, even though they were a bit of a nuisance up at the event in Whiterock, tripping over themselves and everyone else and poking their cameras here, there and everywhere. We can't complain about that, I suppose. That's their job.

No, the ones to blame for all the fuss are the people of West Belfast. The cheek of them!

Imagine poor John Major's predicament. Here he is, the most unpopular British prime minister since the beginning of unpopularity, beleaguered and beset by one scandal after the other, and the demons of West Belfast, without one thought for him and his troubles, the barbarians and savages whom he thought were safely marginalized, go and invite. . .not him, not his Queen, not even one of his ministers, not even a Dublin minister! No, the upstarts go and invite President Robinson. How dare they!

And then think of poor Taoiseach Albert Reynolds. If John Major had a problem he wasn't going to keep it to himself. Of course not. He was going to put Albert on the spot. And did the people of West Belfast think of that? Of course not. How irresponsible can people be? Do they not know their place! And the Unionists? Poor souls. What about their feelings? And the talks? How could they ever get started if the people of West Belfast refused to accept their status? It just isn't right.

The *Irish News*, our daily "Nationalist" newspaper, spelt out its disapproval loud and clear. The Social Democratic and Labour Party (SDLP) proclaimed its opposition also. Today, over two weeks later, one local Sunday paper claims that Cardinal Cahal Daly contacted the President's office at Aras an Uachtaráin and sought a cancellation of the visit! You see! Everyone was against it! And can you blame them? Look at it this way. If everyone was able to have a celebration of culture and creativity, then where would we be?

Let me explain. That's what the people of West Belfast did. They're at it all the time. You couldn't be up to them. They invited Mary Robinson to, and I quote, "A CELEBRATION OF CULTURE AND CREATIVITY." See! In a school, of all places!

So what was poor John Major to do? What could he do? He's not the most unpopular British prime minister for nothing. He wanted the whole thing called off, canceled, done away with, scrubbed. He asked Albert Reynolds to sort it out. Major's minister in charge over here, Patrick Mayhew, asked Irish Foreign Minister Dick Spring to sort it out. The British ambassador (whose name escapes me, for this I am truly sorry) sent a diplomatic note. The stiffest one possible, we are told, and who could blame him?

Albert didn't go just as far as that. He sent a letter. Dick Spring sent himself. Twice! The Unionists phoned. Wee Sammy says the whole place was in a state of chassis. The comings and goings must have been mighty.

Did the people of West Belfast care about that? Did they show any concern for all the trouble they caused? Not so that you'd notice. They went on rehearsing their celebration.

Men from Dublin who had never come to see them before, men from the Maryfield secretariat and protocol officers – or ossifers, as wee Sammy calls them – they all came to say the visit might be called off and you have to do this and you have to do that.

And the people of West Belfast, what did they do? They gave them tea and biscuits and smiled and talked and gave them more tea and biscuits and talked among themselves and said to the men from Dublin who had never come to see them before that they were going to have their celebration anyway, that Mary Robinson had told them she was going to be there and of course they didn't mind a wee change here or there but a celebration was a celebration.

And the men from Dublin who had never been to see them before were mortified by how reasonable all this sounded but they were determined to do their job because John Major and Albert Reynolds and Dick Spring and Patrick Mayhew and Sir What-youmaycallhim, and the Cardinals and the SDLP and the Unionists were depending on them. So the talking went on until the wee small hours and the men from Dublin drank a lot of tea and ate a lot of biscuits but that was all.

The worst fears of John Major and Patrick Mayhew and the Cardinal and elements of the SDLP and the Unionists and the Dublin government were confirmed. The people of West Belfast were as reasonably unreasonable as ever. They were refusing to behave the way marginalized, alienated, excluded people should behave. No self-respecting government could put up with that kind of subversion. No self-respecting President could be a part of it. Once Mary Robinson saw what was going on she'd see sense. Or so ran the logic of the establishment opinion makers and spin doctors.

But she didn't! Things were getting out of hand. It was necessary to mobilize public opinion. That's where the media came in. Leak followed leak. The visit was off/on/off/on. The pressure mounted. Would she or wouldn't she?

The morning of the visit dawned. Media and government distress was now hysterical. The end of the world, as wee Sammy McClarnon said, was near. The sanest, safest and calmest place to be was the Whiterock Road, in the College of Further Education. That's where I went. Mary Robinson went there also. The media followed. Even the men from Dublin who had never been to see the people of West Belfast were there.

Francie McPeake of the famous McPeake family and his friends welcomed us all. They were wonderful. *Go h-iontach ar fadh*! The nerve of them! In front of the world's media! Then the legendary Sean Maguire and his crowd let rip. Pipes and a harp, and fiddles and squeeze boxes. Such subversion. Wild, beautiful, haunting music. And young Finnegan danced on top of it all. Such defiance. And everyone cheered and clapped. The shame of it! Mary Robinson and the local community activists and the children and the men from Dublin who never came to applaud us before. They cheered along with the rest.

And then what did the West Belfast ones do? Just for badness. The renowned Saint Agnes Choral Society went and sang bits of Madame Butterfly and other such arias and the media didn't know what to do. When Sean Maguire started again they tapped their feet also and clapped their hands and then, just when they were starting to behave like real people, they were asked to leave the room, and Mary Robinson and the rest of us had a bit of *craic* on our own.

Well, you can see how that went down. As wee Sammy said, it was about as popular with the British government as the Pope would be in an Orange lodge. The men from Dublin who never came to see us before, they said nothing. They were humming *diddley owh dowh dowh* to themselves. And then to crown it all. Afterwards, Mary Robinson said she didn't regret a thing. She even went so far as to say she enjoyed it.

Well, let me tell you this, to paraphrase wee Sammy McClarnon, that really put the cat among the pigeons. There were great protests from the Unionists and the British Ambassador, Sir Thingymebob, and Patrick Mayhew and...well, nobody else really! The rest of the people of Ireland thought it was just great.

That's the thing about the plain people of Ireland. They are easily duped. You can see just how justified all the concern was about the visit. More importantly, you can see what a scheming, calculating crowd there is in West Belfast. Even the men from Dublin were moved to say the visit was a great success, and that they'd been behind it all the time and what was the fuss about and they'd told the British where to get off and wasn't Mary Robinson great and weren't the people of West Belfast wonderful?

Now you see, don't you. It's them West Belfast ones, as John Major said from the very beginning. Fair play to them, wee Sammy McClarnon says. But you can't pay too much heed to him, of course. He's like the rest of them. He thinks he is somebody. Nobody could shift him on that. Especially all the ones who always treated him like he was a nobody. None of them could move him at all. Not John Major, not Patrick Mayhew, not the Dublin government.

Maybe wee Sammy's right. If him and the women of West Belfast and the children and the rest of us and Mary Robinson want to get together to celebrate our survival and creativity and culture, why shouldn't we? Who could stop us?

You Can't Expect Much From RTE Wallies

RTE, the Irish broadcasting organization, and the Independent Radio and Television Commission (IRTC), placed a ban on advertising The Street, *a collection of short stories by Gerry Adams. The High Court in Dublin upheld the ban. But in West Belfast the annual festival offered an opportunity for some uncensored cultural activity.*

I F CONOR CRUISE O'BRIEN had his way, you, dear reader, would not be permitted to read this. Conor, for ye who know not, is a former Dublin government minister, a writer, broadcaster and censor extraordinaire.

In his heyday, he admitted to keeping a file of the letters pages of newspapers here, particularly the *Irish Press*. Cruiser reckoned the *Press* – at that time its editor was Tim Pat Coogan – was much too easygoing about publishing the opinions of its letter writers, especially those which did not echo the neo-Unionist and anti-Nationalist line favored by the Cruiser himself.

I offer you this morsel of historical information in order that you can see where the man is coming from. In the USA, whatever its faults, I am reliably informed that such messing would not be tolerated. I can make no independent judgment on that but as I mention above, if Cruiser had his way he would not permit you to read this.

In Ireland he might just get his way. In the USA? Well, I'd need a visa to check that one out . . . oops. That slipped out. Sorry, Bill. I digress. Forgive me.

Cruiser was in the Dublin High Court recently. He was there as a witness for the Independent Radio and Television Commission in a case brought by my Irish publishers Brandon against the refusal of RTE and the IRTC to carry a twenty-second radio advertisement for my book entitled *The Street and Other Stories*. The advert was as follows:

"This is Gerry Adams speaking. My new book is called *The Street and Other Stories* and it's on sale in good bookshops in the Thirty-Two Counties. Most of the stories are about ordinary people and everyday events and there's a fair bit of *craic* in them also. That's *The Street and Other Stories* and this is Gerry Adams. I think you might enjoy it. *Slán*."

In his submission, which was full of big-brotherisms, Cruiser argued that while the advertisement was not political, the opening words would offend and corrupt the Irish public.

"I have in mind the opening words 'This is Gerry Adams speaking,'" O'Brien said.

So there you are. No thoughts about my finer feelings on the matter. I was mortified. How could I ever say my name again? My parents have a lot to answer for. Why couldn't they have named me Sammy or Seamus or Cedric . . . or Sue? Why wasn't my da called Smith or Hussein or . . . or Reagan?

God be good to Brandon. What chance had they? You probably know the result. In a reserved judgment, Justice Paul Carney ruled that it was not proper for the court to interfere in the decisions of the broadcasting organizations as to whom they should or should not interview.

In the meantime, it has cost Brandon an awful lot of money and effort in the so far unsuccessful defense of its rights to publish and promote its material. Brandon are to be commended for their efforts which included, irony of ironies, the publication, within days of the High Court challenge, of a new book of poetry by Michael D. Higgins, the Dublin minister responsible for Section 31, the censorship law under which the Brandon advert is banned! It is indeed a funny old world!

A Celebration of West Belfast

I F ANY OF YE are in Ireland during the first week in August, it would do you no harm to partake in Féile an Phobail, the Peoples' Festival in West Belfast. It's the largest community festival in Ireland and Britain and it highlights the positive nature of the West Belfast community in a wide range of diverse cultural, sporting, dramatic, musical, educational, artistic and drinking activities.

This is the sixth year of the festival. Its roots lie in the aftermath of the Gibraltar killings and the Milltown Cemetery massacre when the Gibraltar funerals were subjected to bomb and gun attacks, leaving three dead and over sixty injured; also the mass show trials of those accused after the killings of two armed, undercover British soldiers who drove into the funeral of Caoimhín MacBrádaigh, one of those killed at Milltown Cemetery.

For some time before this, a few of us had talked about organizing a festival as a substitute to the annual bonfires and ballyhoo which marked the anniversaries of internment morning, August 9, 1971. The weeks of vilification and demonization which the people of West Belfast endured after the killing of the two British soldiers became a special incentive to get a festival going. The main motive was to lift community morale in the face of protracted onslaught from church and state, from local political parties, from the media and from many who should have known better. The peoples' response was tremendous. Thousands of events were organized. Street parties for children, glamorous granny competitions, mill-workers reunions, historical tours, debates, lectures, art exhibitions, hurling and camogie games, soccer and handball tournaments, plays, rock concerts, traditional music *seisiúns*, photographic displays, mountain walks and many, many more activities combined to enlighten, entertain and uplift us.

Since then, Féile an Phobail has gone from strength to strength. Ulick O'Connor's *Executions* played here, as did Toby McMahon's *The Second of September*. Charabanc has showcased all its contemporary works, and Frank McGuinness' Broadway hit, *Someone Who'll Watch Over Me*, had its Irish premiere in West Belfast. Most of Moving Hearts have been here. And Black '47. This year Stephen Rea and Robert Ballagh launched the Féile program and poster. Robert designed the poster, and drama on offer includes Gogol's comedy *The Government Inspector*, adapted by Marie Jones, McMahon's *Three Card Trick* and the Ad Hoc Theatre Group's *Ní Thaitneoidh Seo Leo*.

Music lovers will be aware of the phenomenal success of *A Woman's Heart*, the album which has sold over 200,000 copies in Ireland and is almost a year in the Irish charts. The album features top Irish women artists, including Mary Black and Dolores Keane, who have both played Féile an Phobail. This year Eleanor

McEvoy, the singer and songwriter of the title song, will star along with the people of West Belfast. Plus Marxmen, Deiseal, Brush Shiels and Jimmy McCarthy. And you too?

Talks, in Irish and English, include a discussion on the 1981 hunger strikes involving former hunger strikers, and a lecture by Kenneth Griffith and Ronan Bennett and Tim Pat Coogan on contemporary Irish writing.

The Féile runs each year during the first or second week of August. Why not join us? You will be very welcome. For programs or tickets and information on limited local accommodation, contact the festival office at 011-44-232-313440, or Teach na Féile, 473 Falls Road, Belfast. Be there or be square!

Belfast Says Yes!

August 8 saw the first Nationalist rally in Belfast's city center since the partition of Ireland.

IN 1967 I WAS working in a downtown Belfast pub. It was a watering hole – some would claim *the* watering hole – for local and visiting playwrights, broadcasters, poets, writers, journalists, rakes, musicians, communists, trade unionists, judges, subversive drunkards, drunken subversives, hangers-on and Salvation Army choirs.

It was the best of times. Bill Craig was the minister of home affairs at Stormont. It was the worst of times. Unlike Bob Dylan, for Bill the times were not a-changing. Or so he thought.

Me? I was enjoying the Beatles and the Dubliners. Music was king and the *fleadh ceoil* its most exciting servant. The *craic* was ninety.

One fine March day myself and a friend went off on a protracted lunch break around the city center in search of tin whistles. We had decided to form a folk group (what a strange term, folk group!). Our time had come. We were young. We were confident. We were also tone deaf. But this was a mere detail, a trifle. It was a brisk, intoxicating uplifting spring day. The very day to launch our musical careers. We hummed our way merrily around the music shops.

At Belfast City Hall, our City Hall, a throng of people had gathered. They were shouting and chanting. Most of them wore the uniforms of the RUC, the state police. Others were disguised as civilians – but they were the Special Branch, the secret police, Bill Craig's men. They faced a motley crew of mostly young people, students who were protesting against Craig's suppression of Republican clubs a few days earlier.

Republican clubs were formed to thwart the ban on Sinn Féin imposed under the Special Powers Act by the Stormont regime, with the blessing of the London government. They almost immediately suffered the same fate. As myself and my friend were both members of Republican clubs, or at least their musical wings, we decided to linger in solidarity with the protesters. It was the least we could do under the circumstances.

"SS RUC, SS RUC," the students yelled. We took up the cry. Outside our City Hall. In our city center. . . on the wrong side of the RUC lines. My friend was arrested. I escaped with a torn jacket and a bruised back. And we never got our tin whistles.

Later that year we broke the ban on the Republican newspaper *The United Irishman* by selling it in the center of town. It was to be an all-day protest. And if any of us were arrested we were to be replaced by colleagues. Otherwise we were to do two-hour relays.

I was one of those chosen to do the first stint. The rest of the sellers gathered in a nearby hostelry. They hadn't long to wait. The RUC arrived almost as soon as we commenced to flaunt our publications. We had our speeches ready as the RUC approached us. It had taken two days to agree the speeches and another day to learn them by heart. They were important – the basis of the court cases which would surely follow our arrest and the subsequent highlighting of the suppression of the right to freedom of expression, etc.

Pacifism was to be our watchword. No problem! Civil disobedience was the order of the day. Only no one told the RUC. They beat us up. They had us into the back of a land-rover before we even got out a syllable of politically correct, collectively agreed, properly cleared protest. They were like lightning. And not a camera to record it for the masses. Such indignity can be endured if a cause can be advanced, if the cameras are rolling or the flash bulbs are flashing or if Martin Luther King is the victim. A bit of a pain otherwise.

And then they didn't even charge us. An hour or so in the cells downtown, our downtown. Then they threw us out contemptuously. Out of the barracks and into the street. We valiantly returned to rejoin our comrades only to find after the ferocity and speed of our arrest, that the RUC had seized all our papers and threatened our successors. Paperless, our protest had fizzled out, out of our city center, back home or pubwards.

Almost twenty years later a group of us gathered at the Housing Executive Office in our city center. We had journeyed there from the Divis Flats. The majority of our group were women, mostly middle-aged mothers of large families. We were from the ghetto, seeking decent homes and an end to the Divis slum. I had graduated from tin whistle aspirant to MP for West Belfast. It was two decades since my first City Hall experience. Two decades of death and destruction.

We were less naïve. Bill Craig was long gone. But he had taught us important lessons. We knew the city center, our city center was off bounds for us. So we trod carefully. Our protest was quiet, subdued. We handed a petition into the housing chiefs and then our little group paraded sheepishly up and down on the pavement – for all of three minutes. That's how long it took the RUC to arrive, to baton and arrest some of us and shepherd the rest back into the ghetto and out of our city center.

We went back again, of course. Or we tried to. Mostly we were stopped. On International Woman's Day some of us got through, to our surprise. A handful of sisters and fellow travelers outnumbered and dwarfed by hordes of RUC men and herds of British soldiers. A statue of Queen Victoria staring down stonily at us. Outside our City Hall. Surrounded. Out of place. Unwelcome.

All of these thoughts came back to me a few weeks ago as I stood on the same spot among tens of thousands of cheering, happy, singing, weeping Belfast citizens. It was August 8. We had been joined by people from all over Ireland and abroad, including the USA. Our demonstration had followed a month of brinkmanship by the RUC and their political bosses. Would we be banned? Would we be given the go ahead? No one knew, and the clearance for the demo was only eventually made public as we approached our city center in our thousands from the north, south, east and west of our city in a huge colorful surge of men, women and children.

I felt a bit detached at first. I was listening to the All-Ireland hurling semi-final on my Walkman. When we left the Falls Road it was half-time and Antrim was ahead. By the time we got out of Divis Street, Kilkenny had turned the tables. And we had turned into Belfast city center. Every laughing, crying, cheering, tricolor-waving one of us. And everyone was applauding. Spontaneously. In waves. As they moved down in front of the City Hall, the people applauded themselves.

I noticed my father crying as he stood below the Victorian dome of our City Hall in his city center. Then I saw that he wasn't on his own. Throughout the cheering throng people hugged each other and cried tears of joy when Councillor Pat Rice sang *Amhrán na bhFian* and thousands of throats echoed it around the grey grimness of our city streets. Later, as Cruncher sang of the hunger strikers, tears of emotion and sadness flowed as well.

It was a great day. A peaceful, joyous celebration. I'm glad I was there. Afterwards, I asked my Da why did he think the parade wasn't suppressed? Why had it been permitted to go ahead?

"They couldn't stop us," he said. "Belfast is our city also."

A New Climate for Peace

SDLP leader John Hume and Gerry Adams began talks in 1988, which continued over a period of five years. The document emanating from their initiative outlined the right of national self-determination, the importance of earning the allegiance of the different traditions on the island, and identified the responsibility of the British and Irish governments in framing all-party talks. Although it was not welcomed initially, it represented a major breakthrough in the quest for peace in Ireland.

SINCE JOHN HUME and I released our joint statement on Saturday, September 25, there has been a tornado of reaction in Ireland. Anyone who was not aware of what our statement said may have thought, given the negative responses, that we had committed ourselves to some heinous offense. Everyone, or nearly everyone who was anyone, was against us or wasn't sure or had to wait and see. But every negative has a positive, and, while disappointing in many ways, this reaction has served to identify those who want peace and those who don't.

For the record, it is my opinion that the negative attitude of the usual suspects on this issue is actually out of step with grassroots opinion. This is a major consolation for anyone in the position that John Hume and I find ourselves.

One of the consequences of our statement is that Dublin politicians, leader writers and opinion makers now have to look beyond the rhetoric. They are being faced with the possibility that it may just be possible to design a process upon which peace can be built. It is clear that few of them have ever considered this before.

There was a major and contrived distraction about John Hume's absence in the US, and about the manner in which a report on our discussions would be put to Dublin. At the time of writing, this "confusion" appears to have been set to one side, and there is at least some discussion about the real issues.

The Dublin government is not a spectator, and cannot dodge its responsibility to help bring the conflict to a democratic resolution. The belated statements of support from Dublin ministers, while helpful and welcome, are not enough. Dublin must seek to move this initiative forward. Albert Reynolds said the Irish people would expect nothing less. He is right.

The response from the Unionists has been predictably negative. In many ways, one can identify with the trauma facing the Unionist leadership. They have campaigned for so long for "the croppies (Catholics) to lie down" as a means of ending the conflict, that it is not surprising they find it so difficult to even contemplate any other scenario. But the croppies are not going to lie down. That much must be obvious after all these years.

But, while the Unionist reaction is predictable, it is worth pointing out that it is also a source of some comfort to the British and sections of Dublin opinion. In many ways they use the Unionists as scapegoats, and the fear of a Loyalist backlash is touted abroad by elements in the Dublin media and political establishment who are in no danger whatsoever from any Loyalist backlash. The British, of course, blame the Unionists for everything. Indeed, if we are to believe Patrick Mayhew, it is only his affection for Mr. Paisley, Mr. Molyneaux and their followers which justifies the British connection.

Having said that, Mr. Hume and I have made it clear in our joint statements that an agreement which emerges from our initiative must win the allegiance of all sections of our people. The dilemma facing the Unionists or created by them and the British government needs a three-pronged response. This means that those of us who profess to be democratic and who want to build an agreed Ireland must, while standing up to the Unionist dogma, take on board their fears, both real and imaginary.

The responsibility is also on the British government to recognize that Unionism is a child of the British connection which is fearful of being orphaned, and which needs to be brought around to the point where it realizes that its natural family is the Irish one. A responsibility rests on the Unionists themselves to produce someone who will say something other than "No."

Returning to the question of a Loyalist backlash, it is important to remember that there has been a Loyalist backlash since the 1920s, and that you cannot rule out British responsibility for this. Of course, the Unionists have their own agenda which at times may not suit the British, but the relationship between Unionism and the union is central. Thus it was that this state was established, and that Ireland was partitioned. It has never worked. This is so in every decade since then.

When I was a teenager we were told that we couldn't have the right to vote, that the "B Specials" would not be disbanded. Our history is filled with the Unionists saying "No," and all the while the world has been moving on. The Unionists have to be faced up to, but they must also take responsibility for their own situation. What kind of future do Paisley and Molyneaux have in mind? A perpetuation of conflict, of more deaths, of prison camps and division? What is their peace strategy? Have they a peace initiative?

The British government's response to the joint statement has been a negative one. Patrick Mayhew's reaction is arrogant and offensive.

The British government must find the courage to change its policy. It can play a constructive and positive role in developing the peace process. In fact it has a primary responsibility to do so. British policy guarantees Unionist intransigence and violence. Mr. Mayhew's reaction has underpinned this.

Whether he likes it or not, John Hume and I represent the non-Unionist electorate of the Six Counties. Our joint statement deserved a more welcoming response from him. To say as he did that the main thing was to get his "talks" going and that Articles Two and Three of the Irish Constitution had to be amended to permit this is arrant nonsense. Successive British governments are directly responsible for perpetuating the conflict here.

There is only one initiative at present with the potential to move us towards a negotiated settlement. That is the one in which John Hume and I are engaged. It cannot work if Mr. Mayhew maintains his current position. In fact, it can only work if the British government play a constructive role based upon the reality of the situation here, and not upon their propaganda version of it. Mr. Hume and I had said that we recognize that the broader principles involved in our initiative will be for wider consideration for the London and Dublin governments. These governments need to seize the initiative, and move forward in a positive manner.

The IRA leadership has welcomed our initiative. Its statement, the first on this issue, is a significant development.

It says that if the political will exists or can be created that the initiative could provide the basis for peace, and that volunteers and supporters of Óglaigh na hEireann (the IRA) have a vested interest in seeking a just and lasting peace in Ireland. It makes it clear that the IRA remains committed to its objectives, "which include the right of the Irish people to national self-determination."

In a recent interview, I made it clear that all questions about the IRA's attitude to this initiative were a matter for the army leadership. I went on to point out that my priority as president of Sinn Féin, and the central function of the party was to develop and evolve and to be involved in a peace strategy to develop a peace process. In relation to the IRA I have made it quite clear that I am prepared to go to it with a package if one can be produced.

I would of course be seeking a package which would allow me to make definitive proposals to the IRA in relation to the future conduct of its campaign. Whether I can do that, whether this initiative can have that effect, or whether indeed the outcome would be acceptable to the IRA is a matter for all of us to apply ourselves to.

I entered into this initiative conscious of the difficulties facing Republicans, and my own responsibility in this regard. Whatever advances can be made, my commitment is clear. I will not mislead the IRA on this. Neither will I mislead others about the IRA.

There is a need for other influential elements to create a climate for peace, and there is an important international dimension to this. In particular, the Clinton administration can play a positive role by creating a climate for peace. Censorship and visa denial prevent a proper scrutiny of how Sinn Féin policy has evolved over the last decade. The Republican objective remains as it always was, but there has been an evolution of policy and strategy for some time. Sinn Féin were never simply a "Brits out" party at any time in our history. But we have adopted a different approach which is more in keeping with the reality of Ireland in 1993 than perhaps harking back to Ireland in 1918.

We have two different political realities on the island. Sinn Féin are trying to deal with this reality. The leadership of the parties have been very patient with me in the handling of this initiative. Republicans need to be cautious given the history of this island, and the many instances in which the Republican position was diluted or diverted or defeated. But making peace is a risky business. It is easy to make peace with your friends, not so easy with your enemies. So the process which we seek to design will be slow and problematic and difficult. It will require give and take.

As I have said above, this is not merely a responsibility for John Hume and myself. It needs everyone else on board. It especially needs the British government and the Dublin government to fulfill their responsibilities. Bill Clinton can help them to do this.

The Irish in the USA also have a role to play. No matter what way we look at it, US government policy has favored the British. This must be changed.

The Irish in America have played a major role in the history of the US. Sections of Irish America have played a constructive role in the quest for freedom and justice in Ireland. There is room for many, many more people in this struggle, and there have been some worthy developments recently in this regard. Visa denial needs to be ended. The Clinton administration needs to support peace in Ireland.

I am asked if I am optimistic that this initiative will make headway. I am realistically hopeful, given the problems we face and given what appears to be an intransigent attitude by the British government. There are only two choices. We are at the crossroads in this country's history. Either we take the pathway towards peace or we are put off it by those who are interested in maintaining division and conflict. My hope is that we take the path to peace.

The Irish Peace Initiative Must Not Be Ignored

The Irish and British governments in a joint communiqué on October 29 rejected the Hume/Adams peace talks. On October 23, the IRA attempted to kill the leadership of the Loyalist death squads. Instead they killed ten civilians and injured fifty-eight.

O N SEPTEMBER 25, John Hume and I stated our belief that our discussions "aimed at the creation of a peace process which would involve both governments and all parties, have made considerable progress." We agreed to forward a report on the position reached to Dublin for consideration, and we recognized that "the broad principles involved will be for wider consideration between two governments."

We were then, and we remain convinced, that from our discussions "a process can be designed to lead to agreement among the divided people of this island, which will provide a solid basis for peace." In effect, we, as leaders of Nationalist opinion in the North reached agreement on a process which, if adopted by the two governments, could lead us out of conflict and towards a real and lasting peace on this island.

After decades of conflict this is, clearly, a significant development. It has been warmly received by Nationalist opinion in Ireland. The very positive response, last weekend, of delegates at the Fianna Fáil Árd Fheis (national conference) is proof of this. One public opinion poll estimated public endorsement in the South at seventy-two percent. On October 3, the leadership of the IRA welcomed the initiative and pointed out that it could provide the basis for peace. It reiterated this position again last week. International political opinion has also been positive.

The response of the two governments to the Irish peace initiative was contained in a joint communiqué issued in Brussels on Friday, October 29. This rejected the process.

I am asked was it the Shankill bombing which had this effect on British government thinking. The killing of the people on the Shankill Road was wrong, and this has been cynically exploited by those opposed to the peace process or as an excuse by those who wanted to walk away from it, but the British government's attitude was clear before that fateful Saturday.

British Prime Minister John Major rejected the offer of peace as long ago as the Tory party conference. He has had a number of opportunities since then to change his mind. He and his colleagues, despite their protestations to the contrary, have been aware for some time now of the contents of the Irish initiative. They do not wish to admit knowledge of this because then they will have to spell out their attitude to the substantive issues involved. So they tell lies.

When Mr. Hume asked John Major in the British House of Commons why the British Prime Minister had rejected his initiative without even talking to him, Mr. Major bluntly replied, "I reached the conclusion, after having been informed of them by the Taoiseach . . . that it was not the way to proceed." He was given the opportunity again last week by Mr. Hume in an hour-long meeting in Downing Street to review his position.

All indications so far are that Major still says "No." So what now, in the light of British intransigence, is the future of the Irish peace initiative? That depends on the British government being moved from its current position to the democratic one. Will Dublin do this? Does it want to?

I had hoped to have met with John Hume and received his assessment of his recent meetings with the Dublin and London governments. Unfortunately Mr. Hume has been taken ill, and this has delayed our meeting. While I have tried to resist the temptation to prejudge Mr. Hume's assessment of John Major's response, I am satisfied that the British government has no real interest in developing a genuine peace process.

I am also certain that Major is out of step with British public opinion on this issue. He cannot and must not be permitted to reject this opportunity for peace.

In all of this it is important to avoid being fooled by, or party to, perceptions being falsely created by the British government about its real intentions. For example, further evidence of Britain's rejection of a real peace process can be seen in the speed with which it seized upon some of the six points outlined by the Irish Foreign Minister Dick Spring – points which reinforced the

Unionist veto. British support for some of Mr. Spring's remarks, and Mayhew's welcome for them is a cynical effort to divert attention from London's refusal to be involved in a genuine peace process, and to disguise its rejection of the Irish peace initiative.

The Unionist veto is used today as a political justification for the perpetuation of the problem. This bogus concept is created and maintained by the British government.

Mr. Spring also appears to have committed the Dublin government, in the context of the double veto he accorded the Unionists, to change the Irish constitution. A Dublin government, particularly a Fianna Fáil or a partial Fianna Fáil one, could not with impunity acquiesce to this, and Dick Spring has been forced to claw back, while Albert Reynolds has distanced himself from Mr. Spring's remarks.

Mr. Spring, even amid all the hype about his remarks, avoided describing his points as the basis for a peace process. They obviously are not. A peace process, to be successful, must be based upon principles which address the substantive issues and contain the dynamic required to move the situation forward. These are contained in the initiative taken by myself and Mr. Hume. They are absent from Mr. Spring's points. He knows this.

Unionists have understandably grasped the negative power which the veto bestows on them. It locks them into a "no change" mindset. Unionists will not change because the veto makes it plain that they don't have to change. Major's desire is to hold onto power. Party political interests, the Tory party's accord with the Unionists, and the reaffirmation of the Unionist veto have London dancing to an Orange tune. Quite clearly the Unionists see their alliance with the Tory government as strengthening their negotiating position. Hence the preconditions from them.

The rest of the Irish people, on the other hand, do not have any option. Our consent to partition is not even part of the equation, and while this affects all of us, for those of us who live in the North of Ireland, the sense of abandonment is acute. This was palpable within Nationalist areas in the Six Counties following the launch of Dick Spring's six points and the Brussels communiqué. I am sure it was the same in Irish America.

I want to appeal to our friends in the USA. Are you comfortable with a policy which appears to isolate and ignore the agreement which exists between the two leaders of Northern Nationalist opinion? Do you support a policy which surrenders Irish Nationalist interest to the narrow interest of a British Tory government; a position which cuts adrift Northern Nationalists while conceding every major point to the Unionists? Do you support the rejection or abandonment of an Irish peace initiative?

The answers are obvious. Most of the Irish in the USA are there because of the failure of the government in Ireland. You know the score. A real opportunity does now exist to build a new future for the people of Ireland, but it requires political courage, open-mindedness, and flexibility on all sides. Such qualities are rarely found in governments. They need to be moved by public opinion. You can help to do this by lobbying, by letter writing, by supporting the search for a lasting peace in Ireland.

The Irish people want peace. We deserve it. There is no doubt about that. We need alternatives to partition, not excuses for it. As I have said, I am convinced that John Major does not want a real peace process at this time.

All of this puts an onerous responsibility on Taoiseach Albert Reynolds. He must be aware that the seriousness of the situation demands urgent action from his government to focus the attention of the British government on its responsibility to play a leading role in removing the causes of conflict and division in Ireland.

Major and Mayhew must be told that there is no point in them cobbling together an "Anglo-Irish Agreement Mark II" for the sake of it, or because John Hume and I forced them to focus on the issue of peace in Ireland.

There is a real opportunity for a peace process now. That opportunity will not exist forever, and it will not be satisfied by mere formulations of words, by rhetoric or a *Pax Britannica*.

Finally, the Irish peace initiative is not about getting Sinn Féin a seat at the conference table. The mandate for that came from our electorate. And as Mr. Spring said "Peace is more than an end to violence." He also said that "political courage must come from the British government and from the Unionist leadership." Quite right. And from Dublin also, Mr. Spring.

Peace at What Price?

On December 15, 1993, Taoiseach Albert Reynolds and British Prime Minister John Major issued the Downing Street Declaration.

I DON'T KNOW exactly how the Anglo-Irish conflict is viewed in the US. The media wall built around Ireland, with its distorted information siphon through London, obviously gives a distorted, pro-British view, though the US media is much more open, so that when its representatives come here, they have no problem reflecting the Republican and democratic position. No actors' voices needed.

Still, despite the sterling efforts over the decades of many organizations and individuals, I'm sure the question of Ireland is only occasionally a big issue outside of Irish America, and although we mightn't like to admit it, many people had developed a grudging toleration of the ongoing conflict here in Ireland.

In this context, the successful campaign to make Ireland an issue in the US presidential elections is a significant advance and one which can be built upon, and which needs to be built upon, if the peace process is to achieve a durable, negotiated settlement.

Most people in the US will not have read the Declaration in full, and I am sure it is being hyped to the heavens by London and Dublin. But many of us in Ireland have been through such initiatives before. The hype surrounding this one is not a new experience. Every such initiative is presented as the last great opportunity.

This Declaration came at a time of real opportunity and widespread support for an inclusive peace strategy that tackled the core issues. From the beginning the Major government has been devious and mischievous in its approach to the Irish peace initiative. Even though the full story has yet to be told, and the Dublin newspapers' revised version is not quite the full story, everyone knows how unwilling the Brits are to grasp the peace nettle.

The governments are putting it up to the Republicans that we cannot afford to reject their declaration. But when the hype has died away, and the details have emerged, if it is judged that both governments have squandered an opportunity for peace, then the sense of disappointment and disillusionment will be greater, especially in the North, than at any time since 1969. If there is a gap between what is now proposed and what is required, will the governments refuse to bridge this gap. If so, why?

In Irish politics today, and especially the politics of Leinster House, it is the politics of illusion, of the grand gesture, of the spin, which have become the norm. Politicians, even the best of them, have grown used to reducing real politics to a sound bite or a photo opportunity. Occasional rhetoric, a wink and nod, or the politics of the last atrocity verbalized to suit the mood, were deemed to be enough. And hadn't Dublin enough worries of its own to be getting on with? All of this needed to be changed, and it is changing, though some politicians are slow learners, and are struggling to catch up with "ordinary" citizens.

However, no matter how advanced Dublin's project is – and I will deal with this below – a real peace process cannot be built without the co-operation of the British government. By now that must be self-evident to even the most prejudiced observer. Whatever any of us do, short of setting aside our positions, there can be no real movement unless London plays a central and positive role, and no matter how reasonable or facilitating we are, nothing can move unless London joins the persuaders. Ask the Unionists. They know how to make the most out of their historical and contemporary relationship with the British. The establishment of a British House of Commons Select Committee is the most recent example of that. The Rev. Ian Paisley (DUP leader), James Molyneaux (UUP leader), and Mr. Major may have different styles, different ways of saying no, but the message is the same. Why is the Unionist veto reiterated repeatedly in the Downing Street Declaration? Why is the Government of Ireland Act not mentioned even once? This is the act of the English parliament that claims British jurisdiction over this part of Ireland.

The British hold the power to keep the Unionists locked in a negative mindset forever, or abandon them to their fate, or persuade them along the road to an agreement with the rest of the people of Ireland. British ministers have stated repeatedly over the past few weeks that they will not join the ranks of the persuaders. Why not?

Clearly, what is required in this situation of political deadlock – particularly when there is on-going conflict – is an initiative to break the deadlock, allied to a process that moves in the direction of a durable settlement and a lasting peace. Does Wednesday's Downing Street Declaration do this? To get the answer to this may take some time, and we certainly need to see beyond the hype, and to reflect on how far the Declaration advances the peace process.

Proper and full consideration requires of necessity that these deliberations be thorough, and this will require clarification from Dublin about some aspects of the Declaration. Mr. Reynolds has been fully informed about the Sinn Féin position. Apart from this, he knows what is required for a durable peace strategy, and everyone knows that the building of a peace process that will remove the causes of conflict in our country will be a difficult one.

Sinn Féin's peace strategy took years to evolve. Our dialogue with Irish religious, business, community, and political representatives is a protracted one. One aspect of this, my initiative with John Hume, took months to develop into an agreement. Indeed, this week's Joint Declaration was the product of frenzied activity by both governments after we had focused them on this issue.

All of this must be taken into consideration as we seek to find what part the Joint Declaration can play in this phase of the peace process. What are the questions we will be asking? Any scrutiny must include the following:

- Is the Declaration evidence of a real political will to build a genuine peace process, or is it the best that could be put together by two governments conscious of the popularity of the quest for peace but unwilling at this stage to deal in a real way with the core issues?
- Is this as far as the British government will go?
- Is it as far as Dublin wanted them to go?
- Does the Declaration contain any evidence of a dynamic to move everyone significantly in the direction of peace?
- How does it match up to the initiative launched by John Hume and myself?
- Will the IRA's positive and open attitude to Hume/Adams apply also to the Downing Street Declaration?

There is Nationalist rhetoric in the document, but even here have the British merely conceded the wording of certain irresistible concepts, and then, by qualification, rendered them meaningless? Can these generalities be reduced to practicalities? One commentator called the Declaration a masterful piece of ambiguity, which would be fair enough if we are dealing only with words, but we are dealing with a life and death situation that affects all of the people of Ireland. Do these words signal a process? If so, what is it?

We also need to consider the commentary that runs alongside the Declaration. Nationalist disappointment is not only because heightened expectations in the build-up to Wednesday's announcement were swamped in ambiguity, but also because we listened keenly to what the players were saying. For example, John Major, speaking in the British House of Commons after the announcement, said: ". . . the declaration does not assert the legitimacy of a united Ireland in the absence of majority consent. It does not either. . . commit the British government to joining the ranks of the persuaders for a united Ireland. That is not the job of the British government."

The Declaration does not set any timetable for a united Ireland. It does not commit the people of Northern Ireland to join a united Ireland against their wishes, and it does not establish any arrangements for joint authority. . . "For so long as the majority of the people of Northern Ireland wish to remain within the Union, they will have the total and complete support of the government in doing so . . . The Declaration in no way weakens the constitutional guarantee that was first set out in the Northern Ireland Constitutional Act 1973. There is no weakening of the constitutional guarantee, and nothing agreed today in the Joint Declaration gives the government of the Republic of Ireland any additional say in the affairs of Northern Ireland."

This weekend, as part of the pressure, both London and Dublin hinted that if Republicans refused to accept the Declaration there would be a crackdown. The London media quoted British government sources on the need for internment north and south, and the sealing off of the border. At the time of writing, the British have rejected any notion of an amnesty for political prisoners. Last week London told us that exploratory talks with Sinn Féin, after a reasonable period of "decontamination" would be about the IRA surrendering its weapons, which is not the business of Sinn Féin. The issuing of ultimatums from London and Dublin while we are considering their documents is unhelpful.

We have been around for too long now for this kind of Lloyd Georgian approach. Republicans will not be intimidated. Sinn Féin is committed to building a peace process in our country, and has been doing so for some time before the governments applied themselves to any of the issues involved.

There is quite a lot of maneuvering going on at present, and it is important if we are to move towards a durable settlement that the core issues are not obscured in the current frenzy of speculation and rumor. One of these core issues is the need for the governments to recognize and acknowledge the right of Republican voters to have their views unconditionally represented in the broadcasting media and in direct dialogue.

The release of political prisoners must also be part of a negotiated settlement that will remove the symptoms as well as the causes of the conflict.

These then are the matters that Republicans will be applying ourselves to over Christmas, and for some time after that. No matter about the hype of any particular position, there are no quick fixes in this situation. The challenge facing all political leaders is to establish a basis for a lasting peace that brings to an end all conflict in our country. Sinn Féin is totally committed to this, and it remains a personal and political priority for me. Republicans will be considering last Wednesday's Declaration in the context of Sinn Féin's peace strategy. We will approach it positively, and seek to move the peace strategy forward.

A Nice Two Days in New York

After years of being unable to get a visa to travel to the States, Gerry Adams was granted a special forty-eight-hour entry on January 31, 1994 by the White House, on the basis of furthering the peace process.

THE FIRST PERSON I met when we arrived in the US was a huge black man. He was standing in the plane doorway. (Yes, the plane had landed!) He had gray hair and a gray suit.

"Mr. Adams?" he said, looking at me quizzically. "Welcome to America."

"Thank you, " I said.

"You're welcome," he said.

"Thank you," I said.

"You're welcome." He looked at me again and continued quickly, "I'm from immigration. Follow me."

Outside was a posse of peelers – New York's finest – who all looked like they were from *Hill Street Blues*. They talked that way, too.

"Good t' s' ya," they said. They were the friendliest policemen I've met.

"Hi," one of them greeted me outta the corner of his mouth. "Welcome t' New York."

"Thanks," I drawled.

"You're welcome."

"Thanks."

"You're welc. . ."

He looked at me quizzically also. Outta the corner of his mouth. I was soon to learn that everyone in New York says *you're welcome* as often as you say *thanks*. A nice habit. And *"have a nice day."* Everyone says that too. I liked that as well. I thought I wouldn't cos some people here mimic "have a nice day" as an insincere Yankeefacation, but I like it.

Cab drivers, bell hops, waiters, journalists, New York cops. . ."Have a nice day," they say.

"Thanks," I say.

"You're welcome," they say.

"Thanks," I say.

They all look at me the same – quizzically. Like Mickey Spillane.

"You're welcome," they say.

"Than. . . s," I conclude. . .lamely.

What was it like to sleep in the Waldorf-Astoria? Far from it I was reared, you say. Begrudgery, how are you? So what was it like? I don't know. Sleep wasn't included in my schedule. I tell a lie. I never slept at all the first night but the second night I was allowed five hours and by that time anywhere would have done. I'm told I was very relaxed in the midst of all the hullabaloo. Now you know. It was caused by sensory deprivation. Try it.

And food? It was the second day before I was fed. There just wasn't the time the first day and when we had some space in the wee small hours of the next morning, as myself and a friend worked on my conference speech, I couldn't open the mini-bar in my room.

No, not for a drink! No way, José. For a snack. Honest.

Why didn't we call room service? In the beginning it seemed less trouble to go to the mini-bar. It was late. We were busy. The bloody thing was there, all innocent in the corner. But it wouldn't open. Not for anything! I poked it. Pleaded with it. Knelt before it. Begged it. Shouted, "Open Sesame." Kicked it. In vain. It would have been easier to get holy water in an Orange Lodge.

Ian Paisley would have been proud of my intransigent larder. It gave "Not an Inch." Its door was like the Derry gate and not a Lundy in sight. So we settled for a jar of jelly beans between us. One for me and one for him. The yellow ones were lovely.

Okay, so the mini-bar won. You needn't gloat. He who laughs last, laughs last. I got my own back the next night. But that's another story. . .

American journalists? The British establishment and the Unionists and other reactionaries here are giving US journalists a bad press. Which is a sure sign that they're doing something right.

But that to one side, the interviews I did in the US were much more assertive, probing and balanced than the sound bites reproduced here suggest. I am sure there are marginalized and silenced people in the US but I think there is also a genuine free speech ethos which is totally alien to the censored and closed media we endure here. Journalists appear to have much more independence. Certainly I found no trace of the self-censorship which is so prevalent in Ireland and Britain.

And some broadcasters talk like characters from Damon Runyon. Y'know what I mean?

One evening at about seven o'clock I am sitting in XYZ television studios putting on the make-up, which is something I'm not very fond of, when in comes a party from the Bronx wearing a cap as follows – Larry the King.

Now Larry the King is not such a party as I will care to have much truck with, because I often hear rumors about his interviewing techniques that are very discreditable, even if the rumors are untrue. In fact, I hear that many citizens of the Bronx and Brooklyn will be very glad indeed to see Larry the King take up another occupation, as he is always doing something that is considered a knock to the local establishment, such as challenging bad practice or corruption, and carrying on generally like he was the Real McCoy.

I am really not much surprised to see this party in XYZ studio in makeup, as it is well known that he owns the joint and as I am there to be interviewed by him, and here he is and there I am, so of course I give him a very large hello, as I never wish to seem inhospitable, even to working hacks.

Right away he comes over beside me and sits down and reaches out and spears himself some of my baby wipes with his fingers, but I overlook this, as I am only a visitor and he owns the joint and besides I am tired on account of being up most all of the night fighting with a mini-bar.

He sits there looking at me without saying anything, and the way he looks at me makes me very nervous indeed. Finally, I figure that he is a little shy so I say to him, very polite:

"It's a nice evening."

"What's nice about it?" he asks.

Well, now that it is put up to me in this way, I can see there is nothing so nice about the evening, at that, so I try to think of something else jolly to say while Larry the King uses up all my – his – baby wipes. Finally he finishes dabbing his moniker and gets up on his pins and looks at me again.

"See you in the studio," he says. "Everything will be very kosher. You need not be afraid of anything whatever. I have a very bad disposition and there is no telling what I may say to you. But I will say what I want and you will say what you want. Okay? This day I hear that a lot of English dudes do not like the idea of me talking to you and I do not like that, that they should tell me who to talk to in my own television studio, in my own town, in my own country. It is old fashioned, I know, that I should behave like this but that is the way I is made. So we will have a good discussion? Okay?" he says.

"Okay," I says.

And we does.

Squirrels? I saw squirrels twice in Ireland. Once while walking the road from Ughtyneill to Moynalty I passed between great banks of primroses beneath a canopy of trees and there in the upper branches were two squirrels. That was two years ago. More recently, last year on a frosted unapproved cross-border road on a beautiful Irish spring morning I turned a corner and there they were, two different squirrels, in the sunshine frolicking in the middle of the bohareen.

Last week myself and Debbie McGoldrick, Ciaran Staunton and Gerard McGuigan escaped for ten minutes and parked our Cadillac and went walking in Central Park. Squirrels? There was an epidemic of them. And a woodpecker! My first.

I didn't see the Statue of Liberty or Times Square. Central Park was ample compensation and the squirrels and Woody a special bonus.

People? The people were great. The Irish were everywhere and proud of it. So was I. It was quare *craic*. And despite all the shenanigans and doomsday warnings, New York was still where it had been as I left it, accompanied once again by my faithful coterie of cops.

"If you can make it here you can make it anywhere," one of them said to me. "Well done."

"Thank you," I replied quizzically. Like Mickey Spillane.

"You're welcome," he drawled.

"Have a nice day," I concluded.

Heathrow Incidents Must Not Derail Peace Efforts

March 1994 saw the IRA mount three days of mortar-bomb attacks, using mortars which did not explode, at Heathrow Airport.

A S I HAVE said on many occasions, all sides to the conflict here must accept their own particular responsibility for the situation. That includes Sinn Féin, which has, with every other party, a responsibility to find a peace settlement. This is particularly so at this point in the peace process, in the wake of events at Heathrow and continued killings and attacks in Ireland.

Let me restate Sinn Féin's position. We are committed to building a peace process. Of all those involved in this process, I have been most consistent in my realistic assertion that there are no quick fixes, no deadlines, and that the search for peace will be difficult and dangerous. It will also be open to exploitation, as each side or faction seeks to advance its own position.

Depending on what has occurred the pressure may, at times, be on the Republicans or the Unionists or the British. There is no doubt also that some events may cause particular problems for the Dublin government. In this context, most attention recently has focused on the IRA operations at Heathrow, and there have been efforts to present these as the end of the peace process.

When I tried to explain, in the course of an RTE radio interview, that the contrary should be the case, this was misrepresented in an attempt by some to seek what they saw as some sectional advantage for themselves against Sinn Féin. There is always this danger in oral exchanges so it is important to be particularly selective in the words chosen, lest one's opponents put their "spin" on it.

Thus for a period last week, the distorted version of my comments received as much attention and reaction as the more serious events of that week. However, opportunism, no matter about its immediate effect, has little relevance in the longer term. This is borne out once again by last week's experience, because when these distractions are set to one side those engaged in armed conflict

before the distractions are still so engaged. The distractions have
solved nothing.

Why? Because the causes of conflict remain. These causes still
need to be removed. How? By patiently building a peace process
which does this. That was my message last week. It is my message
again this week. The message of all armed actions, whether at
Heathrow or in Ireland, whether by the British forces, their Loyalist allies or the IRA, as I have said many times before, is that there
has not yet been an end to the Anglo-Irish conflict. Tragic and
intolerable though it may be, this is the reality.

The message from Sinn Féin is as valid now, if not more so, as at
any time in recent years. Sinn Féin is not engaged in armed actions,
either at Heathrow or anywhere else. We are engaged only in
unarmed activity and neither condone nor encourage armed actions.
We seek a demilitarization of the situation. The challenge remains,
not only for Sinn Féin but for others also. It is to find a formula for
a lasting peace. The events of last week should serve to spur all of
us to redouble our efforts and to accelerate the peace process.

Whilst all involved have to make a contribution, the British government, more than any other party, ultimately holds the key to
progress. They are the major player; they have the biggest army in
the field, and most importantly, they exercise the most influence
within the Unionist community.

Sadly, the British government, whether because of their cynical
and short-sighted "arrangement" with the Unionists in the House
of Commons, or because of some anachronistic belief in their own
imperial standing, have as yet proved unwilling to take, or even
consider, the measures that would transform an understandable
desire for peace into a genuine peace process.

Despite this hard-line posturing from British politicians, real-
ism and accommodation are not impossible. These qualities have
been exhibited on occasions in the past when it suited the British
to show flexibility, for example in the process which brought peace
and democracy to Zimbabwe.

As I reiterated recently, "Sinn Féin has accepted that the
Hume/Adams talks (the Irish Peace Initiative) could form the basis
for a lasting peace. Nevertheless, we are politically and morally
bound to consider the Downing Street Declaration in the context
of our own peace strategy with a view to determining what contri-

bution it has to make to the development of a peace process aimed at delivering a lasting peace."

Should there be a general consensus that the Irish Peace Initiative and/or Downing Street Declaration are, or are perceived to be, flawed, incomplete, or incapable of producing movement, they too can and should be changed, especially if the end result will produce the peace that all parties are theoretically committed to achieving.

The Irish and British governments, their respective Parliamentary oppositions, Republicans, the SDLP, the Unionists, the political and community representatives of all the people on this island, the church, the cultural and social bodies – are all pieces in the Anglo-Irish jigsaw. They must all be involved, they must all be part of the negotiating process that will, hopefully, slot the pieces together.

The British, to give them the benefit of the doubt, may find it difficult to talk to Republicans. We Republicans too have a decided reluctance to deal with the British government, whose every previous action has reeked of dishonesty and prevarication. But peace is worth any risk.

It is worth pointing out once again that Sinn Féin has no great concern to be engaged in bilateral discussions on constitutional matters with the British government. That government should recognize our rights as a political party, the validity of our mandate and the rights of our electorate. This is not an attempt to place conditions on talks. It is an obvious requirement if progress is to be made. Indeed, it is a logical consequence of London's conditional, half-hearted and impractical offer of talks with us.

As far as such talks are concerned, I have no doubt that Sinn Féin and the British government will be involved in dialogue. The British have conceded this in principle. Unfortunately they have stalled on the conditions.

These issues are not the point of the reasonable call for clarification being made by us. Clarification has been provided to all other parties on request. Sinn Féin and our electorate have the right to equality of treatment. Neither is clarification required as a means of negotiation. Clarification is necessary so that we properly explore how the peace process can be moved forward. It should be provided on that basis.

There will be negotiations, of course, in the future as part of this process, but these matters are more properly the business of all-party talks including the British government and with the Dublin government as the principle representative on the Irish side.

The Irish and British people are, in my opinion, when the process is managed properly, going to establish a lasting and democratic settlement. For all of us the prospect is at the same time exciting and frightening. Republicans are ready to play our full part in the most momentous moment in our history. If we all, working together, can get it right this time we can demilitarize our country, take the gun out of Irish politics and witness the final end of violence and war in Ireland. But we must be careful and patient. Making peace is a difficult business, and we can expect set-backs, disappointments and diversions.

At our Árd Fheis last month, Republicans were asked if we could really grasp what it is like to be born into the culture of Unionism and it was suggested that many of us in similar circumstances might have behaved in exactly the same manner as Unionists and Loyalists throughout the history of partition. We were reminded that a deep and genuine fear of abandonment by the British government has colored both the actions of Unionists and their motivation. The Unionist people of Ireland have, since partition sought to cope with a psychic paradox that has virtually destroyed their sense of independence, democratic radicalism and intellectual rigor.

We in Sinn Féin have a duty to develop our contacts with the Unionist community. We must recognize, be sympathetic and positive to what Unionists are being asked to consider and commit themselves to, if a peace dialogue is to develop. I am calling on Nationalists and Republicans to be aware of what it means to be a Unionist as this century draws to a close. All I ask is that the Unionists and the British government make an equal effort to recognize the validity of the Nationalist experience in Ireland.

I do not seek to minimize the depth of Unionist fears, but, and I would be dishonest not to say it, Unionists must recognize that there is no going back. There will be no more Stormonts, there will be no more Protestant parliaments for a Protestant people.

There need be no surrenders or partisan victories. Not by the British, not by the Republicans, not by the Unionists and their allies. The possibility for real and lasting peace still remains. Its achievement will be a victory for all.

I remain convinced that the IRA is willing to deal with any new eventuality. It has repeatedly made its position clear. To the best of my knowledge, despite the present level of activity, their stance has not deviated from that of last year, when they responded positively to the intensive talks between Sinn Féin and the British government. Given the IRA willingness to take such considerable risks in the search for a permanent settlement, it is literally incredible that the British, after negotiating such a favorable advance, should have walked away. If they really believe that the Downing Street Declaration represents a viable alternative to the Irish Peace Initiative, then let them re-open discourse and convince Republicans of that.

Nonetheless, despite the current impasse, Sinn Féin must attempt to move the situation forward. The peace process needs to follow a carefully plotted course if it is to avoid all the distractions, many of them unforeseen. It must lead to a negotiated settlement which can involve all sections of the Irish people, including the significant and necessary contribution of Unionists.

Sinn Féin is willing to set aside all that has occurred up to now. I ask John Major to do likewise. I have frequently said that a new beginning is needed. I call upon all who are concerned to end conflict, to redouble their efforts to move this situation on in a manner which takes account not only of all the sensitivities and difficulties involved, but more importantly, of the prize of peace which must be the basis for our commitment to this process.

Republicans want peace, we want to see the gun taken out of Irish politics forever. If the British government is willing to examine openly the proposition we have outlined to them, then Republicans will commit all our energies to reaching such an agreement.

Reynolds' All-Ireland Speech On the Right Track

In a speech on April 16, 1994, Albert Reynolds proposed an all-Ireland solution to the North's problems. In the same week, a young mother was brutally killed by a Loyalist death squad.

O N SATURDAY NIGHT Taoiseach Albert Reynolds addressed a conference of Ógra Fianna Fáil. A soundbite of his comments regarding an all-Ireland power-sharing government received widespread media coverage and the Sunday papers gave fuller accounts of his remarks.

Politically, Nationalists were for what he said. Emotionally, many people were disappointed that Mr. Reynolds missed an opportunity to reflect his concern at the Loyalist killing campaign, or even to mention the murder two days earlier of the latest victim of Loyalist violence, Theresa Clinton.

While this is obviously not Mr. Reynolds's intention, it causes profound disquiet to this section of our people. It cannot be stressed enough how important it is to reflect a consciousness of the reality of the Nationalist experience in the Six Counties.

At the same time, Nationalists recognize the need for the battle of ideas to be advanced. A united Ireland obviously needs a foundation of inclusiveness if it is to truly reflect the diversity of all sections of our people. Nationalists and Republicans agree with Mr. Reynolds that what is needed is a process of reconciliation through which the agreement and assent needed for an agreed Ireland can emerge.

The idea of a national partnership government is a useful one. The Unionists will have more democratic input and a more positive influence in an all-Ireland situation than they can ever have within Westminster or even within the old Stormont regime.

The realignment of Irish politics which will obviously follow the end of partition and its distorting effects will mean, for the first time perhaps, the emergence of the political forces along lines of left and right. This will have a profound effect on all the political parties. The union with Britain has smothered democracy in Ireland. Conservatism reigns. Yet within all the main parties there are more progressive elements.

This is especially so among the Protestant section of our people. Republicans need to assure Northern Protestants that the demand for British withdrawal is not aimed at them. It is directed solely at the British government's control in Ireland. It is a demand that the people of Ireland – and that includes the essential contribution and participation of Northern Protestants – be allowed to control our own destiny and shape a society which is pluralist and reflective of the diversity of all our people.

Mr. Reynolds' remarks were rejected by the Unionist leaders. His speech was aimed to some extent towards the Ulster Unionist Party (UUP). He will not be surprised that UUP leader James Molyneaux's dismissal differed only in tone from Democratic Unionist Party (DUP) leader Ian Paisley's. Yet he was right to argue that satisfactory arrangements can be made within an all-Ireland context. Grass-roots Unionism may not be rushing headlong towards an Irish republic but there is a growing realization among significant sections of Unionism that the British will dump them and that the future of all the Irish people is within an island context.

Republicans have long accepted that Northern Protestants have fears about their civil and religious liberties, and we have consistently asserted that these liberties must be guaranteed and protected. Sinn Féin seeks a new constitution for a new Ireland. This constitution would include written guarantees and a Bill of Rights.

What is required is an approach which creates political conditions in which, for the first time, the Irish people can reach a democratic accommodation, in which the consent and agreement of both Nationalists and Unionists can be achieved, in which a process of Nationalist reconciliation and healing can begin.

Republicans have never argued that Unionists should be coerced into a united Ireland. We have consistently demanded an end to the Unionist veto. Our proposal that the British government join the persuaders is the logical extension of this position. It is our firmly held belief that the consent of the Unionists is realizable in the context of a clear policy change by the British government.

There is an onus on all of us, on everyone interested in achieving a lasting settlement to join in this process of democratic persuasion. Mr. Reynolds' speech is a welcome contribution to that debate.

****

Theresa and Jim Clinton have two daughters. Roseann is aged thirteen and her baby sister Siobhán is three. The family live in Balfour Avenue in the Ormeau Road district of South Belfast. They live in an all-Catholic enclave, sandwiched between the river Lagan and the Ormeau Road, in what is a natural and growing hinterland of the Nationalist Markets area.

Ormeau Road has been in the news here a lot recently. Readers may recall the controversy about Orange marches particularly following the Loyalist mass murders at Graham's bookmaker's shop. The Clintons' house is close to Graham's bookmakers.

Last Thursday night Theresa was shot in the living room of her home. She was thirty-three. Her killer broke through the front window of the downstairs room with a large concrete block. Jim was upstairs. Theresa was locking the house for the night. Minutes earlier Jim had been putting coal on the fire. He heard the battering noise and knew instantly what was happening. He screamed a warning down the stairs to Theresa. As he shouted the shooting started.

Jim Clinton had a sense of everything happening at once. The battering noise, the sound of his own voice, the shooting, the noise of a car driving off at speed. When he got downstairs Theresa was slumped on the settee. She was dead. She had been shot fourteen times.

Her killers had a clear view of their target through the hole they had shattered in the window. Later they said that they had mistaken Theresa for Jim. No one believes them. The attack on the Clinton family was the fifth in as many days by Loyalists on Catholic families. A few nights earlier, eleven children narrowly escaped death or injury when, in two attacks, grenades were hurled into their homes. A middle-aged man and his invalid son were seriously wounded in another attack on their home similar to the one on the Clintons.

In these cases none of the victims had any political involvement. Neither had Theresa Clinton. But Jim Clinton has. He is a member of Sinn Féin and a former candidate in local government elections.

In the last four years the Loyalists have killed more people than anyone else. Out of ten deaths so far this year Loyalists have been responsible for eight. This escalation of Loyalist attacks can be traced directly to the large arms shipment in 1988 which was smuggled into Ireland for the Loyalists, involving British military intelligence and their agent, Brian Nelson. Since then 203 people have been killed by Loyalist death squads. Theresa Clinton is their latest victim.

In the past two years, thirteen members of Sinn Féin have been killed and seven former members or members of families of Sinn Féiners have been killed. Scores have been injured, some seriously. Sinn Féin offices have been attacked, in some cases with rocket launchers and heavy automatic weapons. Homes have been bombed and families targeted. In all of these attacks there is a clear pattern of collusion. The Nationalist community knows this, as do many in the media. Anyone who spends even a little time investigating collusion will accept that it is a fact of life, and death, here. Despite this overwhelming evidence of collusion, nothing is done to end it. Where is the outrage in Southern political circles or within the British political establishment? What have the churches to say?

The collusion takes a number of forms. In most cases where heavy weapons were used they were part of the Nelson shipment. In many cases the Loyalists are acting on information, albeit sometimes inaccurate information, from British files. On other occasions they appear to have advance notice of British crown force patroling patterns.

Theresa Clinton's murder brings some of these issues into focus. One of the realities of living in a police state is that intelligence files are kept by the state on a very large number of citizens. Files on Nationalists regularly find their way into the hands of Loyalist murder gangs. Jim Clinton had been told on at least a dozen occasions that his files were in the hands of Loyalist death squads. There was never any explanation of how this had happened. There never is.

The attack on the Clinton family was based on prior information. Balfour Avenue is a narrow, one-way street. Detailed knowledge of the area was required by the Loyalists. Theresa Clinton's killers also obviously knew that the door of her home was strengthened. They ignored it and went straight for the window. The attack was a discriminate one. Like the other attacks on women and children, the purpose is to terrorize and to provoke a reaction.

Such a reaction – which must be avoided at all costs – would benefit British counter-insurgency efforts to depict the conflict here as a sectarian one of Catholics vs. Protestants. Of course the Loyalists have their own agenda. This doesn't always coincide with the British one, but one can be sure that British intelligence have their agents in the Loyalist death squads, influencing and directing operational policy in the same way as Brian Nelson did.

Today we buried Theresa Clinton. During the wake at her Balfour Avenue home her coffin had to remain closed. She was too badly shot up for the lid to be removed. There was an angry mood among the mourners and among the crowds who thronged the pavements. Anger and tears. Anger at her killers. Of course! But also because of their sense of being abandoned. Theresa was shot for being a wife and a mother. To terrorize other wives and mothers. To frighten the rest of us.

As a fitting postscript I learned that Jim Clinton's brother, David, a political prisoner here, had been refused parole to attend Theresa's funeral. This time we can't blame the Unionists. That petty extra hurt didn't come from Ian Paisley. Or James Molyneaux. No, that was Northern Ireland Secretary Sir Patrick Mayhew's gesture of sympathy to the Clinton family.

Breaking the Deadlock

After the British government had refused for five months to give clarification to Sinn Féin on matters within the Downing Street Declaration, the Irish government intervened by passing a document outlining Sinn Féin's queries to London.

L AST YEAR, BEFORE the revelations of my meetings with the SDLP under John Hume, the political landscape here was frozen over. News of our dialogue broke on Easter Sunday 1993 and the political glacier started to thaw. Our initiative kick-started the peace process and for all of last summer and until December, despite many attempts to derail it, the Irish peace initiative pushed everything behind it and focused Irish as well as British public opinion on the core issues required for a lasting peace settlement.

As all of this developed, international attention was alerted to the opportunity for peace in Ireland. The onus was clearly on the British government to engage in a meaningful way in the search for a negotiated settlement. It is important to remind ourselves that the British government was not inclined towards such a settlement. It had its own strategy which was briefly aimed at the pacification and containment of Irish Nationalism and Republicanism, and any settlement envisaged by London as part of this strategy was far short of the democratic and inclusive arrangements required as a foundation for a lasting peace.

Despite this, Sinn Féin has consistently maintained a positive and flexible approach to the efforts to build a peace process. The British government showed a persistent reluctance to do likewise. There are many obvious reasons for this, not least John Major's own leadership difficulties, and for all of last summer he maneuvered his way around the Irish peace initiative. The path to a negotiated peace settlement which favored a democratic option was a political minefield for Mr. Major. He needed to win respite from the demands coming from Ireland. So it was that the British government seized upon the Downing Street Declaration and Mr. Major retreated behind it and sought to use the Declaration as a counter to the Irish peace initiative.

Of course, the Downing Street Declaration marks an important stage in the peace process, but the British attitude has made it difficult to make progress since the Declaration was launched. Mr. Major's own utterances were particularly unhelpful. His demand for the "decontamination" of Sinn Féin, his studied "take it or leave it" outburst, and his dogged refusal to authorize clarifications of the document stalled the search for peace.

I have frequently said that the delay caused by these tactics is intolerable. Sinn Féin has made a number of efforts to break this logjam. These were rejected arbitrarily by Downing Street. Despite this we kept trying. It was in that context that I forwarded to Taoiseach Albert Reynolds, for transmission to the British government, a document detailing the clarification of the Downing Street Declaration which Sinn Féin requires from London.

It is important that the British government responds positively to this initiative and answers the questions put to it in a direct and comprehensive manner. Clarification is more than a formality. Peace requires change. Our questions require unambiguous answers.

John Hume has been fully informed of this initiative and has a copy of our document.

Sinn Féin has a clear view of what is required to achieve a lasting peace founded on democratic principles. We have a peace strategy aimed at moving the situation in that direction and we will continue to build on the conditions created by our peace strategy and the Irish peace initiative. Proper clarification and appropriate responses to our questions will permit us to ascertain what role there is for the Downing Street Declaration in the search for peace.

There is a simplistic notion encouraged by some political opinion here that Sinn Féin's response to the clarification provided to us will make or break the peace process or that peace will break out once clarification is provided. Hype like this is counter-productive. It runs contrary to the way the peace process has developed so far and it defies the experience of peace processes in other countries, particularly South Africa. As I said above, the achievement of a solid basis for peace in Ireland requires change and a political process to bring that about. It also requires a clear understanding of the British government's political interests and long-term intentions toward Ireland.

So it is necessary that the replies from London to our questions properly and honestly clarify these issues. The Republican desire to have the Downing Street Declaration, and Britain's intentions, explained to us, have been dismissed by some in the past as cynical. It is gratifying even five months later to note that there is now an admission that our questions are genuine and that clarification is required.

All of this points up the reason why the search for peace is described by Sinn Féin as a process. There are no quick fixes, no easy answers.

An inclusive process of dialogue aimed at a negotiated settlement based on democratic principles is required. Everyone involved will seek to come to this or to ignore it or wreck it based on their own analysis. So the process may become convoluted and subject to distractions but despite this, and perhaps because of it, the search for peace must be relentlessly pursued and the process must be established upon a solid foundation.

Republicans want to see the clarification debate brought to an end. We want it out of the way so we can all move the peace process on to the next stage. Until now, London has chosen to concoct one pretext after another to refuse our reasonable request. Mr. Major needs to adopt a more flexible position if his claim to be interested in peace is to have any credibility.

The Declaration has been variously described as a masterpiece of ambiguity and a document which can mean many things to those who read it. This is not good enough. If we are to bring an end to the cycle of violence which has bedeviled our history it must be on the basis of clarity and a successful resolution of those issues which lie at the heart of this conflict.

Sinn Féin has many detailed questions which only the British government can answer. However, these can be grouped into three general areas.

Firstly, matters of text in the Downing Street Declaration itself. Secondly, the differing interpretations placed on the Declaration by both governments and the conflicting commentary around it. And finally, what are the processes and structures which both governments envisage will develop from the Declaration.

There are twenty questions in the document presented to the Dublin government for transmission to London. Having sent this document to London, it would not be fitting to publish it before the British government has the opportunity to study and respond to its contents. It is, however, useful to elaborate on the areas involved.

If the British government doesn't seek a pre-determined outcome and if it is for the Irish people to freely determine our future without external impediment or interference, how can these positions be reconciled when set against the continued existence of the Government of Ireland Act? The Government of Ireland Act claims sovereignty over this part of Ireland and yet doesn't merit a single mention in the Declaration. What is the British government's position on this?

The British government says it wishes to see agreement between all the Irish people but what are the means and within what time-scale does the British government see this happening? In view of the failure of the present constitutional structures, what are the constitutional options which the British government see as being a realistic alternative and which could lead to a balanced constitutional accommodation? Furthermore, the British government's interpretation of the Irish people's right to self-determination and particularly how and within what time frame it will give legislative effect to this right, are all clearly areas which require explanation and clarification.

There are also a number of matters of particular concern arising from the British government's interpretation of and commentary on the Declaration. For example, these include: What are the long-term political objectives of the British government in relation to Ireland? We need to know the answer to this and so do the Unionists. We also need to know on what basis does the Unionist veto exist and how far does it extend over constitutional change and political policy.

One benign interpretation placed on Britain's claim that it has no "selfish economic or strategic interest in Northern Ireland" is that this is a statement of "non-interest" and "neutrality." It is an analysis which, when linked with words like "facilitate" and "encourage" presents a particular image of a government which is prepared to act as a neutral facilitator for agreement.

It is a view which has been encouraged by British Ministers. How does the British government reconcile this with its stated objective of maintaining the union? Again, what of the Government of Ireland Act? How should one interpret British claims that the Irish constitutional claim is "anachronistic"? And how does this "neutrality" fit in with Michael Ancram's recent view that "as we have insisted, we are acknowledging that we do have interests in Northern Ireland?"

The Downing Street Declaration is described as "the starting point of a peace process designed to culminate in a political settlement." In reality this process started with John Hume and myself and with a series of initiatives from Ireland. The Downing Street Declaration was a response to this.

This to one side, what are the subsequent steps which the British government sees as arising from the Downing Street Declaration? What are the structures and processes which the British government envisages will be developed from the Declaration? Is acceptance of the Declaration a precondition for involvement in talks on the development of new political arrangements? And what is the process which will lead to a demilitarization?

Last year, the British government talked to Sinn Féin. It refuses to do so now when it claims to have the basis of a settlement. Where is the logic in this position?

Sinn Féin has a democratic mandate. We speak for almost forty percent of Nationalist opinion in the North. Sinn Féin has a clear view of what is required to achieve a lasting peace founded on democratic principles. We have a peace strategy aimed at moving the situation in that direction.

The document which the Dublin government has now passed to the British government spells out in detail our areas of concern and asks specific questions. The British government should respond positively to this initiative and it should answer our specific questions in a direct and comprehensive manner. It is vital that London's response is honest and forthright.

Sinn Féin is convinced that the creation of a permanent basis for peace requires change and a political process to bring that about. Any effort to develop and advance the peace process requires a clear understanding of the British government's political interests and long-term intentions towards Ireland.

It is important to record the positive influences that US opinion and Irish-American opinion have played in moving the peace process forward. This has been noted by Irish Republicans. Positive influence was exerted on Patrick Mayhew during his recent visit to North America. I welcome this. Mayhew has learned that he could not easily dodge the need to address the issues raised by Sinn Féin and that he could not ignore the rights of our electorate.

Let me repeat myself once again. There is a paramount need for everyone committed to peace in Ireland to be clear about British policy and intentions towards our country and our affairs. This is not a formality. It is of grave concern to the people of Ireland and the people of Britain. It is serious business. The document which the Dublin government has transmitted to the British government for Sinn Féin deserves a serious, thoughtful, unambiguous and comprehensive response from London.

Since I have written the above there has been growing concern among many Irish Nationalists that the British government may yet squander this opportunity to advance the peace process. This concern arises from the comments of a number of sources, including Downing Street, whose spokespersons are quoted as saying that Britain's response to the Sinn Féin document will not amount to clarification.

If this is true then everyone concerned to promote the search for peace must seek to persuade John Major that this is not the way forward. Albert Reynolds has identified the gap of distrust between the London government and Irish Republicans. That gap needs to be bridged. The Dublin government knows that Sinn Féin has sought to bridge that gap and remove the distrust. Major must be persuaded to do likewise.

An Important Step Forward

In his first public comments on the clarification given by the British government, Gerry Adams believed that the answers would move the peace process forward, though he raised concern over increased Loyalist violence and collusion, such as the bombing of the Widow Scallon's pub in Pearse Street, Dublin in May 1994.

I'M JUST BACK in Ireland after fulfilling a number of speaking engagements in Italy. There, a number of Irish people turned up at each of the meetings, proof, once again, of how scattered the Irish Diaspora is. The Irish in Italy, of course, have concerns other than political ones. The World Cup in the US is of great concern right now because Ireland plays Italy in the first round. This dominated all of the small talk.

The British response to the Sinn Féin questions reached me while I was in Turin. All twenty-one pages of it. Whatever about the quality of the clarifications, the quantity was certainly at odds with London's previous assertions that no clarification for Sinn Féin was necessary, or indeed possible. The provision of clarification, therefore, marks another step – a small one, some might say, but in my view an important step in the slowly evolving peace process.

The British document is a response to the initiative by Sinn Féin to break the deadlock in the peace process, and was facilitated and assisted by the active and creative role played by the Dublin government. After the IRA suspension of activity last month, I pointed out that the significance of this initiative lay not in its seventy-two-hour duration, but in the fact that the IRA had undertaken it.

At that time I said that this would not be lost on the policy makers at Downing Street. So also was the recent development on the issue of clarification. Its significance lies as much in the fact that the British government responded to the initiative from Ireland, as in the substance of the response itself.

I have not yet had an opportunity to discuss the British clarifications with colleagues here in Ireland. Of the few people I have met since my return on Monday night, all have acknowledged the significance of this latest development, though many registered disappointment at some of the British responses. This is a problem which Republicans will have to deal with as we conclude our assessment of the Downing Street Declaration, as part of moving forward into another phase of the peace process. It would obviously have been much more helpful if the British government had responded in a direct, unambiguous and comprehensive manner to *all* the questions we put to them.

All political parties here are in the last two weeks of the election to the European parliament. So Sinn Féin will not meet formally to consider how the peace process will be advanced until after these elections. The Sinn Féin Árd Comhairle (National Executive) will meet this weekend and, of course, the British clarifications and how we proceed from here will be one of the matters up for discussion. As always, we will be seeking to do this in a positive way, and to address the British responses in a flexible manner.

By then, I, of course, will be more fully briefed on the situation than I am right now. A lot has happened in the short time that I was absent from Ireland. The Unionist death squads have returned to Dublin again, leaving one man dead and one seriously wounded. It should not go unnoticed that the death squads are most active when there is a perception of Nationalism moving forward.

Twenty years ago, bombs in Dublin and Monaghan caused the greatest number of fatalities in any incident in the Troubles. If the weekend bomb had exploded, a new grisly record would have been set. There was a British military intelligence involvement in previous attacks in Dublin, and there is no clarification required about the intentions of the bombers, or their sponsors. Like the campaign against Catholics in the North, actions in the South are aimed at terrorizing and intimidating popular opinion.

There was also a bomb in the Sinn Féin office in Belfast City Hall. This seriously injured two workmen. As I pen these lines, there is a news report of another bomb at the Newry Sinn Féin office. All of these actions point towards further collusion between elements of the British forces and the Unionists.

The newspapers provided by Aer Lingus on my flight home were filled with speculation about a possible Loyalist ceasefire. I think this is most unlikely, although the IRA have said in a statement that a Loyalist ceasefire will bring an end to its targeting of Loyalists.

The Unionist leaders' response to the Dublin bombing was ambiguous. They obviously see it as an attempt to weaken the resolve of the Dublin government in pursuing the peace process. Republicans will not be intimidated, nor will we be diverted from our commitment to establishing a peace settlement. The Dublin government should not be intimidated either from its efforts.

The increase in Loyalist activity hasn't happened by chance. It began six years ago with the South African arms shipment which was procured with the help of British intelligence. The Loyalists are not reactive. There is a co-ordinated effort to kill Nationalists or Catholics, in furtherance of Unionist political objectives.

This is the background against which we all must move towards a negotiated settlement. Of course, this must also involve the Unionists. Twenty-one pages of carefully crafted British responses to the Sinn Féin questions will mean little to Nationalist "Seán" or "Sinéad Citizen" if they think that the stick of Loyalist terrorism is being wielded more energetically than the carrot of British clarification. But, of course, converting the rhetoric of peace into tangible and demonstrable results is a challenge facing us all.

Important questions were put to the British by Sinn Féin. They may have fudged some of the answers, but they also have undoubtedly addressed some of the issues involved. These included Sinn Féin's mandate, the veto, the Government of Ireland Act, and that acceptance of the Downing Street Declaration is not a prerequisite for negotiation. Are these responses adequate?

I have long pointed out that a lasting peace must be carefully and patiently constructed. Peace needs change. It must have a solid foundation. As we have seen, there is a yawning gap of mistrust between Nationalists and the British government which must be bridged. This will happen more effectively and with more likelihood of permanency as a result of small but sure steps. Undoubtedly the provision of clarification constitutes one of these steps. Therefore, this in itself is helpful. After all, we are dealing with centuries of history. The peace settlement in South Africa came after patient and persistent efforts by both sides.

The actions of the Unionist death squads and their allies in the British crown forces shows that a peace process cannot focus only on one source of armed actions. A process which aims to tackle only one source of violence is in its conception and construction flawed and ineffective. The last twenty-five years of failed British initiatives aimed at crushing the Republican struggle demonstrates this. We have moved beyond this. We are clearly at a new and, for everyone, a challenging situation. I remain confident that with commitment, imagination and patience, the peace process can be advanced and a peace settlement constructed which will deal with the causes of conflict and lead, therefore, to a real and lasting peace in Ireland.

Time For a Sinn Fein Response

After European elections, Sinn Féin awaited a report from its Peace Commission before responding to the British on the Downing Street Declaration.

A S I AM penning this piece, the final counts in the European elections are coming to a conclusion. There were two elections here of course: one in each State. Sinn Féin was the only party to contest these elections nationally and this, as you may guess, was a considerable undertaking for such a small party. We also contested some local government seats throughout the Twenty-Six Counties and one by-election in Dublin. We consolidated our position and overall our vote increased, which is a tribute to the resilience and hard work of our activists and supporters.

Although Sinn Féin, like all the other parties, fights elections to win seats, the European one is a particularly difficult contest for us and I have to admit that at this stage in our development the election results in the North, as far as European Parliament seats are concerned, are a foregone conclusion. The interest of course was in how the voting was going to go.

It is too soon for me, or anyone, to analyze all the voting trends. Ian Paisley topped the poll, as was expected, though his vote decreased slightly, but in a significant development, John Hume recorded his largest vote yet, only a few thousand behind Paisley. This, allied to the rise in the Sinn Féin vote, is a clear endorsement of the peace process and of the Irish peace initiative.

Now, with the elections behind us, the Sinn Féin leadership will be applying ourselves formally to considering how this process can be moved on in the wake of the recent British response to our queries about their long-term intentions in our country. By the way, it is worth noting that US opinion played a significant role in getting the British government to change its mind after five months of London stubbornly refusing to clarify these matters for Sinn Féin. The initiative which led to this came from Ireland of course, once again, not from London, but the breakthrough was a welcome one and long overdue. As I have pointed out to people here, Patrick

Mayhew's visit to the USA and the grilling he received, privately and publicly, by those he met as well as the media, for his government's refusal to deal with Sinn Féin, went a long way to changing his government's attitude. There is a lesson here, not only for London; but for Irish America as well as Nationalist Ireland.

As part of our deliberations the Sinn Féin Árd Comhairle will be considering a report from the Peace Commission, established as part of the process of consultation undertaken by us in the wake of the Downing Street Declaration. The Peace Commission received submissions from community activists, religious groups, trade union officials, campaign groups and individuals, including Irish language and cultural rights activists. Submissions came also from party political elements, including quite a few anti-Republican groups and individuals. This process of consultation – of providing a platform for all – was conducted in tandem with a separate and internal process of consultation with Sinn Féin members.

Sinn Féin's desire to hear the views of citizens is not new. Over the years we have consistently solicited views on how to establish a durable and lasting peace in Ireland. All of our recent documents – for example, *Scenario for Peace* and *Towards a Lasting Peace* – were discussion papers which were widely distributed to our political opponents as well as our allies.

None of these documents were set in stone. We offered clarification on the issues involved and at all times we were willing to take into consideration the views of others, while grounding our own analysis on the principles of democracy and the right to Irish national self-determination.

The public interest in these matters was heightened considerably when SDLP leader John Hume and I kick-started the peace process over a year ago and I received several papers from groups and individuals outlining a variety of views on how progress could be made. This continued after the Downing Street Declaration and so earlier this year the Árd Comhairle of Sinn Féin decided that a formal channel or forum through which these views could be expressed would help to democratize and formalize this process of consultation. The Peace Commission was set up. Its objectives were:

- To assess the Downing Street Declaration in the context of Sinn Féin's overall peace strategy;

- To consult with the widest possible spectrum of public and private opinion on how to establish a lasting peace in Ireland;
- To create a dialogue around these issues;
- To publish a report.

In order to consult with the most representative range of opinion in the shortest possible time the Commission organized a hearing in each of the four provinces. The Ulster one was held in Derry, the Leinster one in Dublin, with Galway the venue for Connacht, and Cork the venue for Munster. Due to public demand an extra hearing was held in Belfast. This could have been repeated throughout the country, especially in the rural areas, but we were conscious of the need to complete this stage in the process as quickly as possible and the Commission Secretariat had to apologize to a number of people who were disappointed that hearings were not held in their areas.

The first hearing was held on January 22 and the last one on March 11. The report should be published within the next week or so after the Árd Comhairle receive it and although I can't preempt this, in my view this project was a very worthwhile and valuable one.

I attended only one of the hearings, the Belfast one, and I found this a particularly interesting discussion, not least because it was attended by a number of Northern Protestants, including some who argued the Unionist case.

The sight of the panel of Sinn Féin commissioners, restricted to asking questions and refraining manfully and womanfully from responding otherwise to the points put to them, was a wonder to behold. They did a great job. So did those who made submissions, friends and foes alike. There was a total of 230 submissions. Some were in writing, others were made orally to public sessions and there was the option of private hearings for those who requested this facility. Incidentally, there was a small number of submissions from the USA and a larger number from Britain.

All of the submissions presented to Sinn Féin through our Peace Commission have helped to inform the debate within our membership, particularly at leadership level, where there has been an opportunity to study the submissions. It is obvious from the views presented to us that there are diverse views on how to move the situation forward. These views will be included in our deliberations as we determine how to advance the peace process.

It is my intention that we should conclude this as quickly as possible and the Árd Comhairle will be meeting over the next few days to formally receive the report of the Peace Commission, to authorize its release and to begin the task of responding to the British clarifications. We will do this, of course, within the context of our own peace strategy, and it is my view that we must apply ourselves positively to these matters in order to move the peace process forward. Whatever way we decide to do this we will be informing our own members first and democratizing our response within the party before making our definitive views public.

Thank British Intelligence for World Cup Attack

On June 18, 1994 a Loyalist attack on soccer fans in the North left six people dead.

I WAS IN DUBLIN on Saturday at the Sinn Féin Árd Chomhairle meeting, at which the leadership discussed in a very positive way how we see the peace process developing. The Árd Chomhairle will be meeting again, perhaps a number of times, within days in order to move as speedily as possible towards a conclusion on how to move the situation forward.

Afterwards, I drove to a friend's house to watch the Ireland/Italy match. Bar staff were on strike so the city center had a deserted look, although the back streets were a frenzy of color with tricolors and banners everywhere. Whatever else Jack Charlton has done, one of his great triumphs is that it is now possible to fly the Irish flag in Dublin without the Special Branch interfering. I am not a soccer supporter – as Páidí O'Sé once said, *"Níl suim agumsa in soccer"* – but the rousing Irish brand of soccer is very entertaining, and Saturday's match was brilliant.

When the final whistle blew, as all of Dublin erupted in a volcanic roar of car horns and yahoos, I got a phone call from the North. Six Catholics had been killed in a public house in Loughinisland in Co. Down. The enormity of the atrocity stunned me. As I was given the details, I could hear in the background the sound of rejoicing as Belfast also celebrated Ireland's victory over Italy. They obviously hadn't heard the news of Loughinisland.

Most of the commentary, especially from politicians, has projected this atrocity as being the work of psychopaths or maniacs. This misses the point. This attack was premeditated and deliberately planned. It was also predictable. Most Nationalists were waiting for such an attack. It didn't come out of the blue. Of course, none of them would have guessed what target would have been chosen but in Nationalist Belfast, as in other parts of the Six Counties, people took precautions. They knew that the prospect of large groups watching the World Cup in pubs and clubs throughout Nationalist areas was too good an opportunity for the Loyalists to ignore. The people of Loughinisland, a quiet, rural hamlet untouched until now by the Troubles, could hardly have guessed that they would be chosen.

The brutality of the attack was also premeditated. Like attacks on Republican women, mothers and wives, or on children of Republican families, or like the mass murder attacks on book-makers' shops, funerals or Catholic homes, the intent is to terror-ize. The nature of the attack, and its connection with the World Cup, has once again focused media attention internationally and particularly in the US on the conflict here. But in the days before last Saturday, had the Loyalists been successful in a series of aborted or failed bomb attacks on Sinn Féin offices in Belfast, scores of people could have been killed or seriously injured.

One thing should be clear by now. The nonsense that Loyalist actions are reactive should be set to one side. Loyalist violence has never been reactive. Loyalism has always had its own agenda, and has always been capable of the most horrible, premeditated atroc-ities. Its business is terrorism. Its victims are Catholics. Better if they are Republicans, but failing that, any Catholics will do.

The British government cannot absolve itself of responsibility for Loyalist actions or for the attack at Loughinisland. The Loyal-ists have a capacity to operate now because they have the hard-ware. This was supplied to them by British military intelligence through its agent, Brian Nelson. Forensic investigations into the weapons used over the weekend will identify their source. Since Nelson brought in the arms shipment from South Africa, the Loy-alist killing machine has stepped up its activities.

If ever there was any doubt of the British involvement with Nelson's activities in directing the death squads of the UDA and the other Loyalist gangs, the facts prove otherwise. A senior British officer, identified only as Colonel J., who had been in charge of military intelligence from 1986–89, appeared in court to testify on Nelson's behalf; British defense secretary Tom King sent a letter to the Director of Public Prosecutions saying that Nel-son had been a valuable agent; Colonel J. and a woman who had been Nelson's main handler were given meritorious service awards.

Nelson's trial exploded the myth that Loyalist gangs are inde-pendent of outside direction and control. Of course, they have their own agenda, but they have also formed an integral part of British Army strategy since the early 1970s. British general and chief counter-insurgency strategist, Frank Kitson, has used pseudo-gangs in Africa and Malaysia; during his two-year tour of duty in Ireland in the early 1970s, he set up the Military Reaction Force (MRF). Other colonial wars had taught the British the value of using local groups whose activities would achieve Britain's political aims but whose actions would not be attributable to them.

The MRF was at the center of the creation of such pseudo-gangs. British soldiers with Northern Irish connections were brought from various regiments to train the pseudo-gangs; many of the gang members were still in the British Army. A former British Military Intelligence officer has explained that one way of recruiting gang members was "to use whatever means, legal or illegal, to blackmail the source into acting out of fear for his or her own safety, then force them to carry out operations that cannot be traced back to the handler."

While refusing to acknowledge that they are at war in Ireland, the British military and political establishment authorized the use of pseudo-gangs as a military tactic. Employing Loyalist gangs as their surrogates has enabled the British to wage war invisibly in the Six Counties, and when it suits them, in the Twenty-Six Counties as well.

While Co. Down has been until now one of the quieter areas of the North, it is worth noting that one of the most sustained controversies over collusion was triggered off by another killing in that area. That was the murder of Loughlinn Maginn by Loyalists who released a British intelligence file on Maginn as justification for their action.

The question of collusion is not a new one. It is a fact of life and death in this state. The British crown forces at an official as well as at an unofficial and personal level have always supplied the Loyalist death squads with information.

We should be careful also about accepting the propaganda assertion that we are in the throes of a tit-for-tat campaign. There is no evidence to support this RUC and British-sponsored myth. Premeditated attacks on ordinary Protestants, unlike the Loyalist attacks on ordinary Catholics, have not been and can never be any part of Republican strategy.

So what purpose is served by the killing of six Catholics in Loughinisland? People here are afraid – especially, I presume, those in areas like Loughinisland who may until now have presumed that they were safe. The intention and the rationale behind this attack is to divert the peace process, to put pressure on those engaged in trying to move the process forward. Those engaged in these attacks and their sponsors do not want to see a successful conclusion to the peace process. They feel threatened by the prospect of a negotiated peace settlement based on democratic principles. They seek to set their own agenda, to cause confusion and fear. They must not be allowed to succeed.

Loyalism is part of this state. That state has failed. There can be no internal solution. A democratic peace settlement will thwart the Loyalists and their sponsors in the same way as the end of apartheid defeated the right wing in South Africa.

None of this will be any consolation to the victims of the Loughinisland attack, to their grieving families or to the many others who have suffered in this conflict, but it is the only way to ensure an end to sectarianism in Ireland. A democratic peace settlement is the only guarantee we have that there will be no more Loughinisland atrocities.

Footnote:
On Saturday, June 25, in Belfast, two members of the British Army were charged with serious offenses. They were Neil Thomas Irwin, a private in the Royal Irish Regiment, and Color Sergeant Maurice James Nicholl of the same regiment. Irwin was charged with the murder of Francis Brown, a Catholic whose killing was claimed by the UVF (Ulster Volunteer Force). He was also charged with four separate murder bids – including one which involved the mother of a former Sinn Féin councilor who had a bomb thrown through the window of her home – as well as possessing explosives, a booby trap and an assault rifle. Nicholl was charged with possession of a booby trap and an assault rifle.

Peace Commission Report Now Public

The Sinn Féin analysis of the 228 submissions to their Peace Commission was published on June 24, 1994.

L AST FRIDAY, Sinn Féin published the report of its Peace Commission. As you may recall, the Commission was established as part of the consultative process conducted by the party in the wake of the Downing Street Declaration.

The objectives of the Sinn Féin Peace Commission as set out by the Sinn Féin Árd Comhairle (National Executive) were:

- To assess the Downing Street declaration in terms of Sinn Féin's overall peace strategy.
- To consult with the widest possible spectrum of public and private opinion on how to establish a lasting peace in Ireland.
- To create a dialogue around the issue of a lasting and durable peace.
- To make our findings public.

The Commission held five hearings and received 228 submissions. The Report is a forty-eight-page document which contains summaries of the different positions outlined in the submissions. The full text of all the submissions are to be lodged in libraries; they make very interesting reading.

There was a vast range of opinion across the submissions about the cause of conflict in Ireland and on how a lasting peace can be achieved. Almost all of the submissions believe that a viable peace process is possible. The difference in the submissions arose over the next step in such a process.

The majority of the submissions viewed the Downing Street Declaration as an ambiguous document and most supported the right of Sinn Féin to clarification.

Together they helped to inform the debate within our ranks and were analyzed in the context of our peace strategy. It is obvious from the views presented that people hold diverse opinions on the role of the Downing Street Declaration in the peace process.

Those who gave qualified support to the Declaration included some who felt that it was a good starting point, that it could be built upon, that British sovereignty had been weakened, that the British government was conceding something new in Paragraph Four on self-determination and that Paragraph Eleven on the proposed Forum for Peace and Reconciliation provided Republicans with a means to pursue their objectives with Irish Nationalists.

Other submissions suggested that the Declaration should be accepted for tactical reasons in the interest of developing the peace process.

Those submissions which criticized the Declaration did so on the basis that it was designed to sideline the Hume/Adams initiative; that it offered nothing to Nationalists; that it was drafted for the Unionists while offering no constitutional guarantee to Nationalists; that it is not a foundation stone for lasting peace and that it is designed to isolate Republicans.

A number of submissions focused on the need for the British government to withdraw its support for the Unionist veto in order to advance the peace process. Some reflected the fears of the Nationalist community regarding British intentions in Ireland and the links between the Loyalist death squads and the British. Many Nationalists, particularly at the hearings in Belfast and Derry, felt that they had no rights in the six-county state and that Nationalist rights and the Unionist veto could not co-exist. They did not trust the British government. There were also submissions which argued for the need to address the structures and institutions of conflict: i.e. policing, demilitarization, harassment, etc.

The positive attitude and involvement of the Dublin government in seeking to develop and then promote a peace process was welcomed. A number of submissions took a favorable view of the Forum for Peace and Reconciliation, although concern was expressed at the preconditions on participation which were being applied. Others expressed concern at what they viewed as Dublin's support for the Unionist veto in the Six Counties and the obstacle and dangers that creates.

Twenty-six submissions, just over eleven percent, specifically mentioned the need to create a process of demilitarization involving all the parties of the conflict. Eighty-five submissions, or thirty-seven percent, held that Sinn Féin should encourage the IRA to call a unilateral ceasefire; or a cessation of offensive military operations; or initiate a three-month ceasefire to enter negotiations; or called on the IRA to take up the offer made by John Major at the launch of the Declaration.

Certain submissions focused on the Hume/Adams proposals and the potential which they held. Some contributors to the oral hearings expressed disappointment that Hume/Adams was disregarded by the British government as they felt that it had the dynamic to resolve this conflict. Others felt that the Hume/Adams initiative should be made public. Views were expressed on the importance of a Nationalist consensus and the need for the Dublin government to continue to take a pro-active role in the peace process.

A majority of submissions which addressed the Unionists took the view that the Declaration had repeatedly reaffirmed the Unionist veto and that this guaranteed that the Unionists would remain inflexible and opposed to any change in the status quo and the existing structures and institutions. In the submissions from the Unionist community the refusal to consider any new arrangements was seen as a major stumbling block. It was also said that the British government should take a more pro-active role in creating the conditions for political change. Submissions from Unionists expressed the view that the concept of national self-determination frightens Unionists and that Republicans must engage in dialogue with Unionists. Others argued that both communities share a responsibility for injustices suffered and both communities will have to make courageous decisions.

A number of submissions took the view that the Loyalist death squads are not reactive, but are working to their own political agenda. It was also felt that they must be involved in any political settlement.

Women's groups and individual women felt that women should be centrally involved in the peace process as equals and that this should be reflected publicly. A feeling was expressed that the peace process is dominated by men and that women are being sidelined. Other submissions argued that women should be involved in promoting discussion on structures, a Bill of Rights, and a new constitution which would have equal rights for all, including women.

The international community, submissions argued, has an important role to play in conflict resolution in Ireland. This was proposed specifically in the form of mediators, intermediaries and guarantors. Others suggested that the Dublin government should harness the good will of the international community, especially the USA and the EU, in support of the peace process.

The Peace Commission was an important initiative. I commend everyone who participated. One theme which is prominent throughout the submissions is the overwhelming belief that a viable peace process is possible. I have never believed that the search for peace in Ireland would be straightforward. Nor will it be achieved easily; centuries of conflict cannot be unraveled easily.

To some extent these difficulties are reflected in the range of submissions Sinn Féin received. But as I've said above, if there is one message emerging from the submissions, it is that a viable peace process can be put in place, and that everyone involved in the conflict must be involved in that process.

To summarize, a number of opinions were expressed on conflict resolution which I hope will lead to further debate and discussion. These are:

- The need for the British government to recognize that there must be political change and alter its policy to suit that reality.
- The need to achieve a total demilitarization.
- The need to discuss the Unionist veto and the issue of consent.
- The need to debate and discuss the steps needed to develop the peace process.
- The need to address the grievances of the Northern Nationalist community, including discrimination, collusion and Irish language rights.
- The need for Republicans to outline their vision of a united Ireland.
- The need for women to play a central role in the peace process.
- The need for Republicans and Nationalists to persuade the Unionists that they have nothing to fear from a united Ireland.

- The need to involve the international community in the peace process.
- The need for Republicans, Nationalists and Democrats to agree to a strategy for the attainment of national self-determination.

The Parade, The Protestants, and The Pope

Each year many Protestants commemorate the Battle of the Boyne during the "marching season."

BELFAST IS A ghost town. At least Nationalist Belfast is. Anyone with the money or the sense is away. To Donegal or Omeath or the Glens of Antrim or further afield. I've neither money nor sense. So I've stayed. Me and the Orangemen. It's the Twelfth, you see. The big day out for the Loyal Orange Lodges. The big day in for the rest of us. Some elements of revisionist thinking in Ireland project Orange parades as a quaint folk custom. If we had a normal society here, that's what they would be. Speed the day.

"What's that?" you ask. "What's the Twelfth?"

Well, now, where will I start? The Twelfth? The Twelfth of July is when the semi-secret sectarian Grand Orange Order commemorates the Battle of the Boyne, and as Orangemen see it, "the triumph of the forces of Protestantism over Rome, and the securing of civil and religious liberty."

The Twelfth actually happened on the First. That is, the Battle of Boyne took place on the first of July. I remind you of this little historical point just to be petty. But it's not the only contradiction. The Battle of the Boyne was not about religion at all. It was about power: European power. In Orange mythology, King Billy is the hero of Protestantism. In fact, he was supported by the Pope. Yup! That's not a misprint. Pope Innocent supported the Dutchman William against James after the English parliament sacked James, and invited William to take on the job. James teamed up with the King of France to try to get the throne back, and he and William fought for it in Ireland. The Pope and the rest wanted to curb the power of France. The Pope paid part of King Billy's expenses. (We're paying for that since.) When news of William's victory at the Boyne reached Rome, a *Te Deum* was sung at the Vatican, and there were celebrations in the other main Catholic cities as well.

So there you are. That's what is celebrated here every year at this time. Of course, the Orange Order tend to ignore all the above.

What they really celebrate is that, after the Battle of the Boyne, the Protestant Ascendancy was established by depriving everyone else. After the Boyne – and the grand alliance 'twixt Pope and King Billy – all religions were banned except the Episcopalian Church. Religious tolerance was dropped when the English broke the Treaty of Limerick. This period marked the point when the old Gaelic system was finally forced to its knees. That's what the Orange parades are all about. That's why they are triumphalist.

That's why the Orangemen march arrogantly through areas where they are unwelcome. That's why the Orange bands play loudest and most aggressively outside Catholic churches. The catch cries and rallying calls are well known, ranging from "We Are the People" to "Croppies Lie Down" to "No Surrender, Not an Inch," to "F— the Pope," and worse. Good *craic*, only, like the Ku Klux Klan, they're not joking. That's why it is no accident that one of the sparks which ignited this protracted phase of the Troubles was caused in Derry in 1969 when the Orangemen parading on the walls of the city threw pennies down at Catholics gathered below in the Bogside area. 1969 was not 1690. The croppies had had enough. We were lying down no longer. The rest is history.

By the way, I have no problem with Orange parades. I have problems at their incursions into sensitive areas, and I have no time for the sectarian overtones of their cheerleaders, but I have defended their right to march, and I will do so again, provided that they are not involved in coat-trailing exercises.

I watched an Orange parade today. They didn't see me, needless to say. I felt sorry for them. However objectionable their sectarian swagger – and it is very objectionable – today they have little to swagger about.

Until the late 1960s the Unionists were permitted – through a one-party state – to get on with the business of protecting British and Unionist interests in the North of Ireland. They did so by repressing dissent. That was the era when Stormont was proclaimed "A Protestant Parliament for a Protestant People," and when the Prime Minister said of Catholics: "I wouldn't have one about the place."

The civil rights struggle in 1968 was the beginning of the end of all that. The civil rights demands put the Orange State to a test. The state failed the test, and reacted with terrorism against the moderate and modest demands being put to it. In 1969 the state died. It was revived by the British government, and since then it has been kept alive on a life support unit of British military force and patronage.

That was twenty-five years ago. How then stands the Orange State today? How are the Unionists?

The Unionist leadership continues to feel more secure with the failed policies of the past and present than with the prospect of building a better, a different future. Yet partition has not only failed the Nationalists; it has failed Unionists. It has encouraged in them a paranoid distrust of all Nationalists. Despite deals between some Unionists and the British government, most do not trust the British. Consequently Unionists face a future of unremitting uncertainty dependent upon the whim of whichever government is in power, fearful of the encroaching tide of history which year by year undermines the artificial majority created in 1921. Part of the tragedy of partition is that the dynamism of the Nationalist and Unionist people was diverted from the creation of one healthy and diverse political unit on this island.

The economic, political, and cultural health of the nation suffered by the division. It is time to heal the wound.

Sinn Féin wants to unite the people of Ireland. We do not seek to coerce any section of our people. The Unionist leadership must demonstrate the leadership that it has sadly lacked to date. How will that happen? What must change to persuade the Unionist leadership to break with the past?

As long as Unionists are assured of a veto over change, then there is neither reason nor incentive for them to move beyond the laager wall. So far, therefore, Unionism hasn't produced an F.W. de Klerk. Yet the failures of their present leadership, their increasingly precarious position within the Union, the very selfishness of their British government, which their votes sustain, are compelling arguments for a new Unionist leadership, a leadership which can secure the rights of the Unionists in the context of changing political realities, a leadership which has the ability to look to the future, to stand on its own feet, to lead its people forward.

The Unionist veto, provided by Britain, is a negative power, the power only to say "No!" It sustains a leadership whose only political vocabulary is "No surrender," "Not an inch," and "Ulster says

No." Whose political program is confined to its periodical "Save Ulster" campaigns.

What is required is a new and imaginative approach that tilts the balance away from this negative power of veto and towards the positive power of democracy, agreement, and consent. The British government holds the veto. Its removal would unlock the situation and create the catalyst for real change.

Nationalists do not trust the British establishment, nor do they trust a Unionist leadership that still argues for a return to the old Stormont days. Nationalists have lived in a vicious and violent statelet for seventy odd years. We were forced, at the point of a gun, into an arbitrarily created Unionist state. We were given no choice. We were not asked for our consent. We had no veto, no domestic or international protector of our rights. We were victimized and discriminated against, oppressed and imprisoned, denied our aspirations and our political validity. We were treated as second-class citizens, dehumanized, and driven from our official history. Yet we are still here, still determined, and still willing to be generous, still willing to embrace our Protestant brothers and sisters. Eager to join with them in building a new beginning for all of us.

The Unionists have fears about their future in a united Ireland. Some of these fears are undoubtedly genuine. Others, like the Orange version of the Battle of the Boyne, may be based on myths. It is time that someone in the Unionist ranks spelled out their fears. So that the rest of us can set about allaying those fears. The Orangemen should have as much right – not an inch more – as all other citizens. That Battle of the Boyne is as much an influence and a part of Irish history as the Siege of Limerick, the Famine, or the Easter Uprising of 1916. It is part of what we are, and no part of what we are should be suppressed or marginalized.

Nationalist Nightmare Must End

On Sunday July 24, Sinn Féin held a national delegate conference in Letterkenny, Co. Donegal to review the progress of the peace process and agree the party's response to the Downing Street Declaration.

THE SINN FÉIN national delegate conference is coming at a crucial stage and at a very delicate phase in the peace process. It is a useful time, therefore, to review the situation, and to consider also the US angle. For peace in Ireland is an American issue – especially an Irish-American issue. There is no doubt that one of the successes of the Irish lobby in the US has been the manner in which this has featured on the White House agenda. Peace in Ireland is clearly an issue for President Clinton and it has the potential to become one of his major foreign policy concerns. He has recently returned from a highly successful and historic visit to a reunited Germany. In the Europe visited by Mr. Clinton, borders and border controls are disappearing.

In contrast, Britain's artificial border in Ireland is being increasingly militarized and British installations are being built higher and stronger. The border which cuts across several hundred miles of Irish countryside divides the Irish nation, separates local communities and families, and is a block on the political and economic development of this island.

The current international climate is conducive to the resolution of conflicts. This must be harnessed in support of the efforts for peace in Ireland. This is particularly important in the US, and especially so in the months ahead.

In our first joint statement in April of 1993, John Hume and I acknowledged that the "most pressing issue facing the people of Ireland and Britain today is the question of lasting peace and how it can best be achieved." We are not the first to identify this as a priority. The absolute failure of past policies and political structures, imposed by successive British governments, has contributed to a bitter conflict which has endured in one form or another for centuries. Nationalists, coerced into the northern state without our consent, have been forced to endure decades of injustice and discrimination, and the Nationalist nightmare continues today to inflict considerable pain.

Out of this experience, Irish Republicans and Northern Nationalists are convinced that there can be no more internal settlements. This has been acknowledged even by the British government. It is clear that the Nationalist nightmare must end. The division of Irish people by an imposed border must also be brought to an end. How can this be achieved? How can we mend the fractured and hostile relationships between Irish people and between Ireland and Britain?

These are the core issues which must be tackled, difficult though they are, if progress and peace is to be achieved. There must be political change, fundamental change. The status quo, which has heaped indignities on Nationalists, has to go. A solution can only be found in a functioning inclusive democracy agreed and established by all the people of this island. The creation of a new agreement which can resolve this conflict is only achievable and viable if it can earn and enjoy the allegiance of the different traditions on this island. This is the real challenge facing us all.

Sinn Féin shares the concern of other Nationalists about Unionist sensitivities. We know that the future from a Unionist perspective is fraught with many uncertainties. We understand and seek to take account of these fears. At the same time, the coercion of Irish Nationalists cannot continue.

Progress demands that there can be no veto providing the British or the Unionists with an advantage behind which stagnation and the conditions for conflict can continue to exist. And both governments must play an active and positive role in shaping new arrangements which can facilitate this. In particular, the British government must recognize that it cannot on the one hand assert its neutrality and say it is for no particular predetermined outcome, while at the same time saying that it will stand by the union.

In this context and as part of future negotiations, the British government should re-examine the Government of Ireland Act and all its provisions. It should facilitate and enhance the search for equality and peace by agreeing, as part of the peace process, to legislate away those provisions in the Government of Ireland Act which prevent political and constitutional change.

As we face into our conference, it is important to restate Sinn Féin's position. In our effort to move the peace process forward positively, Sinn Féin is prepared to put into play what we have to offer. This includes our substantial electoral and democratic mandate, our total commitment to establishing peace, and whatever political influence we have to secure a political package so that the IRA can make judgments in relation to the future conduct of its armed campaign. The reality, of course, is that we are not the IRA and it will take its own counsel on these issues. However, it must be remembered that Sinn Féin has helped formulate proposals which have been enough to move the IRA to say publicly that their acceptance by the British government would provide the basis for peace.

We must build on the positive achievements of the last eighteen months. There is a clear need to press ahead. In addition, and while doing this – and there is clearly a US dimension to this also – we must look at more specific short-term and intermediate term objectives to develop the potential which the process has already provided for addressing issues of immediate concern.

It means ensuring that there is parity of esteem and equality of treatment for all Irish people. In the short to medium term, we need to redress the grievances which are symptoms of the conflict here. For Sinn Féin this means strengthening the Nationalist agenda. How do we do this? In a number of ways.

- We must ensure by our efforts that there is no return to Unionist domination over local Nationalist communities in the Six Counties. What is abundantly clear, and Unionist politicians must tell themselves and their supporters, is that there is no going back to the days of Stormont. There can never again be an internal settlement.
- Sinn Féin activists must be able to represent and speak for our communities in conditions of peace, un-interfered with by the British military or the RUC, free of personal harassment and free from the threat of the death squads. The censorship laws which are an affront to democracy and a denial of human rights must be scrapped.
- It is time that a real effort was made to end job discrimination and economic inequalities against Catholics. British policy has made no significant dent in this fundamental problem.

- The underlying sectarian bias against Nationalist areas in the allocation of economic investment must be brought to an end.
- The rights of *gaeilgeoirí* (Irish speakers) must be fully recognized and an equality of status for the Irish language, including funding for schools, must be secured.
- The speedy release of all long-term prisoners, pending a full amnesty for all political prisoners, must become a matter of urgent concern.
- The repressive legislation which saw over one hundred coercion acts in the nineteenth century, the Special Powers Act for most of the twentieth century, and currently the Prevention of Terrorism Act (PTA), EPA and Public Order Act, must come to an end.
- The links between British intelligence agencies and the Loyalist death squads must be severed. Collusion at all its levels must end.

These objectives are all winnable. But it will mean a hard and difficult struggle, requiring co-operation between Republicans and Nationalists. It will require the support of the Dublin government and our allies internationally. Support, particularly in the US, for justice and democratic rights campaigns in Ireland has been instrumental in moving these campaigns towards their goals.

The obvious and best example of this is the MacBride Principles campaign which attempted to lay down standards for fair employment between Catholic and Protestant. That campaign put the issue of discrimination back on the political agenda here and forced the British government to admit that there is discrimination. The example set by the exemplary work done in the US on this issue can be repeated on all these other issues.

These are achievable goals which can provide a focus for friends of Ireland in the US. This will make a real contribution to the peace process and help to increase the momentum for change and move the search for peace substantially forward.

In pursuit of a settlement and a lasting peace there are a number of elements which I believe are essential for success. Firstly, the policies and structures of the past have failed. There can be no peace based on the failures. The status quo must be fundamentally changed. Secondly, there must be a commitment to a process of inclusive dialogue which embraces all of the parties of the conflict and excludes no one. Thirdly, we need an inclusive political process without preconditions which contains the dynamic towards a peace settlement set within a time-frame.

The road to peace, with justice and dignity, is a difficult one to travel. There are, and there will be, roadblocks along the way. I do not know how well this is understood in the US. It must be difficult, especially given the manner in which British propaganda functions.

One thing, however, remains clear for those who wish to see it. Republicans are committed to the goal of a lasting peace in our country, and the Sinn Féin conference will mark another important milestone on the pathway to peace. There will still be some distance to travel after this conference, but positive action in the US, as in the past, by Irish America will help to shorten the road.

Peace Hopes Are
Very Much Alive

Sinn Féin gave its long-awaited response to the Downing Street Declaration at its delegate conference on Sunday, July 24.

THE LAST YEAR has seen many new political developments, and measurable progress has been made on a number of key issues. Not least among these is the interest in and support for the peace process from Irish America. This is not only welcome and very essential; it could also, in the phase we have entered into, be a major influence in underpinning and enhancing efforts to move the situation forward.

The Letterkenny conference considered three motions from the Sinn Féin Árd Chomhairle. These encapsulated the day's business which was divided into three main sections – a review of the peace process; an assessment of the Downing Street Declaration; the way forward.

At the end of these discussions, Lucilita Breathnach, Martin McGuinness and I summed up our conclusions for the assembled media. In her comments, Lucilita concentrated on the progress which has been made so far. She stressed the need to continue building upon this.

"In the weeks and months ahead let us apply ourselves to using the accumulated experience we have gained throughout twenty-five years of political campaigning," she said.

Martin McGuinness emphasized the unity and confidence of Republicans. He said, "In the past twenty-five years we have faced many challenges together. We have been through much together; we have achieved much together and we should be proud of those achievements. We can and we will bring this struggle to a successful conclusion.

"Our message today is clear. Republicans want peace. Republicans demand peace. Republicans are united, determined, and strong and looking to the future."

In my remarks, I outlined our agreed attitude to the Downing Street Declaration. I appealed to the Unionists to join the search for a settlement, and I called upon the British government to seize the opportunity for peace and not to squander it.

In giving our considered view of the Downing Street Declaration, we were conscious of the fact that the Declaration is a step in the peace process. We are now looking forward to the next steps. These must deal in a fundamental way with the core constitutional issue as well as the secondary issues. In this, we and the two governments are at one. We are all agreed that the Declaration is a step, not a solution. We are in a new phase in the search for a lasting peace in Ireland, and I am optimistic that this phase can advance the peace process.

In the immediate aftermath of the conference, most of the anti-Republican elements here in Ireland and in Britain have attempted to put a negative spin on our views, and this was reflected in some of the headlines. I was asked if I was disappointed by this reaction. I was neither surprised nor disappointed. The coverage, at least in the Irish print and broadcasting media, was much more thorough and balanced than the headlines. My only disagreement is with those headlines which claimed that the peace process was over. This is patent rubbish. The peace process is very much alive.

As for the negative political reaction; it was hugely predictable and from all the usual suspects – that is, from a mixture of politicians who have constantly sniped at the peace process and who have never supported it. On the contrary, their contributions have been consistently begrudging and hostile. They have also significantly failed to put forward any constructive alternative to the suggestions made by Sinn Féin or others engaged in the search for a settlement.

The peace process is on course, and we are determined to move it forward. Sinn Féin's position on the Downing Street Declaration is a balanced assessment. The two governments never said that the Declaration was a solution. The governments acknowledged the right of any party to take whatever views it wanted, and our approach has been to identify the positive elements which can be built upon and to isolate the areas of concern which need to be overcome. This is a positive and considered approach.

The Declaration was the response by the two governments to the developing Irish Peace Initiative. From their perspective the Declaration was an important development, and from our perspective it marked a stage in the peace process. In its positive elements it suggests a potentially significant change in the approach of the governments to resolving the conflict in Ireland, and we welcome this.

The success of other peace accords shows that the necessary dynamic to move out of conflict must be found in the framework, the time-scale, the processes and the objectives of a peace process, and all of these essential elements must be based upon principles which are founded firmly in democracy and justice.

It is my optimistic belief that the situation can be moved on, and I outlined how this could be possible when I spoke at the conference on the need for demilitarization. I am always mindful of the terrible tragedy of this conflict and of the heavy price paid by all of our people, in lives lost and scarred, in justice denied and in families separated. Peace demands change. Fundamental change. An end to conflict will require a process of demilitarization. This is not solely the responsibility of Republicans. I have pointed out many times Sinn Féin's willingness to play a constructive role in this matter.

I welcomed last week's statement by the IRA leadership. I interpret it as a clear commitment that, if the proper conditions can be created, the IRA will be flexible. That is the challenge facing all of us, and particularly those who have invested time and energy in the search for a peace settlement. It is particularly a challenge for the leadership of Sinn Féin. It is one we will not shrink from. That is, to create the conditions in which the IRA can act upon its clearly stated commitments and others will act upon their responsibilities so that negotiated settlement can be agreed and the people of Ireland can leave conflict behind us. The public interest now will be whether or not the situation can be further developed. The answer is yes.

"There Is No Collusion!" Targets Told, "You're on Your Own"

Collusion between Loyalist groups and the British Army and the RUC in Northern Ireland continued to be a very real threat for the Nationalist community, as the tragic death of Kathleen O'Hagan illustrated on August 7, 1994.

A FEW WEEKS ago, the Royal Ulster Constabulary (RUC) warned Nationalists from the Short Strand, a Catholic area in East Belfast, that their details were in the hands of the Loyalist death squads. Readers may ask, "Details? What details?" You are not on your own. Those concerned ask the same question. In vain.

The details are contained in British intelligence files. Unlike their American counterparts, citizens here have no rights to information, so none of us have a clue what these files contain. We do know that most of us have one, or maybe two, or perhaps more. We are never told why we deserve to have our details on British intelligence files.

We do know that these files are passed regularly to the Loyalist death squads. We are never told how this happens. We are never told who is responsible or where the files are stored and who has access or who is investigating these matters or what disciplinary measures have been taken.

Instead, we are told that there is no collusion.

Periodically, an individual member of the British crown forces will be charged with "passing information to terrorists." If it gets to court, he or she may be fined or receive a suspended sentence. Sometimes they are not even suspended from duty. Occasionally, if their offense is a notably controversial one, they may be forced to resign and thus become former crown force members. All very convenient.

This weekend a number of people from the upper Andersontown area of West Belfast have contacted me and their local elected councilor, Alex Maskey. Over the last week they have been visited by the RUC and told that their personal files are also in the hands of the death squads. No explanations given. No apologies offered.

Readers might presume that citizens here may be able to get some means of protection from the state. From the RUC? They can't be trusted.

Perhaps a firearm? Maybe? The only problem is that you have to apply to the RUC for a permit. Yes, the same RUC whose files are given to the Loyalists. Do they normally give firearm permits to Nationalists whose files are in the hands of the death squads? Nope! That's highly unlikely. Why? Because you are a security risk.

"A security risk!" you might exclaim. "I'm on a death list!"

Ah, but you're also on British intelligence files. That means you are a security risk! No permit. And no assistance to defend your home and your family. Oh, and there is no collusion.

****

Ask the family or neighbors of Kathleen O'Hagan. They are gathering now to wake Kathleen's remains in the O'Hagan family home in County Tyrone.

Kathleen O'Hagan was seven months pregnant. She and her unborn baby were shot to death in her isolated bungalow home, near Creggan, about twelve miles from Omagh, Co. Tyrone, in the early hours of the morning. Her husband Paddy was at a family celebration and returned home in the small hours of the morning to find that Loyalist death squads had been there before him. The back door of the house had been smashed down. His wife was slumped, bleeding, in the corner of their bedroom surrounded by her five young sons. The walls of the bedroom were peppered with bullet holes, some of which were close to the cot of their seventeen-month-old son. Eight-year-old Patrick O'Hagan cradled the body of his pregnant mother as she lay dying. A ten-pence coin was found on one of her eyes. It is unclear if this was dropped by the gunmen or the children.

Friends told yesterday how the children of Kathleen O'Hagan had recounted the horror of their mother's murder by the UVF (Ulster Volunteer Force). Patrick, the eldest in the family of five, debated with his six-year-old brother if they should contact the neighbors and tell them that their mother had been shot. They decided against this and the alarm was eventually raised by their father, Paddy, when he returned home.

Parish priest Fr. John Ryder, who visited the family home, described the scene as "an appalling sight."

"I expect the children would have heard the noise as the gunmen broke down the back door. She would have done her best to protect them," he said.

Paddy O'Hagan is a former Republican prisoner. The O'Hagan family were victims of constant harassment by the RUC and the British Army. The family and the neighbors suspect that elements of these forces were in collusion with Kathleen's killers.

****

All of this comes at a particularly sensitive and delicate time in the peace process. Other women have been killed, some by accident and some deliberately, but people here are understandably angry that an expectant mother would be a premeditated target.

The aim of the death squads is to terrorize as wide a section of Nationalist opinion as possible. They have no interest in a peace settlement or in a democratic resolution of this conflict. Undoubtedly this interest is shared by elements of the British military establishment, the intelligence services and their agents.

Collusion must be ended. There is an onus on the Dublin government and on progressive opinion in the US to focus attention on this fact of life and death in Ireland.

Seize the Moment!

John Hume and Gerry Adams made a joint statement on Sunday, August 28, 1994, following which Taoiseach Albert Reynolds also issued a statement. These served to urge the IRA towards their ceasefire which began at midnight on August 31, 1994.

TWO PHRASES DESCRIBE the situation here, as I write. One is the hoary cliché, a week is a long time in politics; the other is an opening line from Bobby Sands in his diary of the hunger strike when he wrote, I am standing on the threshold of another trembling world.

By the time you get to reading this column, the IRA may have announced a complete cessation to its operations. If this happens – and because I believe the IRA has a genuine commitment to the peace process, I am optimistic that it will – then all involved in creating this new situation are to be commended. More important, perhaps, will be the need – a pressing and urgent one – to ensure that this new situation is not squandered.

The recent round of speculation started last week when Sinn Féin invited the US delegation to meet with us to discuss the role of Irish America and the US in the evolving peace process. The delegation, led by Bruce Morrison, represented an important and representative section of US opinion. The meeting, one of a series of protracted discussions, was an important and positive one.

On Sunday, I met again with SDLP leader John Hume. This also was a good meeting during which we recommitted ourselves to the peace process. Afterwards, Mr. Hume and I issued a joint statement. As representatives of Nationalist opinion in the North of Ireland, this statement represents a crucial consensus. In conclusion, we said:

"In any new situation there is a heavy onus on the British government to respond positively, both in terms of the demilitarization of the situation and in assisting the search for an agreed Ireland by encouraging the process of national reconciliation.

"It is our informed opinion that the peace process remains firmly on course. We are, indeed, optimistic that the situation can be moved tangibly forward."

That evening Taoiseach Albert Reynolds issued a comprehensive statement.

On Monday, I disclosed that I had provided another assessment of the developing situation to the IRA leadership, at its request. This assessment updated the one I had provided a month ago in the run up to the Sinn Féin conference in Letterkenny.

All of this movement represents an important, perhaps a vital contribution to the peace process. I want to deal here only with two elements of this process. These are firstly, the role of Irish America and the US administration, and secondly, the role of the British government.

Sinn Féin has always recognized the importance of the international community in helping to create the conditions which can resolve this conflict. In particular, we have pointed to the positive role which Irish America and the US administration can play.

Political and popular opinion in the United States can and must, as the peace process moves forwards, play an increasingly central role in the search for an inclusive, negotiated and democratic settlement in Ireland. There is an onerous responsibility on everyone to seize new opportunities to move the situation on.

Irish Republicans have shown a willingness to look forward. This must be matched by a willingness by others to move forward. Champions of freedom in the US, including Republican supporters and other campaign groups, have given great service to the Irish cause, some for decades. There is a need now for everyone to redouble their efforts. There is also a need for others to come into the struggle. Supporters of the Irish peace process in the US have given a lead. The opportunities that they have helped to create must not be wasted.

When I was in the US, I made a number of commitments. These were not made lightly. In my entire involvement in struggle, I have always sought to honor any commitments made by me or those I represent. Others must now do likewise. Urgently.

So what must be done if a peace settlement is to be built? I am an Irish Republican. I believe that the Irish people have the wit, the intelligence and the right to govern ourselves. I believe that the British government is the root cause of the conflict in this country. I believe that that government has no right to interfere in Irish affairs. I understand the fears and anxieties of Unionists. I have a view of the British government's responsibility for this situation and of the need for London to play a constructive role in resolving these difficulties.

If the peace process is to succeed then the British government must be moved to set aside the failures of the past. There must be a new beginning. Tory party political considerations, leadership problems at Westminster or pacts with the Unionists should not be allowed to prevent the creation of an inclusive, united and peaceful society in Ireland. Mr. Major must take measures to end the deadlock by creating a proper climate for inclusive and meaningful negotiation.

In my view, the IRA has shown a flexible attitude to the peace process. Indeed, all the initiatives of recent years have come from Nationalist Ireland. Mr. Major needs to respond to this. Sinn Féin engaged in the peace process with clear objectives and with our eyes wide open to the dangers of what has been a consistently high risk strategy. The whole approach of the British government to the question of negotiations with Sinn Féin is totally unacceptable and needs to be drastically changed. And rhetoric will not be enough. There must be fundamental, political and constitutional change.

But this is not an occasion for me to denigrate the London government for its policy towards Ireland or towards Sinn Féin or those we represent. And despite the threatening knee-jerk reaction of the Unionists to the current developments, this is not the time to be derogatory about them. It is a time to extend the hand of friendship and to urge dialogue and calm reflection.

Anglo-Irish relationships have reached a decisive moment. I call upon all to ensure that the process towards democracy is rapid and uninterrupted. We have waited too long for our freedom. We can wait no longer. To relax our efforts now would be a mistake which generations to come will not be able to forgive. Seize the moment!

Like Us, Paisley Was Also Unfairly Treated by British

Although Dublin greeted the peace with enthusiasm, British hair-splitting and word games slowed the peace process from the outset. On Tuesday, September 6, while Albert Reynolds, John Hume and Gerry Adams shook hands outside Government Buildings, Rev. Ian Paisley was being told to leave a Downing Street meeting.

THE IRA'S CESSATION is now two weeks old. Governments throughout the world have welcomed this initiative, and there has been universal recognition of the historic opportunity which has been created. In Ireland, and especially in Nationalist Ireland, there is a palpable sense of expectation and confidence. This was given a significant boost by the recent meeting at Government Buildings in Dublin between Albert Reynolds, John Hume and myself.

The Unionists, despite some apparently pragmatic signals from the UUP (Ulster Unionist Party), have protested against the cessation.

The British government? Well, the British government is behaving the way the British government always does on the question of Ireland. I am sure that large sections of British public opinion are bewildered and disappointed by John Major's response. He and his ministers have engaged in word games over the IRA announcement.

For the first week or so of the cessation, I and other Sinn Féin spokespersons sought to reassure Mr. Major when he queried the meaning of the IRA statement. However, despite the best efforts of Mr. Reynolds, John Hume, President Clinton, Dick Spring and US Vice-President Al Gore, London's nit-picking continues. Each time someone from Sinn Féin tries to deal with the British requirements, Mr. Major or Mr. Mayhew or Mr. Hurd change their version of what is required. It quickly became obvious that their confusion is contrived. Britannia waives the rules!

In the immediate wake of the IRA announcement, my colleagues and I were conscious that the British government may have been concerned to allay Unionist sensitivities. We were aware of Mr.

Major's leadership difficulties and of the problems within his own right wing. We knew that the history of the peace process is marked by reluctant and minimal movement by London in response to initiatives which have *all* come from Nationalist Ireland. We have learned to be patient, but this does not mean that we are fooled by the British stance. There should be no doubt but that the niggling and hair-splitting, the claims of confusion by senior British ministers, are nothing more or less than tactical maneuvering.

Other developments – not unconnected to the British stance – include a statement from Loyalist death squads which outlined a number of conditions, including assurances on the constitutional permanency of the Union. This statement was welcomed by some usually voraciously anti-Republican elements. It was followed by a bomb at Sinn Féin Councilor John Hurl's home, and earlier this week by a bomb at Connolly railway station in Dublin. Many people here are concerned by the real threat which these attacks present. There is concern, also, that the death squads which did not have a bomb-making capacity or expertise or resources now suddenly and mysteriously have all these requirements. Given the reality of collusion, many suspect the hand of British military intelligence in these recent operations.

Then there was – on the day of the Dublin meeting of Irish Nationalism – the Ian Paisley debacle at 10 Downing Street. The perception of this incident is that John Major threw Ian Paisley out because Mr. Paisley refused to accept John Major's word. While understandably many people relished the contrast between the London and Dublin events and few felt sorry for Paisley, in my view John Major was wrong. I am implacably opposed to Ian Paisley's mixture of religious/political fundamentalism. But I am also opposed to the British government seeking to demonize any section of our people.

Mr. Paisley – Dr., no – needs to be stood up to. But so does Mr. Molyneaux. Knockabout English political farce in the drawing room of 10 Downing Street is no substitute for a political strategy which aims to deal with Unionism on a democratic basis, and which seeks to bring Unionism and its leaders into this century. This cannot be done by exclusion, by marginalization or by demonization. One only has to look at the failure of these strategies by Britain against Sinn Féin to see the truth of this assertion.

The short-sightedness of the Downing Street farce was brought into sharp relief when Patrick Mayhew, days later, addressed an Orange Lodge. This unprecedented "official visit" – there has always been a relationship between Toryism and Orangeism – was to reassure the Orangemen that the Union was safe. I myself had no objections to Mayhew's visit. He can speak to whoever he wants. But I do know that many Catholics, victims of Orange triumphalism, were hurt by this episode.

I spent a morning in Ormeau Road and the Markets area of South Belfast. These areas are often visited by Orange marches. Indeed there was one particular incident – condemned by Mayhew – when an Orange parade engaged in provocative coat-trailing outside the bookmaker's shop where five Catholics were killed by the death squads.

As well as all of this, there has been a continuous "battle" with the British over border crossings. As quickly as local people open up these blocked or cratered roads, the British Army have been closing them again. Mr. Reynolds has quite rightly called for a programatic opening of border crossings. Hopefully, sense will prevail and the militaristic mandarins of Whitehall will realize that knee-jerking, quibbling or hair-splitting have no positive part to play in a peace process.

Two Mondays ago I went to Belfast courthouse. I had been there before, of course, both in the dock and as an observer. On Monday I was there in the latter capacity for a judgment in the case of the Ballymurphy Seven, young men from the Ballymurphy area of West Belfast who have already spent three Christmases in British custody. Two of them were released earlier this year. The remaining five claimed their alleged confessions were forced from them during interrogation.

On Monday, two more were released and in a contemptible judgment Mr. Justice Kerr ruled that Tony Garland, Hugh McLoughlin and Michael Beck should go to trial. Already they have served the equivalent of a six-year sentence. They have all consistently protested their innocence. The scene in the courtroom was heartbreaking, as the families of the five men were torn between relief at the release of Danny Pettigrew and Stephen McMulland, and disbelief and anger at the continued imprisonment of the others.

Many independent organizations have expressed grave concern about the alleged confessions in the Ballymurphy Seven case. Indeed, in 1991, when these confessions were obtained, the UN Committee Against Torture expressed concern about the legal regime governing interrogation and the lack of safeguards for citizens. These concerns were fully vindicated by yesterday's judgment.

Making peace is not easy. On every front the British continue to drag their feet. Despite all this, Sinn Féin remains committed to moving the situation forward. There is plenty of work to be done and lots of room for optimism. There is also room for US opinion to engage in any of the areas of concern which I have touched upon here. I hope to be there with you to discuss these matters before too long. In the meantime, as well as everything else, I've got to go to an All-Ireland football final. Sorry Dublin. Up Down!

First Major, Then Maguire ...Another Busy Week in the North

John Major's trip to the North was a small move in the right direction that needed to be immediately followed with inclusive talks. But, in the short term, Sam Maguire's trip north after the All-Ireland football final gave plenty of reason for celebration.

SO DOWN WON the All-Ireland. It rained throughout the match and while that restricted the players, it did little to dampen the spectators' expectations. There was a huge crowd of Down supporters in Croke Park, outnumbering the Dubs. Or at least the Down flags outnumbered the Dublin ones. I won't bother you with any lengthy discourse on the match. Suffice to say that the Down forwards won the first half and, despite Dublin's valiant efforts, the Down backs won the second half. While I would have been devastated if Down had lost, I must confess that I felt sorry for Dublin. Undoubtedly the All-Ireland – in hurling, camogie and football – is the jewel in the crown of the GAA calendar. It is a great event. All the more so when the winning cup known as the "Sam Maguire" comes north.

John Major also came north last week. Well, he came to Belfast. He made what was billed as an important announcement. Insofar as the Belfast speech marked the engagement in the peace process by London, Mr. Major's address was significant. It was also unimaginative and ungenerous. Mr. Major announced an end to the broadcasting ban which censored Republican voters. He ordered the opening of some border roads. He announced a referendum in the Six Counties on any outcome of talks.

The removal of the broadcast ban and the decision to open ten out of around 250 border crossings is a small but welcome first step by the British government. But other steps need to be taken by Mr. Major now.

The process of demilitarization must be accelerated. All border roads should be re-opened immediately and compensation paid to local communities whose economic well-being and lives have been detrimentally affected. Militarization, so apparent in the legal and judicial system, British Army and RUC patrols, watchtowers and heavily-fortified bases, should end. The British occupied area is under a permanent state of emergency which is based upon a wide array of repressive legislation. This should be scrapped.

At the heart of the peace process is the need for inclusive dialogue and negotiations. This next step should be delayed no longer by Mr. Major. The British government position is at odds with popular, political and international opinion. In his Belfast speech, Mr. Major has acknowledged the "very different circumstances" which now exist. He should act on his own assessment.

Mr. Major's reference to a referendum in the Six Counties is both premature and presumptuous. The six-county statelet is an artificial and gerrymandered political entity with an inbuilt and permanent Unionist majority. The British government-imposed veto based on this artificial majority is both undemocratic and unacceptable. Discussion on how agreement would be measured, when the search for agreement has not yet begun, is therefore premature. All these matters should properly be the subject of discussion in a process of inclusive negotiations which should begin as soon as possible.

An interview with Taoiseach Albert Reynolds in the English Sunday *Observer* also received widespread publicity here. Two points in particular received attention. In one of these, Mr. Reynolds dealt with the need to cut back on the deployment of the British Army. He also suggested that Irish unity would not come for another generation.

I agree with the thrust of his remarks in respect of British troop levels. British crown forces need to declare a "complete cessation" of military operations. Mr. Reynolds' other comments about Irish unity are a matter of opinion about the time this will take. There is no doubt about the need for a united Ireland.

From Sinn Féin's point of view, the objective of negotiations is to replace British jurisdiction with Irish jurisdiction based on agreement among the Irish people. There are, of course, a number of models upon which such an Irish jurisdiction could be based. Sinn Féin wants to see a thirty-two-county Republic – this is also Fianna Fáil party policy. It will take time to bring this about, and while there may be varied views on the length of time involved, I am sure that Mr. Reynolds would not wish to delay such a development.

There has also been a renewed focus on the US dimension to the peace process. The British government appear to be re-running the old visa battle which preceded my last visit to New York. They are also engaging in some quite silly spin-doctoring. For example, BBC World Service proclaimed that I would not be meeting President Clinton during my trip and that this was a considerable diplomatic breakthrough for Whitehall. I am sure President Clinton was as surprised (and disappointed?) as I was to hear this. We have no plans to meet at this time.

Another "victory" for British diplomacy is the visit by representatives of the Ulster Unionist Party. London is making great play of the fact that the Unionists are going to the US before I do. What they have not made clear is how this sequence is important. It certainly is of no consequence to me.

What all this shows, of course, is how sensitive – some would say paranoid – the British government is about international opinion, and particularly US opinion. At this time, London is clearly isolated. This is because of the universal recognition of the IRA initiative which is in marked contrast to London's hesitant response. However, this development is only useful if it can be factored into the peace process in a positive way so that it adds to the momentum for a democratic and negotiated peace settlement. Britain clearly understands the importance of US opinion and of the need to contain Irish-American influence.

In the period ahead as the peace process develops we will, all of us, get a real sense of the power of Irish-American opinion, with all its constituent parts. There is a need therefore, throughout the US, to consolidate the gains of the peace process by building support for a new and agreed Ireland. There is clearly room for building on the need for the British to demilitarize the occupied area and for London to create parity of esteem and equality of opportunity for all citizens. The good work so far against visa denial and for the right of US citizens to invite Irish Republicans to travel to the US to explain our position can be consolidated by initiating and encouraging inclusive debate at all levels throughout North America. I will return to these issues in more detail in the future.

For now I'm off to welcome Sam Maguire across the border. After that, I'm going to apply for my visa.

An Exhilarating (and Exhausting) US Tour

Gerry Adams visited many US and Canadian cities during October 1994. Writing from Toronto, he recalled some of the highlights of the tour.

THERE WERE SOME poignantly sad moments to my visit to the US – one at Ellis Island and another at Arlington Cemetery.

We were taken to Ellis Island by the New York City Police. It was an interesting voyage across New York Harbor with Manhattan in the background. Ellis Island is the place that used to process all of the emigrants to the US. About one million Irish passed through there. The island is now a national park; the buildings have been developed as monuments, and the entire complex is a fitting remembrance to those who walked through its doors.

People from Leitrim and Dublin greeted me as our party was given a tour of this remarkable place. You get a real sense of the expectation, fear and apprehension of the emigrants as they were herded through a huge shed-like area for medical examination and scrutiny. Amid all the noise, commotion and hullabaloo, they would have been able to see across the harbor to the mainland and the land of hope which they had traveled so far to reach. Of course, some were held back, families were divided, names were changed.

Amid the exhibits of clothes, photographs, family heirlooms from Italy and Germany and Poland and Latvia, is a little delft plate of the four provinces of Ireland. In another section there is a shillelagh. One could imagine that anyone going away for good would take their most treasured possessions – a photograph of parents or family, a favorite item of clothing, a little personal memento. That is how the Irish came to America. Little wonder, then, that the first person processed through Ellis Island was an Irish woman, Annie Moore.

It was almost a week later when we went to Arlington Cemetery. We had spent the previous night at the home of the late Robert Kennedy. It was there that Vice-President Al Gore phoned, and it was a fitting place for me to receive his call. The following morning, Robert's daughter, Courtney Kennedy, took us to Arlington, where we visited her father's grave and the grave of John F. Kennedy.

Arlington might have been Milltown Cemetery. I was filled with thoughts of home and the visits to many other gravesides, but nothing could have prepared any of us for the miles and miles of white crosses of the young Americans who lost their lives in Vietnam in a futile war.

The frenetic pace of events from the time I landed at Boston to be greeted by Senator Edward Kennedy, until I left Los Angeles a fortnight later accompanied by state Senator Tom Hayden, left little room for reflection. My overall sense of all the events is of an intensity of welcome or interest or curiosity on the part of those whom we saw.

I don't think that anyone, apart from the team who accompanied me, will realize how many interviews, meetings, speeches or statements were involved in the trip. Nor will anyone get a sense of the insanity which gripped us at times. But for Richard McAuley, it was a dream come true. Richard has been the Sinn Féin public relations officer for fifteen years. The media were actually queuing up for information as the days went by. Richard became quieter, more self-content, even smug. He also adopted many American characteristics – introducing himself as Rich, for instance, and handing out business cards.

Another male member of our entourage – the anonymous one – took to collecting shower caps, shampoo and hair conditioners, and small bottles of Heinz ketchup. All of us were gravely embarrassed when a routine customs check led to the discovery of seventy-five shower caps in his suitcase.

We also had a corruptible wing to our tour group. One of our members increased his body weight by three stone, dining on clams, lobster, and other cordon bleu foodstuffs. He described himself as a gourmet. Others, who shall also remain anonymous, referred to him as the gorb.

In Springfield, Massachusetts, we met the Irish from the Dingle Peninsula and West Mayo. In Philadelphia, it was the people from Tyrone. In Cleveland, it was Mayo again. And so on and on, from city to city. People from the north, east, south and west of Ireland gave greetings in Irish or in soft southern tones, or in the stronger northern dialect. We also met Italian Americans, the Jewish community, Native Americans, Hispanics, and African Americans. The visit to Mrs. Rosa Parks in Detroit was a personal highlight for me. Of course, I have to mention my visit to the *Irish Voice* offices in Manhattan, which was the only place that we simultaneously received cake and champagne in all of the trip, and even a choice of two cakes, at that. And to meet all the faces behind the voices I've spoken to on the phone was a revelation.

There were also lots of heavy meetings. With Wall Street investors. With White House and State Department officials. With city or state or national legislators. In Washington we met the powerful and influential figures and committee chairpersons, from House Speaker Tom Foley to Senate Majority Leader George Mitchell to Minority Leader Bob Dole.

At street level – whenever we got to the streets – there was also good *craic*, and not just amongst the Irish, although they appear to be everywhere and quite eager to identify with us. But good wishes came also from cab drivers and from others we met on plane journeys and in the streets.

In the US there is, among the myriad of events, a new public focus and attention on Ireland. This is due not least to those who have labored for so long, but also to the new expectation. While this is most enthusiastic in Irish America, it is evident also in civic, political, media and economic opinion right across the US. I received many testimonials and honors during our tour. I accepted them all on behalf of those who struggle for freedom and justice and peace in Ireland. I commend everyone who made the visit so successful.

I'm writing this piece in Toronto on the last leg of the North American visit. As we arrived into Canada and as our plane landed in Vancouver, a group of Native American people met us. Women singers recognized our party and, as our plane landed, they sang a song of welcome. In many ways it was not just a fitting welcome to Canada, but also an evocative and poignant end to the US trip.

Over To You, Mr. Major

The Loyalist ceasefire was announced on October 13, 1994.
Next, it was the turn of London to do the right thing by the
Irish and British people, and engage in the peace process.

W HEN WE ARRIVED in Ireland last Saturday it was to Clare and not to Dublin. Dublin was fogbound. So, courtesy of Aer Lingus, and after a few hours' wait, our plane-load of, by this time, rather disgruntled passengers was dispatched by road to Baile Atha Cliath.

When we arrived there hours later it was to the sight of aircraft landing and departing willy-nilly in bright autumn sunshine. We didn't care. We were home and the long drive overland was a fitting, if protracted, end to a journey which started the previous day in Montreal and which had taken us through New York, Shannon, Limerick, Nenagh, Portlaoise, Dublin and eventually northbound to Belfast. It took more time to get from Shannon to Belfast than it took to get from New York to Shannon.

Canada was good to us. In British Vancouver a handful of Loyalists turned out to abuse me. Before that Gerard McGuigan was feeling homesick. The sight and sound of Loyalists cheered him up. Gerard was to become the last survivor of our tour party – the others had already deserted after Los Angeles. Hollywood was too much for them.

In Irish Vancouver the *craic* was mighty. So were the Mounties. It was the same in Toronto and Montreal. I spent Thanksgiving with my favorite aunt in Toronto. All the Canuck Adamses and in-laws gathered that day. The following night almost a thousand and four hundred people joined us. Not bad for a town which used to host the largest Orange parade anywhere.

The trees in Canada are terrific. They also are orange – or at least their leaves are at this time of the year. Autumn orange and yellow and red and all the shades of rust in between. They are like the Irish. Everywhere!

Quebec has its own Ellis Island but here the story is more tragic. Grosse Isle is where the sick from the coffin ships came. Tens of thousands died there in the fever tents and the quarantine camps.

Thousands of Irish died also in Montreal. The people of Quebec gave homes to the Irish orphans. They also allowed them to keep their own names. So it is till this day that among French speaking Quebecois there are Ryans and O'Neills and MacMahons. Survivors of the famine.

Montreal is a mixture of Paris and Amsterdam with few of the sky-scrapers of its USA cousins and little of the fast pace of these cities; more a cheerful European bustle, especially in the beautiful Indian-summer sunshine. We had, as elsewhere, a very busy time and a hectic schedule. I also had the 'flu. Yeuk! The Montreal variety.

It was while we were there that the Loyalists called their cease-fire. I got wind of it the day before the announcement. It was widely semaphored in advance in Belfast. I was delighted to welcome this development which represents a very important stage in the demilitarization strand of the peace process.

The IRA leadership had taken the first courageous step on August 31. This placed the onus on the British government and the Loyalists. The Loyalist cessation was a result of the IRA initiative. Now the British Army and the other crown forces are the only armed faction engaged in military operations in Ireland. Even though there is now no pretext for their presence, British soldiers and RUC patrols continue to saturate Nationalist areas. I can see such a maneuver now from where I am penning this column.

But if there are moderate noises coming from the "extremes" of Unionism in the wake of the Loyalist announcement the sounds from the "moderates" are as extreme as ever. Last weekend the Ulster Unionist Party (UUP) held their annual conference. It provided no evidence of flexibility or compromise. On the contrary, the triumphalist language and message of the conference was depressingly familiar. The conference slogan: "Our duty to the greater number" spoke volumes of the isolationist and exclusive mindset of Unionism. Despite the dispute between them the difference between the UUP and the DUP is tactical.

The responsibility for this negative attitude which rejects change lies squarely at the door of the British government. The Unionist veto, freely given by London, has blocked political progress since partition. Like partition, it has fostered division and conflict and has failed to bring lasting peace.

Irish Nationalists, political and popular opinion within the international community and elements within the British political establishment all agree that there can be no going back to the undemocratic practices of the past. There is broad agreement that there can be no internal settlement or return to simple majoritarianism. There must and will be fundamental constitutional and political change both in the short term and long term. The current status quo – which has reduced Nationalists to second-class citizens in our own country – must and will end. There is a political dynamic now in place which makes change inevitable. The fact is that all of the issues and all of the relationships are now on the table for discussion.

Britain's claim to sovereignty and its role in Ireland has self-evidently been a disaster for both the Irish people and the British people. In my discussions in the USA and Canada at all levels I found that this single fact is widely accepted and that there is no support for Britain's presence in Ireland.

In our imminent discussions with the British government and with other political parties Sinn Féin will argue for, and seek to advance, the view that the union should end and be replaced by a new and agreed Ireland based on democratic principles. For its part, the British government has already stated that such discussions can have no predetermined outcome.

The British government's efforts to reduce the momentum of the peace process have made it the target of significant criticism from Ireland, the United States, Europe and elsewhere. From the outset of the peace process until now, Mr. Major has lacked the imagination, generosity and courage to grasp the opportunity which exists to build a permanent peace. The onus is firmly on him. The British Prime Minister must recognize that the world has changed and that Britain stands isolated with its Unionist allies in its refusal to accelerate the peace process. It is quite pathetic to watch British ministers vainly trying to explain why they refuse to do what has been required in every other conflict resolution situation – engage in inclusive dialogue.

It's time the British government did the right thing by the people of Britain and Ireland and engaged fully and positively in the peace process. But still, despite British government negativity and my own accelerated jet-lag syndrome, I continue to favor the positive scenario. Who, even six weeks ago, would have predicted what is now happening? Who would have predicted it a year ago?

Forum For A New Ireland

Paragraph Eleven of the 1993 Downing Street Declaration outlined the Taoiseach's intention of setting up a "Forum for Peace and Reconciliation to make recommendations on ways in which agreement and trust between both traditions can be promoted and established." This consultative body invited representation from all sides, though not all parties attended. It met at Dublin Castle for the first time on Friday, October 28, 1994.

SO FAR, THE Forum for Peace and Reconciliation has met twice, once at its inaugural session and then on Thursday last for its first full session. The Unionist parties are boycotting the Forum, which may not be a surprise. What was surprising was that the British Ambassador to Ireland was ordered not to attend. Pressure obviously was also put on Peter Temple Morris, co-chairperson of the British-Irish parliamentary body. He also was absent. The absence of the Unionist parties is regrettable and it is a measure also of the work that lies ahead. The absence of the British representatives was a studied snub to the Forum and to the Irish government by Mr. Major.

The Unionist absence is not because they are disenfranchised or precluded by undemocratic preconditions as is the experience of Nationalists under British rule, but rather because the Unionists feel that the Forum does not serve their present political interests. When I spoke at its inaugural meeting, I appealed to the Unionists to join in the search for a settlement which will leave conflict permanently behind us.

What then is the role of the Forum? The terms of reference make it clear that it is a non-negotiating consultative body. Its remit is to consult on and examine ways in which a lasting peace, stability and reconciliation can be established by agreement among all the people of Ireland. It also seeks to establish the steps required to remove barriers of distrust. The purpose of the Forum will be to provide, as far as possible, an opportunity to identify and clarify issues which will most contribute to creating a new era of trust and co-operation on the island of Ireland. Involvement is entirely without prejudice to the position on constitutional issues held by any party.

But this Forum should not be a talking shop for politicians. It should address real issues and take action to bring about change. I'm looking forward to the construction of an informative debate and discussion. This should not be limited to political parties. It will include other submissions from social, cultural, women's and community organizations and from individuals. Such inclusiveness must be encouraged. There is also a need for the Forum to move beyond Dublin Castle. The possibility of holding meetings outside of Dublin must be explored and there is certainly an argument, which Sinn Féin has put vigorously, for the holding of local forums – under the tutelage of a slimmed-down version of the Forum itself – throughout Ireland. It would be particularly symbolic, as well as a real initiative, for a forum to meet in the Six Counties. The same goes for the west of Ireland and for the far south.

But without the Unionist involvement, can this body play a constructive part in the peace process? Yes. It's worth noting that representatives of eighty-two percent of the Irish people are assembled in the Forum. It is the first time, since partition, that there has been such a gathering. The Forum also gives, for the first time, a voice to a large section of Nationalist opinion. If the sense of abandonment and disempowerment which Nationalists in the occupied area have experienced for seventy-five years is to be overcome, then the Forum must listen carefully to their voices and address the injustices and inequalities which have fueled the conflict for decades. It must be made clear that these are no longer tolerable and that those responsible cannot act with impunity. And the Unionists are not entirely absent. The Alliance Party represents one strand of Unionist opinion and it has been said that there is a strong pro-Unionist ethos among some of the Southern parties. So valuable progress can be made.

It would be interesting if the Forum was able to explore what kind of Ireland we want. What is our version of a new agreed Ireland? And how do we get from here, from the Ireland of today, into that new Ireland?

From the Irish Republican perspective, a transformation of Irish society is required. We need a new national democracy: the quality of life in both states on this island, not only in the occupied area, needs to be improved. On matters of social legislation; of the rights of children; of the right to divorce; of protecting civil and religious liberties but of separating church from state; of the need to reverse decades of unemployment; of emigration and poverty; all of these need to be tackled, for these are all elements and dimensions of the national question – symptoms of partition.

So this is not a matter of just looking at the situation in the Six Counties, though of course that must be a primary focus of our discussions. There are pressing matters on core issues which need to be vigorously tackled and which have been neglected for too long. Cultural apartheid must be ended; discrimination in employment tackled; the entire armory of repressive laws must be scrapped; prisoners must be released; the process of demilitarization must be speedily moved ahead.

The British government needs to be encouraged to engage positively in the peace process. In the Forum, as in our discussions with the British government, Sinn Féin will articulate the need for the British government's jurisdiction in Ireland to end and to be replaced with a functioning Irish democracy. Central to this is the right of the people of this island, without external impediment or influence, to exercise our right to national self-determination. How we do that will be a matter for discussion and agreement.

All of the parties assembled in the Forum want to see Unionist participation. In our deliberations Sinn Féin have argued that we cannot build a new Ireland or peace settlement without Unionist involvement and agreement. Whatever the difficulties in this – or our commitment to overcome these difficulties – the British government's position must also be explored. How do we get London to engage in a meaningful way? How can the British government claim to be encouraging agreement between the people of Ireland when its attitude encourages Unionists to boycott the Forum?

This Forum is itself an argument for inclusive dialogue. Peace and reconciliation only become a reality for all our people when London becomes part of inclusive and substantive all-party talks led by the two governments.

We need to have a view and a vision of this new agreed Ireland. We need to initiate change and action to bring this about. We need Unionist participation and agreement. We need the British government to fulfill their responsibility in all of this.

It's Time to
Start Talking

Three months after the IRA's cessation, Sinn Féin and the British government were preparing to enter into talks.

AT THE VERY heart of the peace process lies a desire for a transformation of Irish society. This transformation must involve people directly in democratic discussion. It is the responsibility of the British government to encourage and facilitate such discussions – to join the persuaders and to move the entire situation forward. For Sinn Féin, the process of transformation will be built on a number of core elements. Political dialogue will be the main vehicle to achieve this.

Negotiation with the British government will be an important next step in this process. These negotiations will not mark the end of our struggle. They are a part of it. Negotiations are an area of struggle for us. For this reason, as we move to re-commence dialogue, I am setting out Sinn Féin's agenda for the next phase of negotiations with the British government. Incidentally, it is worth pointing out that London has yet to contact us about these talks.

The Dublin government, under the leadership of Albert Reynolds, actively and enthusiastically pursued the peace agenda. The Forum for Peace and Reconciliation has also applied itself to its task. In stark contrast, the British government has dragged its heels. Almost three months after the historic IRA announcement, the British government continues to stall.

Sinn Féin refuses to accept preconditions being placed upon us and our electorate. We are prepared to be magnanimous as we face into talks, but we are committed to assuring that bilateral discussions between Sinn Féin and the British government reverse the discrimination which we and our electorate have suffered as a result of the British government's tactical refusal to recognize our democratic mandate. This discrimination must end, and Sinn Féin must be accorded equality of treatment and parity of esteem with all other parties.

We therefore wish to deal with two specific areas in bilateral discussions:

112

- The logistics of all-party negotiations led by the London and Dublin governments;
- The rationalization of contact between our representatives and the British administration at all other levels.

Bilaterals may also discuss issues of repressive legislation, prisoners and other matters. Indeed there may be matters the British want to raise, but I am sure we will both be concerned to move speedily to the next phase of dialogue. To facilitate all of this, I have written to John Major to ensure that there is no confusion or time lost over arranging such matters as delegations, venues and times. All of these matters can and should be sorted out now. I have also informed Mr. Major that Martin McGuinness will liaise on behalf of Sinn Féin with his government. Martin McGuinness is responsible to an Árd Chomhairle sub-committee tasked with dealing with these matters. As the person responsible for three years of contact with the London government, Martin brings to this aspect of the peace process a continuity and a wealth of experience.

Sinn Féin has always advocated open debate and inclusive dialogue as the means by which this conflict can be resolved. Our involvement in dialogue, at a number of levels over recent years, has been central to the development of the peace process. On our own, however, Sinn Féin, and the British government cannot bring a lasting peace, and while I welcome the opportunity for bilateral discussions between our party and the London government, the people of this island and of Sinn Féin are concerned to consolidate the peace process and to move towards a negotiated peace settlement.

To achieve that we need the active participation of both governments and all of the parties. Collectively, we can remove the causes of conflict. We can address, in a comprehensive fashion, all the issues which have given rise to conflict and division in Ireland. This requires multilateral discussions – all-party talks.

Bilaterals are important, but it is in multilaterals that real progress will be made because everyone shares the responsibility of bringing about a real peace. Republicans have demonstrated our preparedness to face up to our responsibilities. We will continue to do this. But the power and the major responsibility to initiate negotiations lies with both governments.

Inclusive negotiations, if they are to be successful, must address all relevant issues without vetoes, without preconditions and without any attempt to predetermine the outcome.

A negotiated political settlement poses no threat to any section of our people. Unionists must be involved. We can't make peace without them. We recognize that their concerns must be addressed and resolved. This process of national reconciliation, beginning with inclusive negotiations, must secure the political, religious and democratic right of Unionists.

We do not yet have peace but we do have a real and unprecedented opportunity which I urge Mr. Major to seize quickly. It is Sinn Féin's view that the British government should play a positive and constructive role in persuading the Unionists to reach a democratic accommodation with the rest of the Irish people. The British government's declared commitment to the Unionist veto is, clearly, an attempt to predetermine the outcome of negotiations.

Britain's claim to sovereignty is self-evidently the cause of political instability and conflict in Ireland. The route to a lasting peace in Ireland is to be found in the restoration to the Irish people of our right to national self-determination – in the free exercise of this right without impediment of any kind. Agreement on how that right is exercised is a matter for the Irish people alone to determine. This issue will be at the center of Sinn Féin's own political agenda.

Inclusive and all-embracing peace talks led by the London and Dublin governments should address these broad areas:

- Political and constitutional change;
- Demilitarization and associated issues;
- Democratic rights for all Irish people, Nationalist and Unionist alike.

Sinn Féin seeks to assist the establishment of, and to support, a process which, with due regard for the real difficulties involved, culminates in the end of British jurisdiction and its replacement by an agreed Irish jurisdiction. We believe that the wish of the majority of the Irish people is for Irish unity. The emerging political and economic imperatives, both within Ireland and within the broader context of greater European and political union, support the logic of Irish unity.

Others may have a different view, but few will deny that we are all faced with an unprecedented opportunity to build a real and lasting peace settlement. There is an onus, therefore, on all political parties on this island to look beyond their narrow sectional political interests and to seize the potential to create a new and better future which now exists. There is a special onus on John Major.

Nelson Mandela, speaking last year in the United States, said, "History has placed a challenge at our doors and commends that acting together for the common good, we must make an outstanding success of the historic processes of transforming South Africa into a democratic prosperous and peaceful country."

This observation applies equally to Ireland. This peace process remains a fragile and delicate one. It cannot be taken for granted but it does give all of our people our best hope for the future. That is the spirit which Sinn Féin will bring to the next phase of this process. We look forward once again to talking to the British, and we look forward even more to being part of building a lasting peace settlement and the beginning of British disengagement from Irish affairs.

White House Visit Brings Process Into a New Phase

On the eve of his historic White House meeting on December 8, 1994, Gerry Adams wrote from Washington about the problems back home with the British government-sponsored economic conference to be held December 13–14.

WHEN I LEFT Ireland on Sunday, the British government had just announced that it would recommence talks with Sinn Féin on Wednesday, the 7th of this month. Because I had been invited by the Clinton administration to come to the White House to meet National Security Advisor Tony Lake, we suggested to London that Friday was a more convenient date for our meeting.

These talks will begin slightly sooner than anticipated. The British had not planned that they should start until after December 15. This was and is a denial of Sinn Féin's electoral mandate, and of course we have always said that these talks should have recommenced much sooner than this. I use the word recommence because the British ended earlier talks with us in November of last year.

The British decision to move the date forward came after they revealed that Sinn Féin was to be excluded from an economic conference arranged for Belfast by John Major's government for December 13 and 14. This revelation galvanized Irish America and Nationalist Ireland. The uproar created by political and economic elements in both countries forced the British to make a u-turn. They moved forward the dates of talks with Sinn Féin. This is a welcome development. However, their position on Sinn Féin attendance at the conference was much more of a fudge.

They conceded that six Sinn Féin councilors – our representatives on economic committees of Derry and Belfast councils – could attend for two-and-a-half hours. This is unacceptable. Sinn Féin doesn't expect to be treated any better than other parties, but we do expect to be treated equally. I say this not through any sense of party political elitism, but because the principle of equality and of parity of esteem for all citizens is a principle which has to be the basis on which justice is possible. This is a bigger issue than Sinn Féin's involvement in a conference – it is an issue which demands that all citizens be treated on an equal basis. Sinn Féin is not a second-class party, and we cannot allow the British to proscribe our supporters as second-class citizens. That is the old, failed agenda. A new agenda is needed.

It is important to note that, for the first time since the IRA cessation, Irish-American influence mobilized spontaneously and moved the British. The perception, however, that the British had opened their conference to Sinn Féin on the same basis as everyone else, may have lulled Irish America temporarily into a false sense that everything was okay. It is not.

Sinn Féin wants to resolve this issue amicably with the British. We are looking forward to talks and to the next phase of the evolving peace process. We don't want to start this phase on a sour note. The British government have made a rhetorical commitment to the principles of parity of esteem and equality of treatment. They should match their words with deeds, and Irish America should once again encourage them to do so. This Belfast conference purports to deal with the problem of economic deprivation. Discrimination is a main source of this deprivation. It would be a sad irony if this conference itself discriminated against citizens, and if any section of US opinion was tricked into giving credibility to such an event.

Incidentally, the British stance on this conference is not the only negative signal they've sent in recent times. Last week they refused funding to an Irish language college (Meánscoil Feirste). This college has one hundred pupils. All of their parents pay taxes. Yet the British government turned down an application for grant aid. Welsh speaking schools in Wales are grant-aided, as is right. In Scotland, where one percent speak Gallic, the funding is substantial. In the North of Ireland, such aid is refused. As some leading *gaeilgeoirí* said last week, "So much for the British government's commitment to the peace process."

Despite all of this, Sinn Féin will approach this week's historic talks with the British in a positive and constructive manner. We have been involved for some time in four main areas of talks – with the British, with the Dublin government, with the US administration, and bilaterals with a number of political parties in Ireland and

Britain. A sub-committee of the Árd Chomhairle co-ordinates our strategy. Rita O'Hare and Pat Doherty head up the party's engagement with Dublin. Lucilita Breathnach heads up our engagement in the bilaterals with other parties, and Martin McGuinness heads up our engagement with the British. In fact, he will lead our delegation into next Friday's meeting.

It is worth noting, for the historical record, that this meeting is the first public engagement between Sinn Féin and the British government in seventy-five years. Martin and his team are this week negotiating an agenda and other matters about Friday's meeting with British representatives. I will return to Ireland for a meeting on Thursday, when we will finalize our arrangements.

In the mean time, I am taking a Sinn Féin delegation to the White House. I consider this to be a very important meeting. It marks another step in the positive engagement by the Clinton administration in promoting the search for peace in Ireland. I look forward to giving an assessment of the developing situation back home, and to recording my appreciation of the efforts of the Clinton administration.

I will be bringing an Irish Republican agenda to this meeting. The British policy in Ireland has failed, and it is important that any future arrangements which will perpetuate a peaceful and stable Ireland are rooted firmly in the right of the people of Ireland to self-determination. The British government's remaining function or central function, should be to dis-involve itself from Irish affairs in a way which leaves behind a permanent settlement, a peaceful and united Irish people. There is a need also, of course, for us to spell out the urgent necessity for demilitarization, for democratic rights, and for the release of prisoners.

Incidentally, while the White House meeting is by invitation of the Clinton administration, today our group had a very useful meeting with the State Department. This was at my request. I dealt with many of the issues outlined above, and we made a submission about the treatment of Irish prisoners here in the US, of Irish people awaiting extradition proceedings or deportation efforts.

There has been some focus, in sections of the press, about fundraising. It is my view that this issue will be resolved, and indeed that it is not the problem that some media – particularly London media outlets – have suggested. It is a matter of practicality.

We have come a long way this year. Who would have predicted this time last year, or the year before, that so much could have happened, or that so much potential could have been created. The last three months have been eventful ones. A peace process needs momentum. A peace settlement occurs when the main protagonists engage proactively and positively. This will take some time, as it did in South Africa and in other conflicts. But when it happens, the momentum, the thrust, becomes irreversible.

We have not yet reached that point in the Irish peace process. In the last three months the London government has failed or refused to respond to the new situation with the generosity and courage which it deserves. Such momentum must be created from other quarters. That is why initiatives by Albert Reynolds' government were so fundamentally important. That is why President Clinton's initiatives were so helpful and necessary. That is why John Hume's commitment has been so important.

These initiatives need to be maintained. Last week John Hume and I issued a joint statement. We called upon the British to stop stalling. We called for a speedy move to all-party talks led by both governments. This is the only way to resolve the conflict fully in a permanent fashion. This is also why US engagement is as important in the time ahead, as it has been in the recent past.

Tuesday's meeting at the White House marks a new and important phase. The credit goes to President Clinton and his administration, it goes also to the people in Ireland who have remained committed to the struggle for democracy, but it goes especially to people in the US who put all these issues on the public and political agenda here. As we face into a new era and into another year, one thing is certain – Irish America needs to keep working and refocusing, so that the peace process can be irreversibly advanced.

Sinn Fein's Influence Can Stretch to IRA Arms Issue

Meetings between Sinn Féin and the British government took place in December 1994 and January 1995.

S INN FÉIN IS represented at its meetings with the British government by a delegation led by Martin McGuinness. To date the delegation has included Árd Runaí (General Secretary) Lucilita Breathnach, Árd Chomhairle members Sean McManus and Siobhán O'Hanlon, and Gerry Kelly. Bairbre de Brún replaced Luici at the third meeting as Luici is tied up with preparations for next month's Árd Fheis.

The British are represented by a group of civil servants. Three meetings have taken place at Stormont to date – December 9 and December 19, 1994 and January 16 of this year.

More than three months elapsed from the initiation of the IRA ceasefire on September 1 until the commencement of talks. Five weeks have elapsed since then. Next week, January 28, marks the 150th day of the IRA ceasefire.

Sinn Féin's agenda for the meetings to date has been straightforward and vital to progressing the situation. That is:

- The need to move to inclusive peace talks;
- The need for London to recognize and accept Sinn Féin's democratic mandate;
- The need to accord Sinn Féin and our electorate equality of treatment as an enabling element to move in that direction.

We have provided the British government with three written submissions outlining our basis for entry into dialogue and arguing the need for peace talks. We have also raised such matters as the release of prisoners and the need for a comprehensive demilitarization. We have spelt out in detail the nature and extent of political discrimination against Sinn Féin and the Sinn Féin electorate.

Our approach has been frank, positive and patient, and takes its broad direction from the joint statement of September 6, 1994, issued by the then Taoiseach Albert Reynolds, SDLP leader John Hume, and myself. It said in part:

"We are at the beginning of a new era in which we are totally committed to democratic and peaceful methods of resolving our political problems. We reiterate that our objective is an equitable and lasting agreement that can command the allegiance of all."

After a three-month delay to the commencement of talks and five weeks into them, the British government has, as yet, failed to introduce political representation into the delegation. Two written submissions have been provided by the British government to Sinn Féin. The first outlined the British government's basis for entry in dialogue. The second is a broad, non-definitive response to a number of questions put to the British government by Sinn Féin in our written submissions of December 19, 1994 and January 16, 1995.

The British government delegation has been quite frank in putting the position that Sinn Féin is not to be accorded equal treatment, despite the acceptance of the delegation leader, Quentin Thomas, that Sinn Féin threatens no one and that Sinn Féin is a "main" political party with an electoral mandate.

While responding to Sinn Féin's verbal submissions on such matters as equality of treatment, prison issues and cultural discrimination, the overwhelming focus of the British delegation, and of the time expended in the course of the three meetings, has centered on the issue of the decommissioning of IRA arms. This issue has dominated the discussions to date. While the British government delegation states that the resolution of this issue is not a precondition to Sinn Féin's involvement in inclusive peace talks, they and the British government ministers, privately and publicly, assert that its resolution is "a matter of both principle and practical reality." British Prime Minister John Major states that there must be "substantial progress" before peace talks can begin.

In the course of the meeting of December 19, 1994, the British delegation sought to provide Sinn Féin with a document on the issue of IRA arms. Sinn Féin declined the offer on the basis that we cannot accept the imposition of a precondition on Sinn Féin or the Sinn Féin electorate, and therefore could not accept a document which deals with the detail of that precondition. The British government has subsequently used this in its briefings of other governments on the progress of the talks. In particular, it has sought to influence the US administration.

I believe the British government is engaged in a strategy which involves, at best, stalling the process through the deliberate erection of barriers to progress on a bogus pretext and, at worst, attempting to create and sustain a crisis in the peace process around the issue of IRA arms. And attempting to accomplish this in a way which portrays Sinn Féin as being the unreasonable and inflexible party.

The entire logic of a peace process is that through peace talks we arrive at a peace settlement which removes the causes of the conflict and removes forever the guns from the political equation in Ireland. Peace talks are the vital issue involved here. The British government's refusal to recognize the right of Sinn Féin voters is the crux of this matter. Sinn Féin is not the IRA. It does not have any guns. In our submission to the British government on January 16, we stated the reality of the situation:

"Sinn Féin is totally committed to bringing about the complete and permanent removal of all guns from Irish politics. To bring about, in the word of the British government the "decommissioning" of all weapons of war. Without this commitment the peace process would not have been brought to its present position. The most important element in bringing the situation to this point, as is universally acknowledged, was the IRA's announcement of August 31, 1994. In our view the British government knows this.

"Attempts, therefore, to link the issue of the IRA's weapons to your continued refusal to recognize the rights of the Sinn Féin electorate are disingenuous. We are concerned, therefore, that the British government's position on the decommissioning of IRA weapons is, at best, a stalling tactic, at worst an attempt to create a situation of crisis in the peace process around this issue. This must be avoided. Our position on this matter is transparent. We wish to use our influence on all matters, in a positive way and with the aim of advancing the peace process. How we use our influence and how much influence we have is a matter of judgment for us.

"Be assured of our commitment, but be assured also that efforts by you to subvert the integrity of Sinn Féin's position on the rights of our electorate as a pretext for stalling the peace process will serve only to undermine and subvert the peace process itself."

So, three months after the IRA ceasefire, real talks have yet to start. The British government is now proposing to prolong artificially this phase of this process by at least five weeks, with no commitment to further progress. The refusal, at this point (five months on), to inject political representation into their delegation is aimed at aiding the stalling strategy; aimed at portraying the eventual introduction of a British government minister to the delegation as being a major move forward. In this period, London has also announced that ministers may meet Sinn Féin elected councilors. The end of this ban on ministerial contact between British government ministers and Sinn Féin elected representatives at the level of local government shows this to be a purely tactical matter, not a matter of principle.

Is the British government telling us that unless there is a surrender by the IRA of their weapons, or "substantial progress" on this, that the peace process is over? What other logic is there to this position?

On the basis of the above analysis, it is crucial that the appropriate political and diplomatic action is taken by all parties – Irish, British and in the international community – who wish to see the positive, effective and timely progression of the peace process. It is time for them to use their good offices to move the British government in that direction.

This is particularly a matter needing the urgent attention of Irish America. I note and commend Bruce Morrison's efforts to lobby President Clinton on these issues. The Americans for a New Irish Agenda group have hit the right note. They and the peace process need your support.

Document Is a Useful New Step

A New Framework for Agreement was published on February 22, 1995. A wide-ranging document, it set out a "shared understanding between the British and Irish governments to assist discussion and negotiation involving the Northern Ireland parties." It adopted a number of guiding principles in the search for agreement, and suggested the setting-up of cooperative bodies between North and South, and between Dublin and London.

THE LAUNCH BY the British and Irish governments of the Framework Document last Wednesday brings to an end one phase of the peace process. It heralds the beginning of a new phase. Sinn Féin welcomes the publication of the Framework Document, which should now clear the way for inclusive peace talks and for the next phase of this process, with everyone at the table and everything on the table.

Republicans will enter these peace talks on the basis of our Republican analysis. We will put forth our view that a lasting peace in Ireland can only be based on the right of all the Irish people to national self-determination.

The Framework Document is a discussion document. But its publication by the two governments is a clear recognition that partition has failed, that British rule in Ireland has failed and that there is no going back to the failed policies and structures of the past. The political framework envisaged is clearly an all-Ireland one, and even though we would like to see this more deeply rooted, Sinn Féin will judge the Framework Document pragmatically and in the context of our objectives, policy and strategy.

Sinn Féin's objective is to bring about an inclusive and negotiated end to British jurisdiction in Ireland. We seek to replace it with a new and agreed Irish jurisdiction. In our view this poses no threat to any section of our people, including the Unionists. However, we know that others hold a different view. It is an understatement to say that some disagree totally with this view. Therefore agreement is required.

One important area of agreement has already emerged. There is already a widespread acceptance that an internal settlement is not a solution. New relationships will have to be forged between all the people of our country. This will be difficult. It will require negotiation. It demands inclusive democratic dialogue.

The British have successfully militarized an essentially political problem. The process of demilitarizing the occupied area has been too slow. There needs to be an end to all forms of repressive legislation and an end to house raids, arrests and harassment. All cross-border roads must be opened. There needs to be a decommissioning of all the British crown forces, including the disbanding of the RUC and British spy posts in housing estates, in sports fields, on farming lands – wherever they are they should be dismantled. All political prisoners should be released.

The peace process can be moved significantly forward by the immediate dismantling of undemocratic measures which have contributed to the conflict. These are present not only in repressive legislation. They are also part of religious, political and economic discrimination upon which Unionist domination was built. They are part of cultural discrimination.

The Unionist reaction to the Framework Document was sadly predictable. Selective parts of the document had been leaked a few weeks ago in *The Times* of London. The leaks clearly came from pro-Unionist elements in Britain. The *Times* leak concentrated on proposals for cross-border institutions, and described these as a sell-out which brought the prospect of Irish unity closer than at any time since partition.

Mr. Molyneaux's Ulster Unionist Party (UUP) immediately threatened to bring down John Major's government. His party held the balance of power in the British House of Commons. His strategy was based upon this and on an alleged close relationship with John Major. But the *Times* leak contradicted all UUP claims that Mr. Major was taking their line. Molyneaux's threat provoked a special House of Commons statement from Northern Secretary Patrick Mayhew, and a much hyped and unusual TV and radio "crisis" broadcast by Mr. Major.

DUP leader Ian Paisley seized the moment to remind the world that he had warned against such "betrayal." Molyneaux had got it wrong! The UUP was swept by rumors of a leadership battle and all the main contenders – William Ross, John Taylor, Ken Maginnis and David Trimble – vied for center place.

"The Framework Document is dead and buried," Unionists declared. What, then, of Mr. Molyneaux's special relationship with Mr. Major?

Mr. Major moved again to reassure them. The union is not under threat; he would not become a persuader for a united Ireland, he proclaimed. In a speech to the Conservative Way Forward group he said, "Northern Ireland is a central part of the United Kingdom . . . for my part I cherish the United Kingdom and Northern Ireland's part in it."

In a frenzied effort to win back perceived lost ground, the Unionists launched a counter-offensive. But the leadership on this occasion appear to be out of step with grassroots opinion.

I have consistently argued that the consent and allegiance of Unionists is needed to secure a peace settlement. But Unionists cannot have a veto over British policy. I am convinced that there is an increasing questioning of traditional positions among ordinary Protestants. Few of them really trust London. Many accept that far-reaching change is inevitable. They are seeking real leadership from Molyneaux and Paisley. Regrettably they also are being told "No."

Unionist allegiance to the British crown is matched by a deep distrust of the British government. The Unionist leadership's desire for an internal settlement with a devolved administration comes from their wish to restore Unionist rule – that is, Unionist domination. The furor over the Framework Document is a case in point. Once again the Unionists are playing the Orange card – this time to impose a veto on the phase of inclusive negotiation which we are about to enter.

Irrespective of the content of the Framework Document – of how much of it Republicans might like or dislike – the Document and the inclusive peace talks which must follow should open the way for new political arrangements agreed through democratic negotiations between, and acceptable to, all the Irish people.

For over two years now, Major has had a minimalist approach to the peace process. Now after the publication of the Framework Document, the strategy pursued by the British government will indicate the extent to which it is prepared to engage in advancing the peace process.

The Framework Document is neither a solution nor a settlement. The priority now must be to initiate all-party talks. The onus is on both governments, but particularly the British government, to move the situation speedily forward into inclusive talks. The Dublin government has a responsibility to ensure this happens.

For our part, we have always maintained the centrality of inclusive dialogue without preconditions in creating the conditions for a just and lasting peace. Only through real peace talks, seeking agreement, can we hope to put the conflict of the past behind us. If the Document succeeds in moving all of us to this point, then it will have served a useful purpose.

The Delights of the Aran Islands

Sometimes, less onerous tasks are called for. . .

I'M WRITING THIS high above the Atlantic, on board an Aer Lingus airbus winging its way towards the US. You may have heard that President Clinton did the decent thing and granted Sinn Féin equality of treatment by allowing party fundraising, so what could have been a routine trip has been given a special impetus, and my first St. Patrick's Day away from Ireland will have a significant quality as the peace process is consolidated.

Irish America delivered and everyone involved is to be commended. The British government don't like it, but I suppose that's par for the course.

I was on a plane last week also. Twice. The first trip was to London, where I addressed the Association of American correspondents in London. It was a good, worthwhile visit, and I also went to the British House of Lords. The second plane flight was to Inis Mór. That was brilliant. Inis Mór is the largest of the three Aran Islands. They are situated far out in Galway Bay. There is Inis Meáin, in the middle, Inis Oírr nearest to Co. Clare, and Inis Mór, the biggest island on the Galway side of Inis Meáin.

I was invited there by the local co-operative of Comharcumann Forbartha Inis Mór to launch their guidebook. It's a smashing wee book, full of information about the eating houses and boarding houses and drinking houses. And historic places. And beaches. And fishing spots. And everything.

The islands are special places. I went to Inis Meáin a few years ago for three days, and stayed for five. It was idyllic. No cars. No noise. Beautiful! Masses of wild flowers on a small island bisected by wonderful stone walls. But it's not that alone which makes the Aran Islands splendid. It's the people!

The islands are living islands. Many of the other Irish islands are deserted, even by the sheep. The Aran Islands are vibrant. They are Gaelic outposts – Irish-speaking communities confidently facing the future, steeped in history, but modern in outlook.

Last week I went there in a wee toddy plane. We boarded on a tiny airstrip in Connemara. The plane was delayed by a hailstorm, so we waited in a comfortable lounge while the wind blew a gale and the snow swirled across Galway Bay. There were two *gaeilgeoirí* waiting for the flight – Colm, a photographer, and Paddy the Poet. Paddy had never been in an airplane before.

When our plane eventually emerged though the snowstorm across the seascape, Paddy and the rest of us smiled in a devil may care fashion at each other. We pretended we weren't afraid. Until the plane landed and the pilot alighted.

"*An sean lad sin*," Paddy gasped. (That ould lad.)

"*Ná bach*," his friend said. (Don't bother.)

"*Ná bach le mac an bachtaigh agus ní bach mac an bachtaigh leat*," Paddy replied. (Don't bother with the beggar-man's son and the beggar-man's son won't bother you.)

But he and we need not have worried. The pilot was Biggles incarnate. He had us up and through the snow and sleet, and before you could say "Bermuda Triangle" the islands were before us and Inis Mór beckoned us earthwards.

It is a beautiful place. I was there before but only for a few hours. We had come off Inis Meáin in a currach and my wife, Colette, and I hitch-hiked back to Ireland on a passing boat. But the boat was going to Doolin in Co. Clare, and we were for Galway, so we had to disembark at Inis Mór until a more suitable craft came by. That time I saw little of the island except the harbor at Kilronan.

This time a reception party greeted us, and led by Kathy O'Bioill and the rest of the co-operative committee, we mini-bused our way around the place, picking up poets and a priest and fishermen and Clara and Sally.

The population of Inis Mór is 950, and the island has three primary schools and one secondary. Many of the old island traditions live on, and the young people are staying there, rather than emigrating. Gaelic is the first language and is in every day use, though most islanders are bilingual. Most island women still knit the traditional Aran sweaters and the currach is used not only for races in the summer but every day for the fishing.

Fishing used to be the mainstay of island life. It is still important, but now tourism is crucial also. That's what *The Aran Islands – A Detailed Guide* is all about. It is published in Irish, French, Italian, German and English.

After our brief tour we adjourned for lunch to P.J. Flaherty's "Aran Fisherman" Restaurant. We were foundered. By now I knew why they wore Aran sweaters.

"*Ar mhaith libh uisce beatha te?*" the woman of the house asked. (Would yus like a hot whiskey?)

Paddy the Poet spoke for us all. "*Sea* – yes," he smiled, and we did.

The islands are mainly limestone and slate, so the people have made the fields from sand and seaweed. They cleared the rocks and built the walls which provided shelter from the Atlantic gales. Over lunch, we learned of and sampled the special organic qualities of this moil (soil).

Inis Mór also has a rich variety of wildflowers. Over 427 varieties. And these flowers have shared the island with humanity for over 4,000 years. The guide describes Inis Mór as an open area museum with monastic and archeological sites. And it is.

So after lunch off we went to the Heritage Center, where the *craic* was fierce and *The Aran Islands – A Detailed Guide*, was duly launched with ceremony and cordiality by your *Irish Voice* columnist. I felt really privileged to be there and humbled to have been asked to launch the guide. I said so in my speech. Comharcumann Inis Mór are making an investment in the future of the islands and in the future of their children.

Unfortunately, we had to leave them to it in full *seisiún*, and we boarded our plane again. The flight back was exhilarating. The pilot let me sit beside him. God Bless Aran. The weather had cleared and we flew without a care into the sun. To our left Galway and Mayo. To our right the hills and cliffs of Clare.

Below me now we are crossing over the snowy Canadian coastlands. In a few hours Kennedy Airport and the media hordes are awaiting me. My heart is in Inis Mór. Go there and you'll see why.

In the meantime, Happy Saint Patrick's day to you all.

The Aran Islands – A Detailed Guide, is available from the Aran Heritage Center, Kilronan, Inis Mór.

A Very Good Week

St. Patrick's week in 1995 was spent in the US where the decision had been made to lift the fundraising ban, and where two historic meetings took place between Gerry Adams and President Clinton.

THE SPEAKER'S LUNCH, the White House, and demilitarization. That was the week that was. I'm back in Ireland again, to mild spring weather, bright yellow daffodils and the prospects of talks between Sinn Féin and British ministers.

Last week was a good week for the peace process and for Ireland. It was a special St. Patrick's Day. The international focus on President Clinton's concern for a just and democratic peace settlement has uplifted many people who had been disheartened by the begrudging British attitude. I commend President Clinton for his consistency and commitment, and I thank all those on Capitol Hill and elsewhere – including the publisher of the *Irish Voice*, Niall O'Dowd – who worked for and succeeded in securing a progressive and balanced US engagement in the search for peace in Ireland.

The main purpose of my visit was to open a Friends of Sinn Féin office in Washington and to launch our diplomatic mission in the US President Clinton's decision to lift the fundraising ban previously imposed on me, and his invite to the White House, enhanced my US visit and consolidated the peace process.

The office was duly opened at Connecticut Avenue where our mission was headed by Mairéad Keane of the Sinn Féin Árd Chomhairle. Mairéad, a native of Mayo who was reared in Dublin, is a former head of the Sinn Féin women's department and a former national director of education. One Irish woman against six hundred British diplomats. London is now at a decided disadvantage.

Congressman Peter King accompanied me to House Speaker Newt Gingrich's lunch the afternoon before St. Patrick's Day. It was a nice lunch. Corned beef and cabbage with potatoes, and green ice cream which was very tart. Indeed, at one point everyone screwed up their faces because of the taste!

The Speaker, Newt Gingrich, was very warm in his welcome. After the first bit of diplomatic choreography, John Hume and I met the President and the Speaker for a few minutes of conversation. We were joined by Congressman King. I was very impressed by President Clinton, whose interest in Irish affairs has been well documented. During our cordial discussion, it became clear to me that his engagement is a genuine and committed one. I took the opportunity of thanking him for his decisive role in the search for peace.

During the formal speeches by the Speaker, the Taoiseach and the President, each of them highlighted the importance of this St. Patrick's Day celebration. Each of them welcomed my presence. As was to be expected, there was no mention of the controversy which preceded this event. On the contrary, it was a light-hearted and pleasant affair. Indeed, either the Speaker or the President – I forget which – noted to loud applause that it was the first time in recent memory that there was unanimity on Capitol Hill. It also emerged that John Hume and Newt Gingrich share a common family name. Both have great grandparents by the name of Daugherty.

Incidentally, unlike most of the Irish visitors, President Clinton used a few words of Gaeilge (Gaelic) in both the speeches that I heard him make. He also declared that St. Patrick's Day permitted him the opportunity to sip a Guinness without anyone objecting!

There was a fine St. Patrick's affair at the White House on Friday evening. Again, the President and I, and the First Lady, had the opportunity for a brief discussion. The funny moment of that evening came when a secret service agent gave his card to my associate, Richard McAuley. This openness was a mark of the spirit of the evening. I had been in the White House for meetings on a number of occasions before, but this time an entire floor had been opened for the St. Patrick's night celebrations.

It is a most interesting place. I have been in what perhaps could be described as more palatial or finer government buildings, but they were always devoid of ordinary citizens. The White House, at least on this occasion, was swarming with men and women moving from room to room, taking in the surroundings and relaxing in the ambience.

One of the White House aides acted as a tour guide, and a senior official described to me how functions were usually quite formal affairs restricted to about one hundred guests. ("We couldn't do that with the Irish. Unless you invited about three hundred you can't get any balanced representation," he said.) In the library, we saw an old implement which had been found hidden in the chimney – undecommissioned. We were also told of how the British burned the building, and how some fine paintings were saved from the blaze.

After the speeches and the entertainment, Eileen Ivers and Joe Derrane led other musicians into a *seisiún*. As the evening wore on, the music became increasingly spirited. In due course, singers joined in from the floor and vied with each other in renderings. It was now almost time for the Irish to evacuate the White House. But there was no sign of them going. John Hume and I decided that there was only one thing to do. We cleared the building with an impromptu rendition of *The Town I Love So Well*.

Normally on St. Patrick's Day I have a few drinks to wet my shamrock. On this occasion I had none until Joe Jamison found a bottle of stout which I quaffed with relish.

During my US visit, I was in contact daily with home and kept abreast of Martin McGuinness's talks with British officials, which he was endeavoring to move into discussions with British ministers. There has been considerable focus by the British on the issue of decommissioning. This has been one of the areas – demilitarization – requiring movement which was pinpointed by Sinn Féin a long time ago. The other main areas are constitutional and political matters, and democratic rights. Movement is required on these issues and on demilitarization, which includes the decommissioning of all weapons.

I was pleased to announce at the Washington Press Club that Martin McGuinness had successfully moved the process on, and that he and the senior British official, Quentin Thomas, were discussing agendas. A few hours before writing this piece. I was in consultation with Martin and at the time of writing we have responded to a proposed agenda for meetings with British ministers in a positive way. These should now happen sooner rather than later.

All in all, a very good week.

Friends of Sinn Féin has since moved to new offices at 510 Connecticut Street N.E., First Floor, Washington, DC 20002.

We're Trying Our Best, But British Won't Budge

The British government refused to recognize Sinn Féin's electoral mandate, and thus prevented the peace process from progressing. And at Easter time, Republicans are mindful of the 1916 Easter Rising which, though now unfashionable, still has a resonance in relation to current events.

AS WE APPROACH Eastertide there is still no sign of movement by the British government to move the peace process into the new and necessary phase of all-party talks. Indeed, London is actively preventing movement to inclusive negotiations and, at the time of writing, the British government is still refusing to introduce ministers into the dialogue with Sinn Féin representatives.

The core of this problem is the British government's refusal to recognize Sinn Féin's electoral mandate and the rights of the Republican electorate in the Six Counties. Media attention has focused, to some extent, on the issue of "decommissioning" vs. "demilitarization." This is a distraction. The real issue is whether Sinn Féin has the right to represent the concerns of our electorate and to proceed on the basis of our analysis and mandate.

We wish to engage in serious, substantive and constructive discussions with the British ministers on all relevant issues, including the decommissioning of arms. As has been made clear in public statements by myself and others, in private discussions between Martin McGuinness and the head of the British delegation, Quentin Thomas, and in correspondence between us, Sinn Féin is ready to discuss all issues with British ministers. It is the British government which is holding up these discussions, seeking to dictate the agenda and to exclude issues.

The British government has attempted to limit discussions to bilaterals with a narrow agenda dealing only with the decommissioning of IRA weapons. The British also change the rules on an ongoing basis and are more concerned with media spins and propaganda than progress. Demilitarization included discussion on the permanent removal of all weapons. How can we have an effective peace process which does not include a discussion on demilitarization?

It is important to note at this point that while the British have a role in initiating talks they are not a neutral referee in the process. They are a party to the conflict and cannot therefore dictate the direction of negotiations.

Sinn Féin is a political party, not an army. Unlike the British government, we have no authority or control over arms. Yet we are prepared to discuss these matters. Members of our party, including elected councilors and their family members, have been killed by those who wish to undermine our mandate. We therefore are totally committed to upholding the rights of our electorate. At the same time, we wish to use our influence on all matters in a positive way and with the aim of advancing the peace process. There can be no single-issue agenda.

No issue should be excluded from these discussions and all matters on the agenda must be there with the aim of seeking their resolution. The objective of the peace process is to remove all the causes of conflict, heal the divisions which exist, and achieve a lasting peace through a negotiated settlement. Everyone concerned should apply themselves to this process, which can only be accomplished through inclusive discussion with every issue on the table involving all of the parties.

Why are the British refusing to discuss demilitarization? The British government has the largest force under its control. Demilitarization involves all the forces – all of the armed groups. The British government has to accept responsibility for the actions of its forces. Sinn Féin and our support base have been targeted and have suffered grievously at the hands of the British forces. Elements of those forces have collaborated with the Loyalist death squads in a vicious murder campaign which has claimed over one thousand Catholic lives. We have a legitimate concern to ensure that there can be no repetition of this.

Our party has also been the target of repressive legislation including censorship and, as can be seen from the current British position, our voters are deprived of their democratic rights.

The British government's ban on ministerial contact with Sinn Féin is applied at all levels and on all issues. For example, in West Belfast where there has been a considerable run down of the Royal

Victoria Hospital, the Sinn Féin councilor for that area cannot discuss this matter with the British minister for health. This has been the case for over a decade now.

Whether it be an environmental issue, a matter of education or a social and economic matter, the British refuse to recognize the rights of Sinn Féin and, more importantly, of those who vote for us. When one considers that one in every three Nationalists in the Six Counties votes for our party and that we are a major force in local government, then one gets some sense of the scale of this undemocratic ban.

On the surface it appears that the British government's position is untenable. Already minor Loyalist groups without an electoral mandate are approaching their fourth meeting with a British minister. I welcome the Loyalist involvement in talks. Sinn Féin has stressed, and we are the proof, that marginalization does not work. So it is good that the Loyalists are talking. But the British stance in relation to Sinn Féin is causing considerable frustration, and not just among Sinn Féin supporters. I have just listened to John Hume on RTE, Ireland's national broadcast network, pointing out the absurdity of London's position. What lies behind the British position?

It is worth pointing out that at other times in the peace process they adopted a similar stance – for example, in the wake of the Downing Street Declaration and after the IRA statement of August 31. Then when they decided to change their position, it was as if the earlier difficulty never existed. Presumably the same thing will happen again, but I could not even attempt to guess when.

We have tried to move the situation forward. Martin McGuinness, on our initiative and at our request, sought informal meetings with British officials in order to expedite matters. On two occasions he and Siobhán O'Hanlon traveled to Stormont and made a number of proposals. For instance, when the British appeared to be bogged down over the agenda, Martin suggested that we proceed without an agenda and that each side put forward whatever points they wished and that every issue of importance to either side should be discussed.

It is worth pointing out that when Sinn Féin entered into these bilateral discussions, we did so with two main objectives. These were to rationalize the relationship between our party and the British administration, and to be assured that the British recognize the rights of our voters. We also sought to expedite matters toward all-party talks and to learn how these talks would be conducted.

It was Easter 1993 when the news first broke of the talks between myself and John Hume. It is unacceptable, two years later, that the British government have yet to engage with the generosity, common sense and courage that is required to advance the peace process.

All of this brings us back to Easter time. Throughout Ireland and the US, Irish people and other freedom lovers will be marking the seventy-ninth anniversary of the 1916 Rising. It will not be marked in a fitting way by the Dublin government. This has been the case for almost twenty years now. Before 1969, of course, there were fitting tributes to the leaders and the men and women activists of that time. Anyone old enough will remember the pageantry of 1966 and the dramatic and other presentations.

The Rising of 1916 was a remarkable event. It shook the British empire and it marked the beginning of the end of that imperial power. It also transformed Ireland. When one considers that the Rising was conducted by only about 1,200 volunteers in Dublin, which was the main center, and smaller groups throughout the rest of the country, one gets the sense of the magnitude of their endeavor.

The British rushed 20,000 troops and artillery and gun-boats into the city. They quelled the uprising. It is possible that the Easter Rising might have joined the list of other failed efforts by Irish insurgents. But the British executed the leaders. Connolly was shot strapped to a wheelchair. Tom Clarke, old and almost blind, was killed with the rest. Joseph Mary Plunkett was married one hour before his execution. The brothers Pearse and others faced the firing squads. Their deaths led to a resurgence of Irish Nationalism and the rest is history.

The unfinished business of that history – the end game – is being unraveled now almost eighty years later. Whatever the outcome – and there is every reason to believe that the vision of the men and women of 1916 can be fulfilled – there is no excuse for the absence of a fitting commemoration and celebration of that period. Imagine the United States without the Fourth of July?

So have a Happy Easter. Think of us here, in Ireland. For our part we will endeavor to move the situation on.

At Last: Serious Talks After Eight Months

In April 1995, the British government finally decided to end the ban on ministerial contact with Sinn Féin, thus raising hopes for the prospect of all-party talks on the future of Northern Ireland.

AT LAST THE British government has been moved to end the ban on ministerial contact with Sinn Féin. The news came in an announcement last Monday, April 24 at 4 p.m. Sinn Féin received a letter from British officials at 2 p.m. on the same day. This letter informed us that the British intended to resume dialogue with a minister leading the British government team. We welcomed the end of the ban. It marks an important new phase of the peace process and an end of the logjam.

In our response to the British announcement, Martin McGuinness outlined the basis for Sinn Féin's entry into this discussion. This is:

a) To bring an end to the discrimination that our party and electorate suffer, and;

b) To work out the logistics of all-party talks, the essential next stage in the peace process.

This has been Sinn Féin's consistent position. For months now we have assured the British of our willingness to discuss all issues. This includes the issue of demilitarization, including the decommissioning of weapons. We have yet to work out an agenda, but Sinn Féin will continue to be flexible. We have always insisted that no issue should be excluded from discussion. Dialogue must be inclusive and unconditional.

Monday's announcement, and the British letter to us was in response to correspondence that we had sent to them on Thursday, April 20. There is really no reason why these talks could not have taken place before this. The British decision to move came because of the increasing pressure for them to stop stalling the peace process.

In recent weeks a range of political leaders in Ireland from SDLP leader John Hume, Taoiseach John Bruton, and Bertie

Ahern to Progressive Democrats leader Mary Harney, Dick Spring and Alliance Party leader John Alderdice have called upon London to move into discussions at ministerial level. Cardinal Daly added his voice to this call, and the fringe Loyalist groups did likewise.

Indeed, the Unionist attitude was an interesting one. Although they would presumably prefer that Sinn Féin and the British government never meet at a political level, a number of senior Unionists have said that such meetings are inevitable, and that London should stop pretending otherwise and get on with it.

The British announcement came at a time when the peace process was moving into a potential crisis. Over the past few weeks I called upon everyone with influence to use that influence to avert any crisis. On Monday I met with Mr. Bruton and Mr. Spring before the British move. We discussed the need to ensure that equality is built into the process. This had become, and remains, an urgent necessity, even after Monday's development.

Equality is a basic requirement for any viable peace process. The absence of equality has created the conditions of conflict that have so bedeviled Anglo-Irish affairs. Any serious effort to reverse this situation, to build agreement and national reconciliation, must have equality as its foundation.

The current concern arises from a recent speech by Sir Patrick Mayhew in which he put forward the London government's intention to proceed on a two-track approach with all other parties on one track discussing the future of Ireland, and with Sinn Féin stuck in a second track, quarantined by writ of British Prime Minister John Major's policy of "decontamination." This obviously cannot work.

Sir Patrick was knocked temporarily off course by a very timely intervention from Mr. Bruton. But since then, and since Monday's announcement, this position has been reiterated on a number of occasions. There is a need therefore for everyone to be vigilant. Monday's announcement was a victory for common sense. But there is still a lot of work to be done. All-party talks should commence with urgency. London and Dublin need to take up leadership positions in order to make the best possible progress following this week's breakthrough. There was no excuse for stalling the peace process this last few months. The IRA cessation is now eight months old. It is disgraceful that the British have delayed political contact with Sinn Féin until now. The end of the ban on ministerial contact with our party must also bring an end of British government discrimination against our voters. Every party with an electoral mandate must be treated equally.

In all of this there is a need to be positive, and to move the situation on. The British have yet to engage as fully as they should in building confidence in the peace process. They have now got themselves off a hook. All of us must ensure that they do not put themselves on other hooks, and that progress flows from this breakthrough. I want to commend all of those who have helped to create this new development. This includes the US delegation of congressmen led by Ben Gilman. I, and others, met with them last week, and I was very pleased with their positive response. The USA and, especially, friends of the Irish peace process still play a considerable role, and will continue to play a considerable role in building a lasting peace in Ireland.

In conclusion, may I convey my sympathy to all those bereaved by the bomb attack in Oklahoma. Everyone in Ireland is shocked at last Wednesday's tragedy. In a letter to President Bill Clinton I conveyed condolences on my behalf, and on behalf of Sinn Féin. People here know only too well and share the sense of grief and loss that is now being borne by the citizens of Oklahoma and across the United States.

Bobby Sands — A Personal Memory

Bobby Sands was twenty-seven years old and sixty-six days on hunger strike when he died on May 5, 1981 in the H-Blocks of Long Kesh prison. During his hunger-strike he was elected to the British parliament as MP for Fermanagh/South Tyrone. By August 1981 ten prisoners had died. The hunger-strikes were aimed primarily at rebutting the British government's attempts to criminalize the struggle for Irish freedom by changing the status of Sands and his fellow cellmates from political to criminal. They were also a response to the failure of the British government to implement an enlightened prison regime as promised in the settlement of the fifty-three-day hunger-strike in Autumn 1980 that had ended without fatalities.

O**N FRIDAY, MAY** 5, I was at the Forum for Peace and Reconciliation in Dublin Castle. It was a beautiful day. I arrived fairly early to meet privately with the Taoiseach John Bruton. The inner courtyard of the castle – the center of British military rule in Ireland in a previous life – was bustling with people dressed in period costumes. I was in the middle of a film set. *Moll Flanders*, someone volunteered.

It was an interesting scene. A few years ago, when camping in the Dingle peninsula, I hiked into the village, all brilliantly disguised in glass fiber and real thatch, erected in the wilds for Tom Cruise's *Far and Away*. Funny, that, isn't it?

In the H-Blocks of Long Kesh, to while away the long evenings, the political prisoners – the blanket men – used to retell films they had seen. Or books they had read. Once, Bobby Sands recited Leon Uris' *Trinity*. Outsiders who learned of this marveled at Bobby's memory. *Trinity*, as literati will attest, is a lengthy tome. Methinks Bobby made up the bits he couldn't remember. He probably also amended the bits he didn't like.

Bik McFarlane used to do that all the time. In his version of *The Quiet Man*, John Wayne doesn't get to marry Maureen O'Hara. In fact, he gets run out of town and Maureen marries Darby O'Gill. Copyright didn't matter in the Blocks.

As I waited for John Bruton, these and other thoughts crowded my mind. Below me in the courtyard, actor Morgan Freeman sipped coffee at a chuckwagon van around which the cast had assembled for breakfast or brunch or whatever it is they have in period films.

Bobby Sands loved a good film. Or a good story. Whatever dramatic form it took. He was no mean writer himself. Mostly political stuff. But two of his songs, *McIlhatten* and *Back Home in Derry*, are recorded by Christy Moore. Bobby would have liked that. He enjoyed singing. Kris Kristofferson's *Me and Bobby McGee* was a particular favorite for a jamming session.

One Christmas in Cage 11, the grand finale for our annual concert was a brilliant group mime of Freddy Mercury's "A Night at the Opera." Stu, John the Joiner and the Dosser took center stage in improvized rock band outfits and brought our evening to an unforgettable conclusion. Igor, the handyman and half-genius of Cage 11, had organized colored smoke to waft itself slowly around the performers. We discovered later that he made it by igniting ground-down table tennis balls. The cast of our night at the opera collapsed, gasping and choking for breath. The cage was enveloped in thick smoke. The prison wardens went on an anti-escape alert. Fire hoses were summoned to the scene.

That was a good Christmas and the subject of some of Bobby's stories. He was also an avid *gaeilgeoir*. In the cages of Long Kesh, students of the Irish language formed little Irish-speaking communities. Bobby was fluent before he left the cages. Later in the H-Blocks he was the catalyst for the Irish language revival which saw English replaced as the language of the prisoners.

There was little other mental stimulation. And no physical recreation whatsoever. Bobby wasn't a bad soccer player. He enjoyed Gaelic football and was a good, tight competitor. But soccer suited his size. He enjoyed sport, *craic*, fun. He was committed to life.

It takes bone-deep commitment to lie naked and alone in a prison cell in your own excreta, systematically beaten and brutalized, scrubbed with yard brushes and hosed with industrial disinfectant. But it is soul-deep commitment to rise above all this to stand at the cell door telling of films or books you enjoyed, and enthralling and uplifting others in the telling.

Yet Bobby Sands was an ordinary man. The blanket men and women in Armagh were not supermen or superwomen. They were ordinary people pushed into extraordinary circumstances who rose to the challenge and went beyond it. Hundreds of them did so for six years, in horrific conditions in the blocks and in Armagh. The British government has no concept of such commitment, even less of the Hunger Strike.

After the 1980 strike ended, when there was an opportunity for a settlement, London sought to turn this against the prisoners. The second hunger strike resulted from that. The British saw flexibility by the POWs as weakness. They were wrong. When ten brave young Irishmen died slow and agonizing deaths one after the other, not for their own sake but for their comrades, they won the admiration of people throughout the world. Even as Margaret Thatcher crowed victory in her efforts to criminalize the political prisoners, their attitude to Ireland and to Bobby Sands and his friends criminalized her government.

These and other recollections continued to crowd my mind until John Bruton arrived for our meeting. And after he and I had completed our business, I returned to my musings as I strolled back along palatial corridors, on the way to another engagement. By now the castle was coming to life, but I was undisturbed in my wanderings. I hesitated for a moment to inquire after the whereabouts of the nearest men's room.

"Nip in here, Gerry," one of the attendants told me. He pointed to a side room. I crossed the room and entered a small toilet opposite me.

On my return two plaques above the fireplace caught my eye. One was in Irish, the other English.

"In this room James Connolly was held before being taken from here to be executed by the British on 12 May 1916." Right where I stood, the sounds from the film set outside vanished as I absorbed the mood, the spirit, the sense of that moment.

James Connolly is one of my heroes. He was also a hero of Bobby Sands. On that Friday, the day when I stood alone in the room where Connolly was held, was the day fourteen years ago on which Bobby Sands died on hunger strike in the H-Blocks of Long Kesh.

Once Again, Irish America Moves the Process Forward

The Irish peace process took center stage in Washington DC when President Clinton hosted the White House Economic Summit on Ireland at the Sheraton Hotel May 25–27. Vice-President Al Gore, Minister of State Warren Christopher, and Commerce Secretary Ron Brown were among those who attended. It showed corporate America the opportunities for investment in the North and in the border counties. On the eve of the conference, behind closed doors and away from media cameras, Sinn Féin President Gerry Adams met for the first time with Northern Secretary of State Patrick Mayhew.

IN PORTLAND, MAINE, two excellent musicians provided a background of slow airs, jigs and reels. They sat in the porch while the rest of us overflowed out into the garden and throughout the rooms of the private home in which one of our two events was held. Later that night a troupe of Irish dancers tapped their way through Maine's own version of *Riverdance*.

That was the start of it.

From Boston to L.A., San Francisco to Tampa, Kansas City, Chicago and Cleveland and half a dozen places in between these, there was music in the air. The fundraising highlight, unprecedented in the Irish Republican history of the US, was in New York's Plaza Hotel where over four hundred people attended a $1,000-a-plate dinner function. It went splendidly, as did all the other engagements. Whether people paid big bucks or a few dollars or nothing, they all have one thing in common – a commitment to peace in Ireland and a desire to make a contribution to the evolving peace process. Irish America is on the march, and the new confidence which permeates the Diaspora is making its mark.

This tour, organized by Friends of Sinn Féin, covered more cities than my last visit to the US, and wherever we went people were warm and welcoming. And not only the Irish. We met Native Americans, Italian Americans, Hispanics, African Americans, the Jewish community. . . all interested in the Irish struggle for justice.

There was a widespread recognition of the positive role played by President Clinton everywhere we visited. Even those who might not agree with the White House's position on other issues freely acknowledge that the President's engagement with the Irish peace process has been even-handed and positive. Irish America also knows of the sterling work of Congressman Ben Gilman, chairperson of the House International Relations Committee. It is also obvious that this engagement has been invaluable in moving the process forward, and it is actually possible to measure developments in the peace process by reviewing the various developments here in the US.

For example, when first I was given a 48-hour visa to travel to New York, my voice and the voices of other Sinn Féin representatives could not be broadcast on the British broadcasting media. US broadcasters were outraged and bewildered by such blatant censorship. The result? The British were embarrassed by the unwelcome focus on this undemocratic practice. They dropped the broadcasting ban.

So too with the ban on my right to travel in Britain. Martin McGuinness and I and others were internally exiled into one part of London's "United Kingdom." We couldn't go to London, but with President Clinton's invitation, I could go to the White House. Again the British were moved to end this source of embarrassment. The travel ban was dropped.

Talks with the British officials, promised by Prime Minister John Major last year, were delayed and delayed. Then Senator George Mitchell announced that he and others, including Commerce Secretary Ron Brown, were to visit Ireland as part of the US economic commitment to the peace process. Sinn Féin was invited to meet with the US visitors. The British moved to announce the commencement of talks between us and its representatives before the White House delegation arrived in Ireland.

That wasn't the end of the stalling, of course. These talks were with British government officials. The ban on ministerial contacts remained. But an economic conference, hosted by President Clinton, was scheduled for Washington at the end of this month. Everyone was invited. This open-door policy, similar to the position of Taoiseach John Bruton, meant that all parties were free to attend. The British strategy is totally different. London prefers a two-track, two-speed approach.

Patrick Mayhew visited Washington just before St. Patrick's week to make exactly this point. The White House took a more enlightened view. Back in Ireland the British announced they would end the ban on ministerial contact, but only with certain ministers. This did not include Patrick Mayhew. Not at this time.

When Martin McGuinness led the Sinn Féin team into talks with British minister Michael Ancram, he stressed the need for equality of treatment for all sections of the electorate. I had previously written to John Major on three occasions regarding these matters, and Martin McGuinness had also raised this issue in the meetings with British government officials. We all need to learn the lesson of conflict if we are to secure the peace. Inequality creates conflict. Peace demands equality.

When I started my visit in the US I reiterated this point. It seemed to me that the Washington economic conference would not only provide a much needed focus on economic investment in the British occupied six county area and the border counties; not only would it provide an opportunity to raise the issue of discrimination, but it would also offer a unique opportunity for the British and the Unionists to show good faith, to break the ice and to enter into discussions with us and the rest of those in attendance. These included all the main players – the London and Dublin governments plus the main Unionist parties and the fringe Loyalist groups; the SDLP and Sinn Féin also; all under one roof.

Patrick Mayhew had a choice. He could seek to avoid contact with us, causing huge problems for the protocol people and embarrassment to his government. Or he could do the right thing and demonstrate in practical terms the British government's acceptance of the rights of the Sinn Féin electorate to have their concerns represented in direct dialogue with the British government on the basis of equality.

I am pleased to say Patrick Mayhew did the right thing. I am writing this in Washington, the morning after a meeting between myself and Mr. Mayhew. Mairéad Keane, head of the Sinn Féin mission in the US, and Richard McAuley, public relations officer, accompanied me. Patrick Mayhew was flanked by James Cron, his parliamentary secretary, and his private secretary. We had a good meeting which lasted for around thirty-five minutes. My engagement with Patrick Mayhew was frank, positive and forthright. The atmosphere was relaxed.

Obviously, the two of us come to the Anglo-Irish situation from very different positions. I want to see an end to British rule in Ireland. I reminded Mr. Mayhew of this. He has a different position. I stressed that each of us has to play leadership roles in bridging the gap between us, and I stressed London's hesitance and responsibility to move all the democratically mandated parties into multilateral talks.

When John Hume and I first initiated the Irish peace process, we spelled out the need to reach agreement between the people of Ireland. We pointed out the responsibility of both governments to encourage this. This remains as valid an achievement now as it did then. My engagement with Patrick Mayhew is an important step in the search for this new accord. It was the first time in over twenty years that a British cabinet minister heard the Irish Republican view directly. He heard Sinn Féin's analysis on resolving the conflict; on the need for demilitarization; the release of prisoners; the urgent necessity to democratize the situation and to consolidate the peace process.

Dialogue is a two-way process, so I listened intently to Patrick Mayhew's views on these matters. We each have a duty to bring a generosity of spirit to these engagements. The process of decontamination of Sinn Féin is over. Inclusivenss is needed.

I was concerned that my discussion with Patrick Mayhew, which happened before the start of the economic forum, should not distract attention from it. As things turned out, it put everyone concerned with building peace in good form for what was a unique and imaginative contribution to the peace process. My engagement with Patrick Mayhew was an important one. The dialogue must be accelerated. All-party talks, led by London and Dublin, are required. Progress on a range of issues is necessary. In this way we will consolidate the peace process.

It is no accident that this first meeting since last I met a British cabinet minister, in 1972, took place in Washington. This has been a good trip, but I'm looking forward to getting back to Belfast again. It will be a good flight, knowing that engagement with US officials and with Irish America has helped move us all, once again, towards freedom, peace and justice.

A Major Crisis Looming in the Peace Process; "Bad Faith" Negotiations Threaten Progress

Continued British inaction seriously endangered the search for peace.

L AST MONTH'S MEETING with Northern Secretary Mayhew in Washington was an important step. The next step is all-party talks and negotiations, led by both governments, at which everyone is at the table. I saw my engagement with Patrick Mayhew, and the meetings between British minister Michael Ancram and Sinn Féin's Martin McGuinness, as movement in that direction.

When I returned to Ireland I wrote to Patrick Mayhew, commending him for his part in our meeting and seeking another meeting to build on the Washington engagement. He refused my request, and although he later spoke ambiguously about not ruling out a future meeting, his refusal to meet again at this time brings us all to a possible major difficulty in the peace process. This is the British government's insistence that there cannot be all-party talks unless the IRA surrenders its weapons.

To quote Patrick Mayhew's letter: "The plain fact is that there will be no substantive political talks which will include Sinn Féin without progress on the issue, not least because other parties will not take part in them."

This brings us to a crux. How can the peace process progress into a peace settlement if there are not multilateral talks or if the British government refuses to play a leadership role, along with Dublin, in initiating these talks?

The entire logic of a peace process is that, through substantive all-party peace talks, we arrive at a peace settlement that removes the causes of the conflict and takes the guns, forever, from Irish politics. All-party peace talks should be initiated as a matter of urgency, and within an agreed time-frame. They need to address three broad areas:

- Political and constitutional change;
- The democratization of the situation;
- The demilitarization of the situation.

No issue should be made a precondition for further movement towards a negotiated peace settlement. Dialogue and inclusive negotiations based on democratic principles are the only viable means of securing a lasting peace settlement.

The British government cannot be allowed to dictate the terms of this accommodation, nor can it be allowed to determine who can or cannot participate in the negotiations leading to such agreement. The peace process does not belong to the British government. It belongs to the Irish people – to all the Irish people. Nor can the British government be allowed to control the peace process itself – its pace, participants, terms of reference, the structure of the negotiations or terms for a settlement. The record of the British government in bringing peace to Ireland is regrettably deficient. It is a record of failure. By and large it has been the Irish people who have paid the price for that failure.

Having stalled the commencement of all-party peace talks over the ten months of the IRA cessation, the British are now erecting an absolute precondition to further movement in the peace process. All those committed to finding a peace settlement are concerned that the British government is demanding the surrender of IRA weapons as a precondition to all-party talks on the future of Ireland. The logic of that position, if adhered to, is that there will be no inclusive peace talks, and no democratic settlement.

The demand for surrender of IRA weapons as a precondition to negotiations was never mentioned by the London government before August 31. In fact, the British were engaged in intensive contact and dialogue with Sinn Féin for two years prior to the IRA cessation, and never at any time was the issue of decommissioning raised. In my view, had a surrender of IRA weapons been imposed as a precondition to peace negotiations prior to the cessation, it is possible that there would have been no IRA cessation on September 1 of last year.

The British government is clearly acting in bad faith and is reneging on its commitments to all-party negotiations given publicly prior to August 31.

Sinn Féin is not the IRA. Sinn Féin does not have any weapons to decommission, a reality accepted by the British government in the course of our dialogue. Sinn Féin presents our views on the sole basis of our electoral mandate. We will approach the negotiating table on the same basis. As democrats we believe that a democratic and lasting settlement must be based on the fundamental right of the Irish people to national self-determination. As Irish Republicans, we are committed to ending British rule in our country. We will bring this commitment to the negotiating table.

We accept also that there are those who have a different view, a view they will take to the negotiating table. We are wholly committed to a process of democratic and peaceful negotiations, and to the agreed political settlement among the Irish people that will emerge from these negotiations. This was underlined publicly in a statement issued jointly by the then Taoiseach Albert Reynolds, the SDLP leader John Hume, and myself on September 6, 1994, which stated:

"We are at the beginning of a new era in which we are totally committed to democratic and peaceful methods of resolving our political problems. We reiterate that our objective is an equitable and lasting agreement that can command the allegiance of all."

The Irish government has accepted this position, and has acted upon it. So too has the US administration which, at its highest level, has engaged in political dialogue with Sinn Féin. The British government alone adheres to impossible preconditions to all-party dialogue.

Sinn Féin is totally committed to the permanent and effective removal of all guns from Irish politics. We have consistently underlined our desire to see a democratic settlement and the complete demilitarization of the situation – that is, the removal of repressive legislation, the release of all political prisoners and the removal of all guns – British, Unionist, Loyalist, and Republican – from Irish politics.

The British government has said that: "The holding of illegal arms and the use of violence and threats have no place in a peaceful, democratic society." We agree. The six county statelet, however, is not, and since its creation, has never been a "peaceful, democratic society." Since its creation seventy-two years ago, the governance of the six county statelet has been a matter of crisis management. It has always been dependent on the existence and exercise of repressive legislation, coercion and discrimination. This lies at the heart of conflict and division both in Ireland and between Britain and Ireland.

Against a backdrop of conflict and violence, often directed randomly at Nationalists and Catholics, the precondition of surrender of IRA weapons is unrealistic. It is necessary to create the conditions in which those with weapons will decommission them. The depth of insecurity for Nationalists should not be underestimated. It arises from the history of the six county statelet from its creation up to the present day, and from a continuing and understandable fear of further attack by official and unofficial British, Unionist and Loyalist forces alike.

Nor is there any room or part in the peace process for the victory/surrender ethos that the demand for a surrender of all weapons represents. This would have a demoralizing effect on many Nationalists and, potentially, a profound and damaging effect on the peace process itself.

These are the human realities of the realpolitik, which have been understood and accepted in other conflict situations. There is no international precedent and certainly no historical precedent in Ireland for the handing over of weapons. The important thing is to build on the opportunity that has been created, to advance the situation to the point where all guns are not simply silent but obsolete.

It has been argued that the British government is simply asking for a symbolic gesture. But it is a gesture that would symbolize an IRA surrender. This is hardly a reasonable or justifiable demand, particularly in light of the British government's reluctance and begrudging response to the new situation. It would be even more unacceptable and reprehensible if the British government were allowed to hold up progress towards a lasting peace settlement over a demand for a symbolic gesture.

Of course, the British government is not simply interested in a gesture. It is, in reality, demanding the start of a surrender process as a precondition to all-party peace talks. It is, in reality, attempting to achieve by stealth what it could not achieve in twenty-five years of military conflict.

The British are treating arms in isolation from all else, and are trying to impose a one-item agenda. The Irish Foreign Minister

Dick Spring, speaking in Washington, DC on March 1, 1995, pointed out that: "If we take the attitude that nothing will happen unless there is a surrender or decommissioning of arms, then I think that is a formula for disaster."

But why is this issue so important to the British in the context of a disciplined and complete IRA cessation?

The British government, or at least the politically dominant elements within it, remain locked in the victory/defeat mindset. They wish to deflect and dilute the national and international support for a democratic and negotiated settlement by creating an unnecessary and divisive argument over IRA weapons. They hope to divert the progressive and democratic dynamic for a negotiated settlement into a side road, a cul-de-sac, in the hope that pressure will go on to the IRA, when what is important is that the IRA weapons are already silent. They may, in fact, wish to cause divisions and fractures within the IRA itself in an effort to undermine the strength of the Republican position. In short, they wish to maintain the status quo.

In pursuing this agenda, the British have, as ever, used the convenient cover of the Unionists. In doing so they are encouraging, rather than discouraging, Unionist intransigence. The Unionists cannot be given a veto over negotiations leading to an agreed accommodation on this island. Such a veto is undemocratic. It must be said, however, that the Unionist people are both pragmatic and intelligent. I am confident they will not allow their representatives to simply opt out of negotiations on issues that fundamentally affect their future. The Washington conference, for example, demonstrated that if they cannot prevent such inclusive debate and discussion, the Unionists will become involved. The Unionist resistance to negotiations, which is perfectly understandable, is a flag of convenience for the British government. The British government must be persuaded to move to all-party talks.

The practical aspects of decommissioning are, of course, an entirely separate matter from all of this. These are matters on which agreement would be required once we create the conditions in which those with weapons will decommission them. In this context we have discussed with and examined closely the British government views on the modalities of a decommissioning process. This may be an effective or acceptable approach to the practical aspects of this issue. Indeed, it is conceivable that other formulas may be advanced. The modalities of decommissioning are practical matters which can be resolved in conditions of justice and democracy which make peace a reality. The most important thing, therefore, is to create these conditions. At that point the "how" and "what" and "when" become relatively simple, practical matters on which agreement can be quickly reached.

It is also important to note that there are many armed groups – British, Loyalist as well as Republican – involved in this conflict, and there are many consequences of this:

- There are approximately 16,000 members of the British Army still involved in military operations;
- There are massive military encampments throughout the six county statelet; an intensive campaign of recruitment for the RIR, the renamed UDR, is being conducted;
- There are 13,000 heavily armed members of the RUC, a paramilitary force that has acted as the armed wing of Unionism and which is totally unacceptable to the Nationalist community, and whose existence Patrick Mayhew has endorsed into the foreseeable future;
- There are approximately 120,000 licensed weapons, most of them in the hands of the Unionist community;
- There are large stockpiles of weapons in the possession of Loyalist paramilitaries, brought into the country through the combined efforts of Unionist politicians, Loyalist death squads and British intelligence;
- There is also a plethora of repressive laws that the British government retains, and which must be repealed as part of a process of demilitarization and democratization;
- And the British government has made no move to deal with the reality that there are hundreds of political prisoners held in British jails. All the political prisoners need to be released. In the interim, the day to day hardship for prisoners and their families need to be improved, and most immediately, Irish political prisoners held in England need to be transferred back to Ireland.

These are all issues that Sinn Féin, if so minded, could, like the British government, create preconditions around in order to deliberately block forward movement. We have not.

It is wholly inconsistent to focus entirely on one aspect of a militarized society while ignoring or ruling out movement on other aspects of the conflict; and more importantly, blocking progress towards a negotiated settlement, which is the only way to effectively and permanently remove the causes of the conflict. The British government is, in effect, demanding the surrender of the IRA. This is a demand that cannot be delivered on, and which, if maintained, can only serve to undermine confidence in the peace process itself. It represents a psychology of war. What is required in this new climate is a psychology of peace.

The IRA has already taken an enormous step, and sustained it over ten months – a step far beyond any mere gesture. The British government has not matched the magnitude or the courage of this decision, nor has it lived up to the rhetoric of Prime Minister John Major, Patrick Mayhew or former Northern Secretary Peter Brooke.

All aspects of militarization are the symptoms of the political failures of the past. They need to be addressed and resolved as part of a political settlement if we are to have a lasting peace. The consequences of the conflict, of course, need to be dealt with, both as part of the peace process itself, and as part of a wider healing process of national reconciliation. But the clear priority is to address and resolve the causes of conflict: the failed political policies and structures that led into conflict and to the militarization that we are now seeking to redress.

Twenty-five years of British political and military strategies did not defeat the IRA. Sinn Féin cannot and will not involve itself in futile exercises to bring about an IRA surrender. Any such attempt by Sinn Féin to do so would undermine our political influence and ability to advance the situation. Sinn Féin cannot deliver an IRA surrender. That is the reality.

Everyone has an influence over this situation. The collective application of that influence through serious and comprehensive negotiations can transform the political climate and put an end to the failures of the past. Sinn Féin's position on this matter is transparent. We wish to use our influence on all matters, in a positive way, and with the aim of advancing the peace process. How we use our influence, and how much influence we have, is a matter of judgment for us.

The British government also has an influence – in fact the major influence – in the present situation. The Irish government and all political parties with the exception of the Unionists have called for substantive negotiations to begin. The British government is refusing to take this essential step and is preventing progress towards an agreed and lasting political settlement.

Peace is not simply the absence of conflict. Rather it is the existence of conditions in which the causes of conflict have been eradicated, and where justice, equality, and democracy prevail; where agreed political structures and institutions are a substitute for political conflict; where diversity is recognized, and democratically accommodated. This task can only be accomplished through all-party peace talks.

At this stage of the peace process – two years after John Hume and I initiated the process, and almost three years since London reopened contact with Sinn Féin, and now ten months into the IRA cessation – we should be discussing these matters. It is the widely held view right across the community that we should be building on the momentous opportunity that has been created through the efforts of many who were prepared to take risks for peace.

By now we should be negotiating our future, striving for agreement, seeking a new accord. Instead, we are stuck in a rut with progress blocked off by an obstacle created by the British government. It is the duty of everyone concerned to find a way of resolving this difficulty. The obstacle must be removed. Failure to move beyond this will jeopardize the entire peace process. This must not be allowed to happen. Failure cannot be allowed to breed greater failure.

Out of Africa
With Some Good Lessons

*In June 1995, a Sinn Féin delegation made their first-ever
trip to South Africa to meet with President Nelson Mandela
and the ANC leadership, and to learn from the South African
peace process.*

MY RECENT VISIT to South Africa was a week-long whirl-
wind of meetings and interviews, of salutations and
sound-bites, of solidarity and speeches. And one rugby
match.

We saw little of the country – Cape Town by moonlight; Preto-
ria, a pretty tree-lined city, Durban Beach on a stormy late night
two-minute stop. Johannesburg was the only place where the sun
shone.

In South Africa it is winter. Weather-wise, that is. Every other
way, it is spring. A sense of a new beginning, of a new South
Africa. Of a near miracle. Of course, there is a lot to be done. A
stable future demands more miracles.

The conditions in the squatter camps are pitiable. No matter
where we went, no matter how salubrious or palatial our surroundings, I was conscious that only a short time ago, black people were excluded.

So the ghost of apartheid stalked us, shadowed us, throughout
our travels, quietly lurking in the background of the new South
Africa as an echo of the past. Everywhere except in the townships
and squatter camps. Here, the obscenity of apartheid howled at us
and the fortitude and patience of the black majority humbled us.

Our delegation – Rita O'Hare, Richard McAuley, Chrissie
McAuley and myself – were guests of the African National Congress (ANC), and from our first boisterous welcome in the early
hours of the morning, after an eleven-hour flight, until the more
subdued tear-filled farewell a week later, we were greeted everywhere with open arms.

There were three reasons for our trip. The primary one was to
learn from the peace process in South Africa, so that the lessons
there could be applied to the Irish peace process. We were also

there to inform people of the evolving situation in Ireland, and finally, on a personal level, our visit was almost a pilgrimage. I have been a life-long supporter of the anti-apartheid cause. My first protest in that cause was in Dublin in 1970 against the Springboks. There was thus a sense of coming home to attend my first rugby match in Durban and in support of the Springboks. And there were lots of other examples of being home. On our first day at ANC headquarters, over lunch we met Walter Sisulu, the grand old man of African resistance. All of us were so familiar with his personal history, and all of us in the delegation – former political prisoners – were bear-hugged by him in what was almost a reunion.

I was very impressed by the ANC leadership. In many ways, President Mandela is a first among equals. We met Cyril Ramaphosa, the secretary general and the ANC's main negotiator with the old regime. We also met with Thabo Mbeki, deputy president, and with Jacob Zuma, national party chairperson. Women were represented in every delegation: at national, regional and local level. In other meetings with Pravan Gordhan, National Executive Council (NEC) member and senior negotiator on constitutional affairs, and with Cheryl Carolus, and with Yusuf Salojae, we learned of how the ANC were plotting the course from conflict to democracy. We also met with a range of cabinet ministers and other NEC members.

Of all the political leaderships which I have met, never have I met a group as cohesive, articulate and far-seeing as those in the ANC leadership.

The meeting with President Mandela was, of course, the highlight of all our meetings. Before we did our formal session, we met informally for a few minutes for what was lighthearted *craic* and banter. The President is self-effacing in his humor; totally relaxed but focused. On the day of our meeting, as with every normal workday, he arose at 4 a.m.

During our meeting, he recalled how he was castigated when he visited Ireland in 1992 because he publicly called for talks between the British government and Irish Republicans. Good-humoredly, he recollected how, while he was being publicly condemned for his audacity, the British were secretly talking to Sinn Féin. His commitment is clearly to a peace settlement in Ireland.

The meeting itself was constructive and friendly, and at the press conference afterwards President Mandela fielded questions with ease. In response to one query in relation to the current impasse in the Irish peace process, Mr. Mandela pointed out that while the ANC suspended its armed struggle unilaterally, it never surrendered its weapons. He added that he was sure Sinn Féin and the British government would find a way to resolve these difficulties.

We also met a range of other political opinion, and in a strange way, the engagement with the Afrikaner representatives was a revelation to us. We met first with the General, Constand Viljöon, leader of the Freedom Front Party. The General came into party politics on the eve of South Africa's historic election. In his own words, he and other generals "were set for war." Then, four days before the election, and following twenty meetings with the ANC, he opted for a negotiated settlement.

In our discussions, he pointed out the need for an acceptance of change by all sides. It is obvious that he and his supporters have not yet decided on how much change they will contemplate, but the need for change was their starting point, and from a right-wing position, he has now moved to being a central, pragmatic symbol of the new South Africa.

Our engagement with the PAC (Pan African Congress) representative, Patricia de Lille, was also interesting as she outlined the peace process from the perspective of a very radical black African group.

Roelf Meyer, who was the chief negotiator for the old Apartheid regime, gave us of his time. This was my second meeting with him, and it is now acknowledged by all sides that the personal engagement between Mr. Meyer and Cyril Ramaphosa was a crucial element in winning the peace.

Meyer also stressed the need for an acceptance of change for all sides. He sketched out how the old administration and the Afrikaner people found it difficult to come to this position, and how many of his associates and colleagues condemned him as selling out or compromising on basic positions. Out of all this, many of the positions which Sinn Féin have adopted were reaffirmed for us: the need for all-party talks, the need for inclusive negotiations, the need for change, the need for a negotiated settlement. We were privileged to get a wide range of views and to witness how parties once in conflict were now working in partnership.

At one squatter camp, Pholar Park, we were surrounded by hundreds of people and our group quickly became a demonstration *toytoy*-ing and chanting its way off a dual carriageway, and into the bush towards the squatter camp. At one point we were flanked by a few hundred warriors semi-naked and carrying traditional weapons. They, all male, took up macho positions during the welcome ceremony and the speeches.

For me, a telling reality of the situation was that one of the women who formed the welcoming committee announced to the assembled multitude that the children needed to get polio injections the following afternoon at three p.m., and children there were in their hundreds. This was probably the most stark memory of our visit. Afterwards, the sight troubled all of our delegation because Pholar Park, the scene of some of the worst killings, is without water or electricity, and there's a collection of shanty huts.

So it was a week of contrasts, of great progress and of many challenges. All of us felt privileged and rejuvenated in our quest for a peace process in our own country. The people of South Africa who sent a message to all humanity for decades were told that the conflict there was intractable. We are told the same thing about the Anglo-Irish conflict, and therein lies the biggest lesson of all.

If peace can happen in South Africa, why not in Ireland?

Despite British Arrogance, Republicans Still Seek Peace

Just one week before the Twelfth of July parades, the British government, in a bid to win party support for John Major's Conservative leadership, released paratrooper Private Lee Clegg. Clegg had served only two years of his life prison sentence for the murder of a teenage girl, who had been in a joyrider car that drove through the checkpoint where he was on duty. Three days of rioting in Nationalist areas followed his release.

LAST MONTH THIS column intended informing *Irish Voice* readers about the plight of Irish political prisoners. The prompting for this came from what appeared to be the inevitability of the release of Lee Clegg. I am sorry now that I didn't get around to writing that piece. It might in some way have forewarned Irish-American opinion about the cavalier way that the London government is treating the Irish peace process, and about the dangers for all of us if the British government continues to behave in an irresponsible manner.

It isn't that we won't get peace. It is my firm conviction that we will have peace in Ireland. But we can't have peace unless and until the British government is also committed to this objective. So the road to peace will be bogged down or obstructed by obstacles or lengthened by diversions and cul-de-sacs – unless and until we get Britain on board.

I still need to write about the prisoners, but the urgency of the current situation demands that I deal with the need now for everyone with influence to persuade the British government to face up to its responsibilities. There is a positive dimension to this. The leadership contest within the British Tory Party and the re-election of John Major as leader has removed the distraction – or the excuse of a distraction – from the British government. Mr. Major can now focus on the Irish peace process.

It is worth pointing out again that this peace process does not belong to London. It seeks to be inclusive and requires the building of confidence and trust to a point where our common responsibility guarantees a shared management of the search for peace in Ireland.

In considering the work ahead of us, it is useful to explore in brief where the process came from. A consensus of views and opinions was developed between John Hume, myself and the former Irish Taoiseach Albert Reynolds – between the Irish government, the SDLP and Sinn Féin – across a number of key political areas. This consensus of views and opinions was supported by mainstream Irish-American opinion. There was broad agreement that the principles of equality of treatment and equality of opportunity would have to apply across the political, cultural, economic, social, legal and security spectrum. There was agreement on the need for a negotiated settlement.

The Irish peace initiative galvanized Irish national opinion, north and south, and focused the Irish and British governments and the White House on the issue of peace in Ireland in a manner unparalleled for decades. The political climate and the search for a negotiated peace settlement was transformed by the IRA cessation and by a broad evolution in Sinn Féin strategy which in recent years has been the catalyst for much of the potential which has been created.

The events of the past week illustrate in a very dramatic way the fragile nature of a peace process. The problem is typified by those who approved of Lee Clegg's release, who defended it and who claimed it has no bearing on the peace process. The British government was well warned about this situation by the Irish government and by others. Typically, London decided to ignore this advice, and it did so in an arrogant way.

This is another slap in the face for those of us who are trying to develop a non-violent way out of the conflict. That is how Clegg's release was viewed by many, many people, especially those who took to the streets to protest. In turn, an element of these protests – the violent element – has been utilized by anti-Republican elements opportunistically and wrongly to attack Sinn Féin. Our party's constructive contribution to peaceful demonstrations and our appeals for calm have been largely ignored by our detractors.

My position on this is clear. Nothing should be allowed to distract attention from what should be the main focus of all our efforts – that is, all-party talks. It is little wonder that frustrations reach boiling point when ten months after the IRA ceasefire, the British refuse to join with the Irish government to initiate real peace talks; when Patrick Mayhew refuses to meet the Sinn Féin leadership; and when London treats all representations from Irish Nationalism with dismissive arrogance.

Some journalists are now painting up alarmist, speculative scenarios about Republican intentions. Republicans, in my opinion, remain deeply committed to the search for peace. The anger at the British attitude is much wider than the Republican family. It is shared by the Sinn Féin leadership, but in a weekend of meetings in Dublin and elsewhere I have been surprised at the depth of annoyance at London's position. Last August 31, a climate of hope was created by the IRA cessation. For the most part, this cessation was viewed as an opportunity to create the conditions which would remove the causes of conflict and lead to a lasting peace in our country.

Today that hope is beginning to dim, and anxiety is replacing anticipation within sections of our people. Those of us in leadership positions have a duty to ensure that we are not unnerved by this development or distracted from what should be the main priority of all sensible opinion makers. I am not surprised by the British government's failings. Historically, it has rarely shown imagination or vision in its dealings with Ireland. When it has moved, it has been because it has served British strategic interest to do so.

The British government engagement with the peace process to date has been a bad faith engagement, not just last week, not just for the last ten months, but going back to when John Hume and I were trying to initiate a way forward. This way forward requires everyone to play their part in creating and agreeing to a solution. It is on this point that I wish to concentrate, because the need for everyone to play their part is a constant one and in this regard, Irish America has a very special role to play.

For some time, elements of political opinion here and in the States argued that the IRA was the problem, that the British government was neutral – that an end to the IRA's campaign would see the prisons emptied, a complete withdrawal of troops, an end to repression and discrimination, and most importantly of all, the commencement of real peace talks.

I have a different attitude to the British government's involvement in Ireland and to its policy. But the problem facing all of us today is that not one person – whether in the Irish government or any of the political parties – has a notion of when Mr. Major will begin talking about peace, talking about a peace settlement. The British government has yet to be moved to build the peace. And they blame the Unionists! We know that we have to make peace with the Unionists, but they cannot dictate the agenda by their absence and Mr. Major cannot dodge his responsibility. This is the Orange card being played once again. On Monday morning, July 10, Unionist leader John Taylor said that the Unionists, and not the British, would decide "when, if ever, all-party talks would begin." That is the challenge facing Mr. Major. Irish Nationalists can make peace with the Unionists, but only when they want to make peace with us. John Major must tell them that the time is now.

Today (July 10), as I write this piece, a small and peaceful demonstration in Portadown is demanding an end to triumphalist and provocative sectarian Orange parades through a Catholic area in the town. A sizable contingent of Orangemen is in its second day of protracted efforts to march through the Catholic area, and the prominent UUP leader David Trimble has just announced that unless the Orangemen can march through this area then there is no peace process. Mr. Trimble has played no part whatsoever in the peace process except to attack it. Leading Loyalists have threatened dire consequences unless the Orange parades go ahead.

It is worth noting that most Catholics in this state tolerate the Orange marching season with great patience. There are hundreds of Orange marches, and I for one uphold the right of the Orangemen to march. So long as they don't march over the rest of us. Only a handful of parades are contentious. All of these are in Nationalist areas. In many ways the intransigence of the Orangemen and the current row shows how the diversity of the people of this island which should be a source of joy and strength, is manipulated and used to perpetuate division and to entrench inequality.

The imperative of peace demands that we move beyond this phase of the peace process. That is the challenge also for Mr. Major, and this must be put to the British government. Peace talks demand compromise and accommodation, and a peace settlement requires fundamental change – political, constitutional, economic, cultural and legal change. The British government is not yet prepared to face up to that reality. They must be convinced and persuaded to do so. They cannot be allowed to stick to their own narrow agenda.

Irish America played a leading role in moving the entire situation to this decisive point in Anglo-Irish relationships. We who have created this opportunity for peace, who have built the peace process and who support the creation of a process of peaceful change, need to remove the obstacles to forward movement. This is our responsibility – in Ireland, in Britain and in North America.

Peace in Ireland cannot simply sit and wait until the British government is ready or willing to move. We need to move the peace process into negotiations – into all-party talks as the only way to secure an agreed political settlement and therefore a sustainable peace. That is the commitment which the London and Dublin governments made publicly prior to the IRA cessation. Most importantly, it is the essential and urgent next stage of the peace process.

It is of crucial importance that this is our agreed position and that the signal we send is a clear and unambiguous one which the British government cannot misrepresent and misunderstand.

Drumcree
Mark One

The peace process continued to teeter back and forth in the summer of 1995, and progress continued to be elusive. The Orange parades created serious tensions and violent disturbances; while the leaked news of a private meeting between Sinn Féin and Northern Secretary Sir Patrick Mayhew caused a minor furor.

IT IS DIFFICULT to cover the many twists and turns of the situation at this time, much of it damaging to the peace process. The behavior of the Orange and Unionist leaderships over the Twelfth of July period, and the deteriorating conditions in which Republicans are held in prisons in Britain, are two matters of serious concern.

The Orange Order used to be an immensely powerful force within Unionism. It brought together all trends of Unionist opinion, uniting the landed gentry and the manufacturing classes with businessmen, shipyard workers and the urban and rural Unionist grass roots. Those were the days when Unionism was one party, when it had a one party state and its own Parliament.

Things are rather different these days, but some things never change. So it is that during the summer there are almost 3,000 Orange marches. Most Nationalists tolerate these parades. In Belfast, those who can afford to evacuate the city for quieter climes. Not so the people of Garvaghy Road or the Lower Ormeau Road.

These are two areas – there are others – where Orange parades are unwelcome. They are Catholic areas yet Orangemen insist that they should march through these districts playing provocative sectarian tunes in a swaggering display of triumphalism. The Orangemen have the right to march, but not in places where their behavior is unwelcome.

In Garvaghy Road in Portadown, thousands of Orangemen gathered and laid siege to the small Catholic enclave. It was a frightening experience for the families, circled by a huge mob led by Ian Paisley and UUP leader David Trimble. For three days the siege continued.

Elsewhere, other Orange mobs gathered in solidarity. There were protests and blockades. In one incident, the port of Larne was blockaded for forty-eight hours, two highjacked lorries were placed across the road and the local Unionist MP, like his fellows elsewhere, joined the mobs.

Not far from Garvaghy Road, where the Orangemen had assembled at Drumcree, Ian Paisley ranted in a display of dismally familiar anti-Catholic hysteria and incited the crowd. David Trimble said the peace process was worth nothing if he could not walk down Garvaghy Road.

Throughout all this mayhem, a small crowd of Catholic residents sat in the middle of their road in protest at the threatening behavior of the Orangemen. It was a very frightening time for them. At different times the Orangemen stormed the lines of the RUC. At one point Paisley and Trimble broke through. Eventually the stand-off ended in silent protest as a silent group of Portadown Orangemen marched down their road.

Everyone breathed a sigh of relief which quickly turned to anger when David Trimble emerged from Garvaghy Road onto our TV screens to declare, his face glowing in delight, that they had won the day, that there had been no negotiations and no compromise and that they would be back again. Ian Paisley and he then strutted in a triumphalist tango through the "victorious" cheering mob.

So what was is it all about? It was about making the "croppies lie down." Telling us who is in charge. It was about "No surrender" and "Not an inch." The politics of no change. During this time, despite the disturbances, rioting, intimidation and mob rule, the RUC made no arrests.

The following day on the Lower Ormeau Road it was a different story. On Garvaghy Road an Orange mob had hemmed in the residents in order to force through a march. In the Lower Ormeau the RUC did it for them. They invaded the area in a dawn raid and placed the small network of streets under effective curfew. The media were barred, residents were denied milk or bread supplies and this situation continued for some hours until, despite the protestations of the local people, the Orange parade had made its way through their area. In marked contrast to their handling of the Orange protesters the previous day, the RUC waded into residents on the Lower Ormeau.

At no point did any Unionist leader seek to reassure the Catholic citizens of this statelet. I use the word "Catholic" advisedly. For me the big lesson of the Garvaghy Road and Lower Ormeau is that the Unionist leadership has yet to accept that to have peace we must have change. I fully accept that Orangeism is a strand of Irish history. I see the Battle of the Boyne or the Siege of Derry as being in their own way as important as the 1916 Rising. We need to create a society in which this diversity can become a source of strength instead of a cause of division.

My intention at this point was to discuss how this can be achieved, and to look briefly at the visit by the Irish-American delegation, led by Bruce Morrison, when one of the twists and turns of the situation which I mention in my opening sentence came to light. Someone leaked news of a meeting between myself, Martin McGuinness, Northern Secretary Patrick Mayhew and Northern Minister Michael Ancram. This meeting, which is big news here as I write these lines, was in Derry last Tuesday.

Earlier this month, Martin McGuinness and Michael Ancram held a separate meeting. The purpose of our discussions was to explore ways to break the current impasse in the peace process. These meetings, which were held at Sinn Féin's initiative, were kept private at the request of the British government, even though we wanted a public dimension to our discussions.

It was a constructive, businesslike, two-hour engagement. It dealt with the current impasse, the need to move it on, and the urgent imperative at this time on the British government to initiate all-party talks. The failure of the British government to play a leadership role has created the impasse. I told Patrick Mayhew that he needed to invite all parties to the conference table if he wished to salvage the peace process and to prevent it from reaching a crisis. Our meeting did not break the impasse, but it did address the need to move the situation forward. Since then we have remained in contact with the British government and will continue with our dialogue. All of us need to focus very sharply at this critical time.

There is a special responsibility on the Irish government. At another meeting, in Dublin this time, John Hume and I made the point to Taoiseach John Bruton and Foreign Minister Dick Spring. Afterwards, the four of us issued a joint statement. We reiterated "our total and absolute commitment to democratic and peaceful methods of resolving political problems, and our objective of an equitable and lasting agreement that can command the consent and allegiance of all."

Today as I finish these lines, Dick Spring is meeting Patrick Mayhew. There will be lots of other comings and goings. There will be loads of speculation. Talk of movement. Illusions of movement.

One thing is clear – there has to be real movement if we are going to have peace. The British government can no longer dodge its responsibilities.

We need real peace talks now.

The Heat Is On,
But Talks Aren't

The sun shone in Ireland during August 1995, but dark clouds still hovered over the North's peace process. Sinn Féin met a third time with Northern Secretary Patrick Mayhew in an attempt to focus the British government on the urgent need for all-party talks where all issues would be up for discussion.

IRELAND IS SWELTERING in a heat wave. Most of the population is basking in uncharacteristically warm summer sunshine. The countryside is very beautiful, lushly green in Mediterranean clime.

There are festivals everywhere from Kerry to Derry, from Belfast to Cork. This week marks the eighth annual Féile an Phobail in West Belfast. There is also a *fleadh* in Ardoyne and a new festival in the New Lodge Road. Despite all our difficulties – or maybe because of them – if the good weather continues, there will be a sense of *mardi gras* about this city. As well as the film festival, and the usual plethora of music, drama, poetry, exhibitions, song and sports, the Féile will include debates, lectures and discussions. "Questions and Answers on the Peace Process" will feature Martin McGuinness of Sinn Féin, Mark Durkan of the SDLP and Ken Newell, a Church of Ireland clergyman, among others. This session is sure to attract widespread attention.

For all the other distractions, there is continuing anxiety about the peace process. This mainly centers upon the British refusal to call all-party talks. There is also concern at the negative stance of the Unionist leadership.

Martin McGuinness and I have had another meeting with British Minister Michael Ancram and Northern Secretary Patrick Mayhew. This was the third in a series of meetings since Patrick Mayhew and I met in Washington last year. Our last engagement was in his office at Stormont Castle. The meeting lasted one and a half hours. It was a very focused discussion and both Martin and I are satisfied that we concentrated Patrick Mayhew's mind on the responsibility of his government to initiate round table talks as soon as possible.

The expectation here in Ireland is that the peace process will be in great difficulty – a crisis – unless it moves speedily to that point. This sense of foreboding is heightened not only by the many provocative examples of British double-think – for example, the release of Lee Clegg, the triumphalism of the Orangemen, the treatment of Republican prisoners in Britain – but also by the fact that the process is now some years of age and the IRA cessation is almost one year old.

The meetings with Patrick Mayhew are evidence that the British government is conscious of the seriousness of the current impasse and of its potential. There can now be no doubt at all in the minds of Patrick Mayhew or Prime Minister John Major that Sinn Féin is totally committed to the peaceful resolution of this conflict. They will also be absolutely clear that making peace is a two-way street. The London government cannot dodge its responsibilities. It cannot pretend to be referee. It cannot blame the Unionists for its refusal to play a leadership role.

Since the IRA cessation, the British government has stalled the commencement of all-party peace talks by erecting the decommissioning of IRA weapons as an obstacle to further movement in the peace process. Herein lies the crux of the current impasse and the core of the crisis which threatens this unprecedented opportunity for all of us to build a new and peaceful future for the people of this island.

It is important, therefore, to have a strategic overview and a firm grasp of the objectives of the Irish peace process. It is in this context that judgment can be made on a continually developing situation. How much, if at all, can the positions taken up by the various parties be dismissed as negotiating stances? This is a vital area. A miscalculation here can cause irreparable damage.

Just before our Stormont Castle meeting, I dealt with some of these points in a well-publicized assessment of the current impasse. I pointed out how the British government have to accept that dialogue and inclusive negotiations without preconditions provide the vehicle to a peace settlement which will eradicate the causes of conflict in our country and remove all the guns permanently from Irish politics. This requires good faith negotiations by the London government. It means an end to preconditions, including the decommissioning obstacles to all-party talks.

The British government and others may be miscalculating the IRA's position on decommissioning, or the Sinn Féin leadership's room to maneuver on this issue. If this is so, they do so with the benefit of having heard at first hand from Sinn Féin that the IRA will not decommission or surrender its weapons to anyone as a precondition for all-party talks. This is not a negotiating position. The reality is that Sinn Féin has no room to maneuver on this issue.

So how is this logjam to be broken? In the first instance, the British government must be persuaded that all issues, including the vexed question of disarmament, will be resolved in the context of dialogue and inclusive negotiations based on democratic principles. They know this. They know that the IRA will not disarm in any other context. There is no expectation within Unionism or even within the British military or security circles that the IRA will surrender its weapons outside of a negotiated settlement.

Apart from anything else, there is increasing disquiet in Republican circles about ongoing efforts by Loyalists to produce weapons. Loyalist arms factories were uncovered in Holywood, Co. Down, and in England, and a British Ministry of Defense official was arrested. Only last week, six Loyalists were arrested in Scotland and charged with attempting to obtain weapons for the Ulster Volunteer Force (UVF). One of those charged included Lindsay Robb, a member of the Progressive Unionist Party's delegation in talks with British government representatives. There are also reports of Loyalists gathering intelligence on Republican activists.

So the issue of disarmament is a complex one. From Sinn Féin's point of view, the weapons of the IRA have been taken out of commission. The IRA cessation provided an opportunity to build and consolidate a peace settlement. We have argued that a lasting peace can be accomplished in agreement with all the parties involved. The British government must accept the rights of all sections of the electorate without preconditions and it must move speedily to convene all-party talks where every issue will be on the table and everyone will be at the table.

In our discussions with Patrick Mayhew and Michael Ancram, Martin McGuinness and I outlined in great detail how the peace process can be moved through the current impasse into all-party talks and towards a negotiated settlement. Patrick Mayhew is to reflect upon the points we made to him. There is no arrangement for us to meet again, though I expect that we will and before too long. In this context, and as I finish, comments by President Clinton in an *Irish Times* interview with their Washington correspondent, Conor O'Clery, are particularly welcome. The Clinton administration has had an even-handed and balanced approach to the Irish peace process. President Clinton's reiteration of his commitment to the process and of the need for movement is timely. The British government must be persuaded to move to all-party talks.

Maggie McArdle,
A Wise and Funny Woman

The life of a very special Belfast woman.

I'M WRITING THIS marooned high in the mountains somewhere in Ireland. A too short but welcome break from the usual frenetic political situation here. It doesn't pass as a summer holiday. That was canceled first during the Twelfth of July shenanigans, and then again last week when Colette's mother, Maggie McArdle, died. So, after all that upset, and before we face into more difficulties, I've stolen these few days away to gather my thoughts, and to recharge the batteries, partially anyway.

You don't know Maggie McArdle. She was a Belfast woman, born and baptized Margaret Walsh in that city in 1911. Maggie lived in Malcolmson Street in what would then have been close to the countryside on the edge of the Falls Road, and at a right angle to the Springfield Road. She didn't remember the 1916 rising, but she did remember Ireland being partitioned, and the Troubles of that time. But, in her reminiscences, Maggie usually dwelt on the uplifting episodes of that period: sing-songs with Lizzie Callaghan, who played the tin whistle and many other musical instruments, the closeness of neighbors, the solidarity of poverty, the scrapes and the escapes of survival.

In 1929, Maggie married Jimmy McArdle, and some years and three children later, they were lucky enough to get a house in the Whiterock. In Malcolmson Street the toilet was in the backyard, along with a single cold water tap, and the houses, tightly backed onto terraces, boasted only two small bedrooms. In the Whiterock there were three bedrooms plus an inside toilet and bathroom and scullery. In this house Maggie and Jimmy raised twelve children, four boys and eight girls. Jimmy McArdle, who was generally unemployed, was a totally dedicated family man. His wife was the politico. Like all working class women of that time, it fell on her to put the food in the bellies of her children, clothes on their backs, and shoes on their feet. The older McArdles, Lily and Seamus, remember these as hard times. By the time Colette came along, the situation had improved. Older brothers and sisters were bringing home a wage, and she recalls a much more settled childhood.

Jimmy McArdle by then was a house husband. In the close community in which they lived, he also moved easily with his peers to the bookies, and more frequently to the illegal pitch and toss school, which gathered regularly among the kilns of the brick yard close to the Whiterock. He loved films. The Broadway Cinema and the Clonard picture house were his escape into the world of movies. At all other times he was at home. He brought Maggie breakfast in bed all their married life. It may have only been a cup of tea, but in later years, when Peter the baker arrived on his daily delivery around 6:30 in the morning, Jimmy was there to greet him, and to prepare fresh bap and butter with hot tea for his wife, sons and daughters. He polished their shoes, bathed the younger ones, and generally played a fuller role than most men of that time.

Maggie worked in the house and outside it. During the great depression of the 1930s, and the Outdoor Relief agitation of that time, she protested with the rest. She was also an active supporter of the Republican cause. Over fifty years ago, when the British hanged Tom Williams in Belfast Prison she with other women gathered outside the jail. The next day she miscarried. Her home was a regular sanctuary for Republicans on the run during the '40s, and the scene of some narrow escapes for herself and the ones she was keeping.

By the time I came into the family in 1971, all the McArdles were adults, and Jimmy and Maggie were beginning to relax into grandparenthood. Their close-knit clan continued to gather regularly in the family home. It was there that Colette and I adjourned briefly after we were married twenty-four years ago this month. Those were days of mighty upheaval. The Whiterock, by then part of Free Belfast, was behind barricades. When the barricades came down, McArdles' was one of the first houses to be visited by the British Army.

"Do you know your daughter has married Gerry Adams?" the British Army officer quizzed Jimmy.

"God help him," Jimmy replied.

When I was in Long Kesh, and Gearóid was born, his mother and he lived with Jimmy and Maggie. Jimmy died seventeen years ago. After his funeral, Maggie told her assembled children: "I'm not like some women, you know. I have no regrets about your father, and I won't be jumping into the grave after him."

Maggie loved to sing. She had a great collection of Belfast street songs: songs of the mills, songs of patriotism, love songs, and funny songs. She played bingo or housey all her life, told yarns at the drop of a hat, and retained a keen interest in current affairs until her death. By then she had accumulated a total of forty-five grandchildren, and fifty-four great-grandchildren.

"Jimmy put on his working clothes when he was going to bed," she used to say.

Six weeks ago, her son Anthony died suddenly. Maggie had long been concerned about Anthony. After the trauma of his death, she busied herself making sure that all his affairs were in order. On the Tuesday before her own death, she and Joe Cahill discussed the campaign for the repatriation of Tom Williams' remains from Belfast Prison.

The following night, Maggie took ill. She was taken to hospital in the early hours of the morning, and died shortly after, surrounded by her family. When the coffin came home to the Whiterock, Joe Cahill draped the Irish flag over Maggie. That's how she was buried. As she left Whiterock for the last time, a piper played "Raglan Road." The priest at her Mass described her as a true patriot, and recited a line from Pearse's "The Mother:" "Lord, thou art hard on mothers/We suffer in their coming and in their going."

None of us has recovered yet from Maggie's death. Some of us never will, Colette especially. I was privileged to know Maggie McArdle. She was a wise and funny woman. She had a good, long, full life, and she lived all of it with generosity. She lived in Belfast through it all, through good times and bad times, hard times and easy times. She died at eighty-four years of age without knowing what it would have been like to live in a peaceful and just society.

Peace Comes Dropping Slow

The first anniversary of the IRA cessation.

T HERE WAS A time when Irish Republicans and Nationalists were told that the IRA was the main obstacle to peace in Ireland. If the IRA would only stop, we were told, the British government would be able to move speedily to address and redress the many injustices arising from its involvement in Irish affairs. The British government, according to this wisdom, was no longer the imperialistic monster. This was the twentieth century. No matter about all its sins in the past, Britain now was neutral in relation to Ireland. Its attitude was now benign, and only the IRA's campaign was preventing a new era of modern and forward-looking cordiality between these two islands.

Against the background of all the things that have happened – and more importantly not happened – this last year, one issue now stands starkly clear. The British government is not neutral towards Ireland.

The relationship between our two countries has certainly changed in this century, but the British government does not have a benign attitude towards its nearest neighbor. A year ago, as the whole world knows, London was handed an opportunity to create a new beginning in Ireland when the IRA announced its complete cessation of military operations. This courageous and brave initiative followed years of careful work to build a peace strategy. John Hume played a central and pivotal role – despite fierce criticisms from anti-Republican elements – and the Irish government led by Albert Reynolds joined the process. Months of dialogue forged a shared commitment between the three of us to shape an alternative strategy. The core of this was a negotiated settlement, all parties on an equal basis seeking agreement on our future. No party was to be allowed a veto.

Every effort had to be made to win the agreement of the Unionists, but they could not be permitted to impede progress. We could not make peace without them, but they could not be allowed to block the peace process. Both governments would have to fulfill their responsibilities to encourage and facilitate agreement between

176

the people of Ireland. While this was proceeding, equality of treatment would be accorded to all sections of people with progress on demilitarization, prisoners and democratic rights, and civil rights issues.

Irish America rowed in to support this position, and the powerful lobbying potential of Irish opinion in the US was harnessed by a group of far-sighted US representatives who traveled to Ireland to volunteer their help.

All of this was the tip of the iceberg. Below the surface there was protracted dialogue with the British government by Sinn Féin, negotiations between London and Dublin, and between John Hume and London also.

Would the IRA assist the process? Towards the end of last August there were a series of statements. From the Irish government, from the Irish Americans, from John Hume and myself. Each statement contained the necessary pieces of the jigsaw required to usher in a new era. Then on August 31 came the dramatic IRA statement announcing its cessation.

It said in part: "We believe that an opportunity to create a just and lasting settlement has been created. We are therefore entering into a new situation in a spirit of determination and confidence – determined that the injustice which created the conflict will be removed, and confident in the strength and justice of our struggle to achieve this . . . a solution will only be found as a result of inclusive negotiations. Others, not least the British government, have a duty to face up to their responsibilities. It is our desire to significantly contribute to the creation of a climate which will encourage this. . ."

A review of events since then will provide evidence of the effort by all involved to honor their commitments. From John Hume to President Clinton to the IRA. Even the Loyalists were persuaded to call a cessation. All contributed to the peace effort. All except the British government. Even when Albert Reynolds' government fell – an unforeseen disaster – the new government defied the predictions and the previous utterances of the new Taoiseach John Bruton to embrace the process.

Now, a year later, because of the British government's stance, the peace process has been severely undermined, and the widespread optimism that there would be a peace settlement has been replaced by an increasing dismay at London's negative and minimalistic response and the allied intransigence of the Unionist leadership.

Irish Republicans should of course be philosophical about London's stance. We never believed that the British government was neutral. We always insisted that peace in Ireland is dependent on the attitude of London. But even though our position has been vindicated, there is little succor in this because the price may well be the collapse of the peace process. That is one of the realities facing us all.

If the peace process is to be salvaged, the notion that London is a referee, or that it can be allowed to behave as if it is, must be ended. Everyone concerned to consolidate the peace process, to make it succeed, must face up to the British government. Whether in the US or elsewhere, progress towards peace in Ireland will only be achieved if and when those concerned face up to the truth. All of us, whether the Irish government, Sinn Féin or the other parties, must use our influence to persuade London to fulfill its commitments and its responsibilities. There is no way over, under or around this issue.

If this best opportunity for peace is not to become another wasted opportunity, then a date for all-party talks must be set. That was the message coming out of a Sinn Féin/Dublin government meeting on Monday of this week. That was the message coming from the Humbert School in Co. Mayo on Sunday which was addressed by myself, John Hume and Albert Reynolds. That was the message of the mass rally last Saturday in Dublin. It was also the message from a joint Sinn Féin/SDLP meeting in Belfast on Tuesday. Nationalist Ireland wants peace. Grass-roots Unionism wants peace.

The message from Britain is equally clear. It continues to seek a Republican surrender. That was the essence of Patrick Mayhew's speech last Friday. It was the essence of Michael Ancram's remarks on Monday. We don't need to speculate on what is behind this British demand. One year on, we need to face up to it. We need to get the British to respond to acts of peace with all the same urgency with which they used to react to acts of war. Sinn Féin is totally committed to this peace process. The peace strategy is the correct strategy. But Sinn Féin cannot make peace on our own. That much, at least, is clear at this important anniversary.

Sheared and Cheered In The US

Further meetings with Vice-President Al Gore and National Security Advisor Tony Lake at the White House, while constructive, couldn't produce the breakthrough that would move forward the peace process. The British government held the next move in their precondition for decommissioning IRA weapons.

THE NEW YORK cops and I get on very well. Especially when my New York bodyguard, Big Brian, is around. "Do you think," I asked immediately after I arrived in New York on Monday, September 11, "that I could get a haircut somewhere?"

The cops looked at me. I looked at them. I explained how I tried to get a haircut at home. I felt guilty. A dangerous feeling. Especially with cops. They didn't notice. My Grizzly Adams look had some advantages.

"TWA International," the cop said. "Let's go."

So we went. Me, Brian, Tom, and their uniformed comrades. I felt even more guilty. Worse still, everyone we passed looked at me as if I was guilty. I tried to look like a cop. That way I figured they would think Brian was the guilty one. He didn't seem to notice. Brian's nice like that. So was the barber's shop, Antonio's.

Me and Brian and Tom and the six cops didn't leave much room for anyone else. Antonio didn't seem to notice. Brian spoke nicely to him.

Antonio found me a chair and a barber. He and the six uniformed cops and Brian discussed my haircut. Tom kept out of it. I let on I didn't notice.

Antonio told me he was a friend of congressman Peter King. All the time the barber clipped and snipped and scissored away. He told me that he came to New York thirty-four years ago and that's when he opened his barber shop. We discussed the Pope's visit next month. And the situation in Ireland. And the UN's fiftieth anniversary. Me and the barber and the sergeant and Antonio. The barber cut the hairs on my head. He cut my beard. He cut the hairs up my nose. He cut the hairs in my ears. I felt like one of

179

Ciaran Staunton's sheep at shearing time.

Brian told the barber to give me a shampoo. He did. Then we got our photos taken.

Antonio refused to accept payment – his contribution to peace in Ireland, he declared.

"Viva Italia," I declared. That's how my visit to the US started this time around.

This time around we were in Washington DC, New York and Mineola, Long Island, which is the real center of the US.

Did you know that Long Island has more Irish than anywhere else in North America? That's what I was told by one of the locals in Eileen and Jack Bingham's house during a fundraiser. The Bingham family organized a reception for Friends of Sinn Féin at the end of our visit. It was very enjoyable.

I am continually uplifted by the hospitality of people in the US. Martin McGuinness was here a week before me. He and I missed each other, but in a series of telephone conversations, I could sense how Martin also had been moved by his engagements here. And he clearly uplifted everyone he met. That's them Derry wans for ye. Jamesie Quinn, how are ye?

Me? I felt a bit like John the Baptist, shorn of his locks, tonsurially spreading the gospel.

In Washington, DC, Mairéad Keane and Ciaran Clifford and all their people have made a huge difference in getting the message across on Capitol Hill. There is still a lot to be done, and they need all the help they can get, but our mission in the capital is up and running. This time around there was a marked difference. For the first time in my series of engagements, I could see how the resilience of those individuals who have persisted in both the Republican and the Democratic parties to raise the issue of peace in Ireland is winning converts.

There is now clearly a caucus in both parties concerned to assist the peace process, and worried at the British government's refusal to match the courage and generosity of the Irish Nationalist and Republican investment in the effort to build a peace settlement.

Our discussions with National Security Advisor Tony Lake and Vice-President Al Gore were equally positive. There has been a British-inspired spin that the meeting in the White House was at the behest of the Clinton administration, so that officials there could pressurize me. This is nonsense. I asked for the meeting. Vice-President Gore's attendance was both welcome and indicative of his commitment and the President's interest. The US government is very focused on the need to consolidate the peace process, and to move beyond the current vacuum.

We had a very constructive engagement, and a number of propositions were explored by both ourselves and the White House. The focus of all our dialogue was to try to clear away the obstacles or impediments, and move the process to all-party talks. But there weren't any firm proposals from the White House. The British are putting up as a precondition the need for the IRA to surrender its weapons. That's a totally unacceptable precondition and it's totally out of character with successful peace processes elsewhere, but I'm encouraged and assured that the even-handed approach of the White House will continue, and that, if a formula can be agreed, the administration will help to work it out.

Sinn Féin wants to find a formula which will salvage the peace process, but all the armed groups have made it clear that there will be no decommissioning of weapons at this time. So if the British keep to their precondition, then it appears to me that what scuppered previous efforts to bridge this impasse will also scupper any future effort to bridge it. The onus is very clearly on the British government to accept that this is a political process, that disarmament is a very necessary part of the overall objective of demilitarization. We cannot have a peace process if we don't seek to have the guns taken permanently out of Irish politics. That objective should not be made an obstacle.

It would be wrong to assume that the Clinton administration is seeking to broker or get involved in the minutiae, or is pushing any particular notion of how the logjam can be broken. Sinn Féin's flexibility in this matter is very limited. A formula must be found. Otherwise the vacuum will end inevitably in tragedy. Sinn Féin is absolutely committed to finding such a formula.

But the reality must be faced up to. The internal dynamics of the situation in Ireland, or between Britain and Ireland, place Britain in the stronger position. The dynamic must come from outside the square; from outside the frame. That's why the US is so important. All roads lead to Washington. That's why you, dear reader, are important, why Irish America plays such a pivotal role.

You helped to create the peace process. It belongs to you. Make it work. Don't let John Major screw up the best chance for peace we have had in seventy-five years.

Me? As I write this I'm flying back to Ireland to watch the All-Ireland. Myself and Sam Maguire will be in the capital city for a day, and then back north again or so we hope! By the time you get to reading this, the best team will have won.

As Antonio the barber might have said, *"Tiocfaidh ár giorno! Viva Tyrone!"*

Outside Dynamic Needed to Save the Peace Process

The peace process continued to flounder.

I'M NOT A very good swimmer. The last time I went for a bathe I was very satisfied or at least reassured by my ability to proceed through the water in a welter of foam and splashes and mini-tidal waves. Then a real swimmer passed me. He made little noise and barely rippled the surface of the pool as he knifed his way to and fro. By the time I had finished one lap I had swallowed whole mouthfuls of water, half choked on chlorine, and frightened other swimmers. The Irish peace process is a bit like that. Like me, it's a bad swimmer. There's plenty of surface action, splashing and splishing, threatening at times to founder everything but progress is laboriously slow.

Since I was last in the United States, Sinn Féin has remained in regular contact with the White House. I have been in constant touch with John Hume; we have remained in contact with the British – Martin McGuinness has met with Michael Ancram once and we will meet with him again; and we have been in constant contact with the Dublin government. Sinn Féin, the USA, the Irish government and John Hume are applying ourselves to finding a way out of the current protracted impasse, and I am assured by the commitment of the others in achieving this goal.

However, while privately applying ourselves vigorously to the effort to advance the peace process beyond British preconditions, I have to say – indeed I have a duty to inform public opinion – that the British government has yet to indicate that it is prepared to apply itself meaningfully to this task.

So like my swimming, the peace process has a lot to do before it reaches Olympian standards. Or even before either of us would dare to traverse open water. Particularly if there was stormy weather. Anyway, before this column drowns itself with overworked metaphors let's take a little look at what's been happening.

The Forum for Peace and Reconciliation reconvened and like schoolchildren at the return of term we assembled under the excellent tutelage of Chairperson Catherine McGuinness to review the events of the summer. I missed most of this as I was closeted for two hours with John Bruton. He emerged to say that a way out of the impasse was "tantalizingly close." I could say no more than "If I heard John Major saying that, there would be room for optimism." Some commentators have questioned the positive spin which the Irish government consistently tries to put on events. In many ways this is understandable. For Dublin to acknowledge that there is a crisis actually deepens the crisis. But the persistently positive line from Dublin has its shortcomings. A number of times in the past, not least the last planned summit meeting, and earlier important meetings between Irish and British representatives, the Dublin government hype backfired leaving many Nationalists anxious and concerned that their expectations were not fulfilled.

Having said this, of course I too want to be positive and I want to see the obstacle to all-party talks removed. That is the focus of all Sinn Féin endeavors at this time. It is the British who have created the obstacle to progress. I am prepared to help John Major if and when he wants to remove the obstacle but I have little room to maneuver if he continues to refuse to budge.

There is no evidence that the British government is yet ready to engage in the search for a formula to end the impasse in the peace process. Whatever formula is required to do this it will only be possible when London engages. The internal dynamics of the political situation in Ireland are not enough to save the peace process. The necessary dynamic must come from outside the frame, from the international community.

Meantime, Sinn Féin met in private conference last Saturday. It was a good conference which was dominated, as was the intention, by contributions from activists from throughout Ireland. The conference has been played up by some sections of the media here as a crunch meeting. It was an important meeting. It was the first opportunity for Sinn Féin activists to assess our management of Sinn Féin's peace strategy. Up to eight hundred members gathered and by the time proceedings came to a close over seventy people had spoken and others were still waiting their turn.

Nearly all the speakers expressed both concern and anger at the British government's refusal to consolidate the process. Some voiced opposition to the peace strategy, and some criticized the leadership, but it was all conducted in an open climate of camaraderie. The conference was organized by us for exactly that purpose. We are not leading sheep and Sinn Féin is not, and never has been, a monolith.

Despite some media spins, the conference was not a review of the IRA's cessation. That is not our business. Sinn Féin is not the IRA. Perhaps if the IRA had been meeting there may have been a different conclusion. The IRA had made its own position clear the day before. Obviously annoyed by the British government's stance, it ruled out any disarmament except as part of a negotiated settlement. It described the British demand as "ludicrous."

The Sinn Féin Árd Chomhairle will be meeting next week to consider the contributions and views expressed at Saturday's conference so that we can work them into the management of our peace strategy.

After the conference I went from Dublin to Glasgow. There, the Scottish Committee for Peace in Ireland hosted a conference at which I was the guest speaker. Despite the best efforts of a mob of Loyalist protesters, we had a very successful session. Unfortunately the proceedings were marred when the Loyalists attacked people coming into the hall. I thought they were only trying to make me feel at home, but I'm sure that others, less used to the sectarian bigotry that they encountered, were disturbed by the experience. Ach well.

In Brighton, at about the same time, the British Labour Party was beginning its annual week-long conference. The leadership's position on Ireland is not a good one. Once, at a meeting with veteran Labour MP Tony Benn, I was presented with a tin of fudge.

"Here's some British Labour policy on Ireland, Gerry," he said with a smile.

Tony Blair, the Labour Party leader will have to do more than echo the Tory party's policy if there is even to be a public debate on Anglo-Irish relations.

After Glasgow, and as I headed from Dublin back to Belfast, the Ulster Unionist Party leader David Trimble was heading from Belfast to Dublin. He was on his way to meet John Bruton and he is the first Unionist leader to meet an Irish Taoiseach in thirty years. The last time that happened was when Sean Lemass traveled north to meet Terence O'Neill. Ian Paisley threw snowballs at Lemass in the grounds of Stormont Castle. This time Paisley was

185

equally frosty and condemned Trimble for his treachery. Some Nationalists may be concerned at the outcome of such a meeting. Whether or not there is cause for their anxiety remains to be seen. I think it is a good thing that Unionists are meeting other people. The more Unionists make their case, the more they leave themselves open to examination and public accountability. The more they engage in dialogue, the better it is for the rest of us. That's why, when I was last in New York and Washington, I argued that David Trimble needed to be there also.

Unionism has not needed a leader since the beginning of this century. After partition Unionism only needed a safe pair of hands. There was no need to modernize or reconstruct or even examine the tenets of that ideology. Its future was secured because the rest of us were powerless. Now that has changed. There is no way that any of us are going back to the old days and Unionism cannot afford to return to the old ways.

Of course David Trimble may feel that he has only to build a more visible and positive profile for the UUP. If this is the case then he too will be squandering the best opportunity on offer to his section of our people.

So there you are – ripples creating ripples and making more ripples. Me? I'm trying to find the time to take swimming lessons. If the peace boat hits a rock it might be useful.

The Impasse Can Be Resolved

Gerry Adams made his seventh trip in two years to the US during November 1995. At meetings in New York and Washington he outlined the real possibility of a serious breakdown in the peace process. The commitment to round-table negotiations had been a key element in bringing about an IRA cessation. The later introduction of preconditions was unacceptable. Also unacceptable to Nationalists was the proposal put forward by UUP leader David Trimble for a new Northern Assembly.

RETURNING TO BELFAST from Washington DC, I was very honored to unveil a monument to the United Irishmen – mainly Presbyterian men and women – who led the rebellion of 1798. It was interesting, on a brisk Irish autumn day, to look from the site of the memorial at the Roddy McCorley Society towards Cave Hill, where the leaders of that movement first gathered over two hundred years ago and pledged themselves to the unity of Catholic and Protestant and dissenter, and to breaking the connection with England.

Sometimes today's Republicans, in moments of dark humor, wonder why Wolfe Tone and his comrades started the whole thing in the first place. Then we look around us and the answer is obvious.

Back in Belfast again from Dublin today, my idle plans to listen to the first Beatles single to be released in thirty years came to nothing. Politics ignores such historic musical happenings.

My meeting at the White House, which in many ways was the main media focus of last week's visit, was not the only reason behind my going to the US. Of course it was a very important element, but the purpose of the trip was so that I could inform representatives of Irish America of the serious deterioration in the situation here, and particularly those who had helped to put together the Irish peace process.

I consider, therefore, that my lengthy meeting in New York with the group led by Bruce Morrison, and later my discussions with Senators Dodd, Kennedy and various congressional members, was crucial. In some ways I felt morally obliged – particularly with the Bruce Morrison group – to spell out to them the worst-case scenario if the British are permitted to continue with the strategy which has subverted the peace process. This is the message that I also took into the White House, and my other engagements as well.

Although some of our friends were alarmed at the possible consequences, I have to say that they appeared not to be too surprised at how the protracted vacuum had created a possibility of a serious breakdown. Everywhere I went – and I also had a very important meeting and luncheon with John Sweeney, new head of the AFL/CIO and his colleagues – people understood that Sinn Féin and other parties had been standing at the negotiating table for fifteen months waiting for John Major to join us.

Since my return, Mr. Major has replied to the correspondence of Taoiseach John Bruton, and I spent today with Mr. Bruton, Labour leader Dick Spring and Democratic Left leader Proinsias De Rossa. John Hume had a separate meeting with them. It would be inappropriate for me to disclose the content of the Irish government's submissions, or indeed their view of the British correspondence. But of course I have no difficulty in setting out Sinn Féin's case.

First of all, as has been clear for some time, and especially at this defining moment, if we are to re-establish the peace process we need a date for the commencement of peace talks without preconditions, as was promised by both governments prior to the IRA cessation. Any proposals which retain the British demand for a surrender of IRA weapons as a precondition to all-party talks, are a formula for disaster. Dialogue and agreement threatens no one. Without peace talks there can be no negotiated settlement; without talks there cannot be peace. This, then was the mood of the Republican delegation, made up of myself, Lucilita Breathnach and Rita O'Hare, which met the Irish government yesterday.

In summary, Sinn Féin's attitude since first we were persuaded that a twin-track approach could be a way out of the current impasse, has been to secure the commencement as soon as possible of all-party talks, an end to all preconditions, and a resolution of the weapons issue to everyone's satisfaction.

On all-party talks, there has been some discussion around the British notion of a target date. Target, in this context, is another word for conditional. What is required is an end to preconditions. The commitment to round-table negotiations was a key element in bringing about an IRA cessation. Fifteen months after this cessation, it should not be more qualified or conditional than it was at the time the cessation was announced.

I don't mind how the British describe those talks, provided there is a firm date and that they start soon. No party can have a veto over the commencement of all-party negotiations. This was clearly stated by the Irish government in discussion with Sinn Féin prior to the IRA cessation. It is a responsibility for the two governments to commence these talks, and the preparatory phase cannot become open-ended.

On the weapons issue, Sinn Féin has made it clear that we would be willing, as part of an agreed package which moved the peace process into all-party talks, to speak authoritatively to an international body on the issue of IRA weapons. We also stated our intention to address the issue of all the weapons involved in the conflict, with the aim of removing forever the gun from Irish politics.

Last week I made it clear, in the wake of a ferocious publicity assault from London during which the British government reiterated its position, that Sinn Féin could not accept the British terms. Our involvement in these matters could only be as part of an agreed package. We could not co-operate with a body which takes a selective view on the arms issue. It is also our view that the remit or terms of reference of an international body should be publicly promulgated. The inclusion of the British preconditions implicit in their "building blocks" paper would undermine the entire purpose of, and therefore Sinn Féin's involvement in, a twin-track approach.

David Trimble's demand for a Stormont assembly is being touted widely by the entire Unionist family. Of course, every party should have the right to put any issue on a talks agenda for discussion. But for governments to single this out would clearly be partisan and would give this proposal, which is anathema to Nationalists, a status above all others.

Having said all of this, I have to repeat my conviction that every single issue of contention at this time can be resolved. It requires only a political will by John Major. All-party talks as soon as possible remain the key.

Some may think that Sinn Féin is exaggerating the difficulties, or for our own purposes that we are playing up the fragility of the current situation. This is not the case. As I said to senior White House officials last week, "What do you think would happen, how do you think people would feel, if the budget crisis here in Washington was to last for fifteen months without significant movement to resolve it?"

****

As a postscript, you may be pleased to know that the Plain Language Commission awarded the British Prime Minister, John Major, its foremost anti-gobbledygook prize when it gave him its Golden Rhubarb trophy for the most baffling document of 1995, *Frameworks for the Future*, which the British released about the peace process. The commission described the document as "rambling, repetitive, jargon-filled and incomprehensible to its target audience."

A Tea Cup in a Storm

President Bill Clinton visited Belfast and Derry on Thursday, November 30 against the background of a flurry of diplomatic maneuvering. The flagging peace process required immediate positive intervention if the President of the United States was to be seen to endorse it. On the evening of the 28th, as the President was already airbound for meetings in London the next day, the British and Irish governments rushed through a Joint Communiqué outlining a "twin-track" approach and proposing all-party talks within three months. A three-member International Body, chaired by former Senate Majority Leader George Mitchell, was to be set up on the issue of decommissioning. Buoyed with renewed hope, Ireland gave President Clinton a tumultuous and emotional reception.

THERE ARE MANY home bakeries on the Falls Road, each one of which is worthy of a visit by a US president. All of them serve bannocks and farls, baps and potato bread, pancakes and pastry.

None of them are talking to me. Talk about the need for talks about talks, and about a healing process? I need to reconcile with my local bakers. Except for McErlean's, of course.

McErlean's is delighted with itself. That, as the world now knows, is where President Bill Clinton went for some tea last week. Just below the Springfield Road corner, and up from the Sinn Féin center. He was dying for a cup of tea, you see. As the whole world now knows also, the Falls Road is the only place in Ireland for a decent cup of tea.

That's the thing I never liked about the States. You can't get tea. Except for Kathleen and Sheila, no one in the US ever gives me a decent cup of tea. So I knew how Bill Clinton felt. Maureen O'Looney gave me tea bags one time in Chicago. No hot water or milk. Just tea bags. They were but a memory of tea. More tease than tea. Tea needs boiling water. It needs to be drowned in a teapot. It needs to be simmered, not stewed, until it's happy, and then it needs to be made even happier in a cup or a mug.

The President's tea in London couldn't have been much fun. Good enough, I suppose, in its own way. Weak and tepid. With lemon. If you like that sort of thing. Which I do every so often. When I have nothing to do. But when I have a ball-breaker of a schedule, tea is your only man. They make such tea down the Falls Road, in all the home bakeries. In Kennedy's and the Tudor, in Ed's and in the coffee shop, in Sheehan's as well as McErlean's.

The CIA obviously keeps an eye on these things. They've got a reputation for stirring things up, for annoying people. Before this, it might have been possible to excuse this reputation by blaming it on enemy propaganda, whoever the enemy is these days. But that's another story. Now, given the open hostilities between Falls Road home bakeries and my good self, I know why the CIA got such a reputation.

I was supposed to go to Mackies. There was a time when Catholics couldn't get into Mackies. The day the President came they were everywhere. It just goes to show you. So were the Secret Service. Well, everyone thinks they were the Secret Service. But they're not, really. The media here in Ireland describe everyone who wears a trench coat and an earpiece as Secret Service, especially if they talk into their sleeves. But down the Falls we know different. Some of these guys are embassy officials. Some go around in their long coats giving US flags to small children. Some are former agents of the KGB who were abandoned by Democratic Left when they left the Workers Party. Some live in Divis Flats. A few might even be Secret Service. Who knows? Who cares? The first Secret Service man I ever met in the US gave me his card. I thought that was strange. But that's another story as well.

As I was saying above, I was on my way to Mackies. I went into the Cultúrlann, to the Café Gleas for my morning tea. They only had coffee. There weren't many people about. Just me. And Eamonn. And Maggie O'Wireless.

And a man in a trench coat. A man with an earpiece. He was talking into his sleeve. "Of all the joints in all the world, this one ain't got no tea," he was whispering. "I'll go to the other location."

I looked at him. He looked at me.

"Did you say tea?" I asked.

"Tea?" he asked.

"Yup," I said.

"Yup?" he asked.

"Yup," I repeated.

"No problem. Let's go," he said.

"Thanks," I smiled.

So he left the Cultúrlann. I followed. Behind me came Eamonn. And then Richard McAuley. Behind him came Allison, one of the pupils from Meánscoil Feirste, the Belfast Irish language high school, and Liz, her mother, and Cahal, the teacher.

"*Ca bhfuil sibh ag dul?*" (Where are you going?) I asked them.

"*Beidh muid a buail leis Uachtaráin Liam Clinton,*" says she. (We are going to meet President Bill Clinton.) "We have a presentation for him about not getting funding from the British government."

"Oh," I exclaimed. "I'm just looking for a cuppa tea."

"Oh," they looked at me warily. And then at your man in the trench coat. We all walked on in silence, except for your man, who was engrossed in animated conversation with his sleeve at this point.

Ahead of us we could see a large crowd. They were gathered outside McErlean's. They were cheering and cheerful. "McErlean's must have a special offer," I mused.

When we got to the front door, the White House convoy drove up alongside us. The President bounded out of his limousine. He bunked the queue. People shouted and gestured at him.

"Hiya Gerard," the President said to me with a smile.

"*Céad Míle Fáilte,*" said I.

"I'm dying for a cup of tea," he said, "but this place looks too busy. I've been going all morning without anything except some herbal stuff."

"It's not usually as crowded as this," I replied apologetically, glancing around worriedly at the encroaching epidemic of local people.

"Let's nip in here," Mr. Clinton said. So we did. Right into McErlean's.

The President got his tea and some bannocks and farls, baps and potato bread and pancakes. Everyone was happy. Except for all the other home bakeries. They were glad to see the President, of course. Of course! But they'd never stop to think that it was he and not me who chose McErlean's. Now I can't get bread anywhere else on Falls Road. All I get is abuse. And all because of a cup of tea? And does anyone stop to consider who paid for the President's bannocks and farls, baps and potato bread?

The Mitchell International Body Meets

Sinn Féin submitted a comprehensive presentation to the Mitchell International Body on Monday, December 18.

YOU WILL RECALL how Brian Nelson was recruited by British Military Intelligence and asked to join the Ulster Defence Association (UDA). He was trained how to collate intelligence by British Army officers, he received practical assistance in targeting Republican activists for assassination, and he was given British intelligence files. In fact, in a two-year period, over 2,600 of these documents were handed over to Loyalists from the British Army and RUC barracks.

However, the most serious aspect of Nelson's work was the re-arming of Loyalists. These weapons were brought into Ireland from South Africa with the active assistance of British military intelligence. Between January 1988 and September 1994, the weapons were used to kill 207 Nationalists, in addition to over 300 other attempted killings.

When I was in South Africa in June, I raised this matter. Earlier, in March of this year, two prominent lawyers from Johannesburg had visited Ireland on my invitation to compile a report on the arms shipment. I also made a written submission to the Cameron Commission, which was set up by the South African government to investigate illegal arms transactions by the state arms corporation, Arm Scor. Representations were also made by the Relatives for Justice group. When the South African Justice Minister Dullah Omar visited Belfast last summer, I and Sinn Féin international affairs chairperson Bairbre de Brún met with him on this issue.

All of this intensive lobbying came to fruition over the weekend, when we received a letter from Minister Omar telling us that he is seeking cabinet support for a proposal by him to appoint an investigator to examine the Brian Nelson affair. This is very good news, especially for the relatives of victims of Loyalists. It is my own view that it is the tip of the iceberg of British dirty tricks and collusion.

These matters also received a special focus today, when Sinn Féin met Senator George Mitchell, Canadian general John de

Chastelain and former Finnish Prime Minister Harri Holkeri. Senator Mitchell kick-started the twin-track process when the International Body met in Belfast on Saturday to receive submissions and to hold hearings on the issue of decommissioning weapons.

Sinn Féin met with Senator Mitchell and his colleagues at eight o'clock this morning (Monday) in Dublin Castle. As it turned out, we arrived at our offices in Dublin Castle at 7:15 a.m., in the dark, and as the mist shrouded part of the cobbled courtyard. It was very atmospheric. "The early bird decommissions the worm," someone said. Probably the last time a group of Irish Republicans visited Dublin Castle at this unearthly hour was in Easter 1916.

We presented the International Body with a comprehensive submission, including a detailed document, entitled *Building a Permanent Peace in Ireland*, and videos. We will be publishing our submission which outlines the background to the conflict, the history of the Irish peace process, and our view on the weapons issue and how it can be resolved. The submission which we made to Mitchell and his two colleagues is itself evidence of our earnest and serious approach to resolving the arms issue and to the International Body. In this submission we have addressed the issue of weapons in Irish politics comprehensively and authoritatively.

In *Building a Permanent Peace in Ireland* we state that the decommissioning issue is a new precondition by London. It is a stalling device and a bogus argument created by the British to avoid the commencement of all-party talks. It stands in stark contrast to the British position on preconditions as stated in a written communication to Sinn Féin on September 1, 1993, which said:

"The objectives of an inclusive process would be the pursuit of peace, stability and reconciliation on the widest possible basis. Beyond that, there would be no attempt to impose prior restrictions on the agenda. On the contrary, it is assumed that each participant would enter such a process on the basis of their separately stated political analysis and objectives. The government's position is well understood publicly."

In our engagement with the International Body, which lasted for over two hours, I formally requested that they should ask the British government for copies of various reports which have been suppressed by the British. These include the Stalker report, the Sampson and Stevens reports, and all other reports which have accumulated over the years on issues such as Britain's shoot-to-kill policy, collusion between the British forces and the Loyalists, Brian Nelson, and torture in interrogation centers. British weapons are a central element in the conflict in Ireland, and it is crucial that Senator Mitchell and his colleagues get a full and proper picture of weapons and their use in the conflict.

It is Sinn Féin's hope that the International Body will clear away the British government's obstacles to all-party talks. I am very impressed by the speed and the urgency with which the International Body have approached their task. These are very busy people who have come from distant parts of the world; in a hectic round of discussions in four days, they managed to meet more people and to receive more submissions than the British government have in the last sixteen months.

It would make a decisive change to the future of the peace process if this urgency was brought to the political tracks element as well. As former South African President de Klerk said during a recent visit to Dublin, a peace process must be played like a one-day game of cricket.

This morning's engagement constituted one track of the twin-track process. This afternoon, the Sinn Féin delegation traveled to Iveagh House to meet with an Irish government delegation led by Foreign Minister Dick Spring. In the course of this meeting, we proposed to the Irish government team that they should join with the British government in initiating multilateral talks as soon as possible for all those parties which are prepared to be involved. The essence of this twin-track approach, we are told, is that it is for parallel talks – one track on the issue of decommissioning, the other for political talks.

Tomorrow, I will be traveling to Stormont to meet with the British government team led by Patrick Mayhew. We will also be impressing upon him the need for his government to bring about multilateral discussions. This current frenzy of activity will continue right up until Christmas, whereupon your columnist will collapse in a heap under the nearest piece of mistletoe. Until I return again in 1996, best wishes to all our readers. *Nollaig shona d'ár leitheoirí uilig.* 1996, here we come!

A Fairy Tale of Christmas

Gerry Adams took time out from the politics of peace to share a Christmas story on the politics of cooking and how to make three go into two. . .

HERE I SIT on this cold wet sleety Irish morning – the last one of this year of Our Lord 1995 – just me and the word processor. We have had a great Christmas. Just after midnight it began to snow, soft dry fluffy snow which marzipanned the Black Mountain and frosted the trees all along the front of the Falls Park. Bing Crosby's dream fulfilled.

We had a terrific Christmas dinner. Me and your man had successfully negotiated the sale of two geese – rustling, wee Jimmy called it. I then brokered a deal with big Ted whereby and whereupon Ted had to prepare the geese for cooking and I had to cook them. That's when the problem started. How do you divide two geese into three?

"Get Solomon," said your man.

"Who?"

"Solomon!"

"There's hardly enough for three without you inviting someone else. . ."

"Don't be so stupid. I mean King Solomon. . ."

"Have another drink," said big Ted.

So we did. Ted made a chestnut stuffing. *Go h-iontach*! We drank to Ted's skill as a stuffer of geese, and after a solemn undertaking by your man that he would dutifully return Ted's portion of the geese, cooked and table-ready for Christmas Day eating, the two birds were released into your man's custody for me to cook.

"You shouldn't be eating geese," said wee Jimmy, "or turkey either. It's not fair on them."

"A foul," quipped your man.

"What?" asked wee Jimmy, sharply.

"You should join my new group, ITAC," said your man.

"What's that?"

"Irish Turkeys Against Christmas. You can be the president."

Wee Jimmy wasn't pleased. Then Paul and Pat O'Dwyer

phoned from New York to wish us a happy Christmas and I asked Paul to be Honorary President of ITAC, and wee Jimmy stopped huffing which was a big relief for everyone. Except the geese of course. They didn't care.

Meanwhile, me and your man set out to cook the geese. No easy task. Neither of us trusted each other enough – even at Yuletide – to give the geese over. And time was running out.

"Look," I told him. "I'll guarantee to give you and Ted your share."

"No," he snapped.

"I promise."

"No."

"Honest to God!"

"No!!!"

"You sound like a bloody Unionist," I told him.

"And *you* sound like a Brit. Promises, promises, promises!"

We glared at each other. Outside, a group of carol singers assembled. As your man and I faced up to one another, the sound of their singing drifted toward us.

"*Silent night. Holy night.*
All is calm. All is bright.
Around yon virgin, mother and child.
Holy Infant so tender and mild.
Sleeeppp in heavenly peeeace,
Sleeeppp in heavenly. . ."

Your man relaxed. He smiled at me.

"Who is this guy Solomon you were talking about? Would he cook them?"

"Would you ever go and. . ."

"No, I don't mean that. I mean let's get somebody acceptable to both of us to cook them."

"Like who?"

"Well. . .George Mitchell."

"That's not funny," I told him.

"All right. All right. I'm only joking. Is there any chance of another drink?" I poured a jar for the two of us.

"This is your last one," I told him. "We better sort this out, pronto."

"Aye, you're right," he agreed. "If I don't get home soon, my goose really will be cooked." He laughed.

We drank slowly and in silence. The two geese lay on the table between us. The choral singers continued their melodious meanderings. Eventually, your man stirred.

"What about," he began, "what about if you cook one goose and I cook one goose?"

"What about Ted?" I reminded him.

"Ted?" he frowned in wonderment, "Ted who?"

I looked at him for a long, reflective moment. His huge innocent eyes stared placidly back at me.

"Oh," he said eventually, "Ted. I nearly goosed the cook there, didn't I? I was only joking of course."

"Of course."

"Well, say you cook one and I cook one and then each of us gives Ted his bit? How does that sound?"

"Do you promise to give Ted his bit?" I asked.

"Of course," he replied. "Do you promise to give him his bit as well?"

"Of course," I replied.

"Well, I'll drink to that," he said.

And we did. Then your man left.

"Remember," I reminded him as he closed the gate. "Remember to have a really good 1996."

"And you too."

"And everyone in the whole wide world," we chorused.

"Especially Ted," your man concluded, as his voice and the goose and he drifted off in the Belfast snowdrops.

"Aye," I said as I put the goose in the oven. "Happy New Year to you too! And to all readers of this column and to friends everywhere – and enemies too – *Bliain úr faoi mhaise daoibh*."

Breakdown No Great Surprise

On Friday February 9, 1996, the IRA ended their seventeen-month ceasefire with a large bomb in the Canary Wharf area of London. Two people died and over a hundred were injured in the blast. Extensive damage was caused, totaling between one and two million dollars. The statement given by the IRA noted that "The cessation presented a historic challenge for everyone and Óglaigh na hÉireann commends the leadership of Nationalist Ireland at home and abroad. They rose to the challenge. "The British Prime Minister did not. Instead of embracing the peace process the British government acted in bad faith, with Mr. Major and the Unionist leaders squandering this unprecedented opportunity to resolve the conflict."

LAST FRIDAY I was in good form. For the first time in months it looked like I was going to manage a Saturday or half a Saturday free from the trials and tribulations of politics. It had been another exhausting week. After our highly successful round of meetings in Washington and a very enjoyable and uplifting overnight visit to Pittsburgh I had arrived home to yet another frenetic, jetlagged week of wearisome journeys between Dublin and Belfast. There was no chance to recover from my trans-Atlantic voyage, so as the weekend loomed it brought with it the hope of a lie-in.

Trivial? I know that now as I write it, but last week it was a big deal. On Tuesday, February 6, I and other Sinn Féin representatives had a low-key meeting with the Irish government. None of the three leaders of the coalition parties, or the Sinn Féin delegation, had any real sense that British Prime Minister John Major was going to keep the commitment he had made to Taoiseach John Bruton the night before President Clinton arrived on his visit to these islands last year. We were agreed that our key strategic aim should be to get him to honor that commitment.

Outside on the steps of Government Buildings, the assembled media were openly skeptical. Briefings from the British government were stressing the difficulties of keeping to the end of February date. There was considerable anxiety among the hacks, reflecting in many ways the wider concerns of Nationalist Ireland that Major was more concerned with playing footsie with the Unionists than with building peace in Ireland. That feeling was also widespread in Republican ranks.

For my part, as I had told people in Washington, I had become philosophical about Nationalist or Republican annoyance at the British strategy of minimal engagement in the peace process. There was once a time when I used to warn publicly of the dangers which were inherent in the British attitude. Whenever I did this my concern was always misinterpreted as a threat. So instead I took to raising my concerns privately, at first with all those with whom I was in contact, and then because it was becoming tedious and because I thought few were listening, unless I was asked I raised the dangers of Major's high risk strategy only with allies or with those whom I considered to be genuinely concerned and open to what I was saying.

The last time I really ran hard at this issue was November, when I thought the peace process was going to break down. Then President Clinton's visit rescued the situation temporarily. Everyone was uplifted by that visit, and although few people had much faith in London's sincerity about the twin-track approach Sinn Féin engaged positively with both tracks. The Unionists did not, and Major made clear his government's attitude to any report from the Mitchell Commission which did not suit London.

Despite this, I and other Sinn Féin leaders spent seven hours with Senator George Mitchell and his colleagues. We spent longer putting together a lengthy written submission which dealt with all the main issues. When Senator George Mitchell issued his report it contained difficulties for Republicans. Notwithstanding this, my response was a positive one. I welcomed the report. I felt it presented a way forward, an avenue into all-party talks.

Major's response was to dump the Mitchell report. A week before this, British Secretary of State Patrick Mayhew, in the presence of Irish Foreign Minister Dick Spring, told me that the response of the two governments to the Mitchell Report would be to consult with all the parties. It would be greeted only with a welcoming holding statement. Some welcome!

The cumulative effect of bad faith upon bad faith, of obstacle placed upon obstacle, of the British government reneging upon one commitment after another, had already stretched the peace process like a piece of elastic. Last Friday night, the elastic broke.

I received no notice that it was going to, but as soon as I heard the rumors and as quickly as I could check them out, I made a number of phone calls. I called SDLP leader John Hume. I spoke to John Bruton's office. I phoned the White House.

By now the rumor had become an IRA statement which appeared to be circulating around the media for some considerable time before it was given air space. I remembered that Dick Spring was in Washington. In an effort to warn him of the developing situation, I phoned the Irish Ambassador in the US. Spring was already airborne, on the way home. By now there was news of a bomb alert in London. As news flash followed news flash and the TV pictures of Canary Wharf and news of the casualties emerged, my sense of sadness at the earlier news turned to sorrow.

Since then I have had little time to reflect on all that has been lost, or on how it can be recovered. My sympathy is with those who died or were injured, and with their families. I regret that an unprecedented opportunity for peace had foundered on the refusal of the British government and the Unionist leaders to enter into honest dialogue and substantive negotiations. There was a year and a half of no war, and neither London nor the Unionist leaders felt compelled to move beyond their own narrow sectarian interests.

The IRA is clearly responsible for the explosion in London. But John Major is responsible for the breakdown in the peace process. He refused to honor the commitments given to Sinn Féin, to John Hume and the Irish government.

For my part, I remain totally committed to peace. Sinn Féin's peace strategy remains as the main function of our party. It is my personal priority.

Tonight (Monday) as I write these lines in an apprehensive Belfast, the establishment in Dublin and London are starting their old agenda of isolating Sinn Féin in an effort to pressurize the IRA. This is sheer folly.

There are two big lessons of the last eighteen months – the potential of that period was created by dialogue. Dialogue makes peace. The second lesson is that for the peace to be consolidated, the British government, and particularly John Major, must be partners in that process.

Where Do We Go From Here?

Within two weeks of the Canary Wharf bomb, another explosion occurred at Aldwych in London. Twenty-one-year-old Edward O'Brien from Gorey, Co. Wexford, was transporting an IRA bomb when it detonated prematurely. He was the only fatality in the burned-out bus. Huge public rallies on Sunday, February 25 in Dublin, Belfast, and other centers called for peace and a restoration of the IRA ceasefire.

THERE IS A need for a peace settlement in Ireland. That need is as urgent this evening as it was last week, last month, last year. The IRA cessation gave an unprecedented opportunity to everyone genuinely committed to conflict resolution. We could have built the peace. Now, regrettably, that cessation has ended.

Does that mean that the search for peace is suspended? No, it does not. On the contrary, it means that we must redouble our efforts.

It was never going to be easy to reach an agreed solution to a conflict which has bedeviled Anglo-Irish relationships for centuries. That requires everyone pulling their weight. It especially demands that the two governments take up leadership roles.

The last year and a half has seen the London government taking the peace process for granted. A cessation of military operations is not a peace process. It is part of it. It is not an end of conflict. That can only be achieved through honest dialogue. Through justice. The harder the British Prime Minister works to avoid these issues, the harder the Taoiseach must work to get these matters addressed and resolved.

That is what the plain people of Ireland and Britain have been saying these last two weeks. Shocked and saddened by the IRA bombs in London and the deaths and injuries which these caused, they have been calling for the restoration of the peace process. While demanding that the IRA cease its operations, the mass demonstrations are also demanding that politicians talk. The plain people find it difficult to come to terms with the refusal of John Major to embrace the peace process. They understand that, while the IRA is clearly responsible for its actions and the consequences of them, the rest of us are also responsible for our actions and the consequences of them. The end of the IRA cessation was caused by the IRA taking that decision. The breakdown of the peace process was caused by British government policy.

John Major chose to treat the peace process like a bicycle which needed only to be kept upright. He decided, as we all wobbled from side to side and as he deepened his relationship with the Ulster Unionists, that he could free-wheel the peace process into the next British general election. Others contributed to Mr. Major's totally misguided sense that he could behave as he has. More of that some other time. For now it is more important to try to get some sense of where we go from here.

One thing is certain. We cannot allow ourselves to become fatalistic or depressed. That is the easy (and understandable) emotion. We still need a peace settlement. There are other certainties in the situation. For example, it must now be clear that it is impossible to get peace in Ireland unless the British government are partners in the process. Last year during a meeting with Patrick Mayhew, as I tried to explain that his high risk strategy was the wrong one, I spelled this out to him. Quietly and sincerely, I asked that he and I form a partnership for peace. "To make peace with an enemy one must work with the enemy, and that enemy becomes one's partner."

The present dynamics in the Irish situation mean that we have to look to our friends outside of Ireland to help us persuade the British establishment that peace in Ireland is more important than any other issue facing the people of these islands. Will we succeed? We have to.

People in North America have taken risks for peace. You must continue to take risks. We here in the occupied part of our country are taking greater risks. For most politicians, risk is measured in terms of popularity, party political concerns or electoral considerations. Peace in Ireland requires much more from political leaders. It is my clearly stated intention to bring an end to all armed actions, to end the war and to take the gun out of Irish politics. That is a formidable and daunting task. It is bigger than any one person. Making peace is the sum total of many acts. It must be a collective effort.

If John Hume and I have done anything, it was to show that there is another way. While we were engaged in putting together the Irish peace initiative, we were subjected to an intense campaign of demonization and vilification. Our friends and supporters were victims of a murderous terror campaign.

We would never have come as far as we have without the help of Irish America. You must redouble your efforts now. I have been uplifted and humbled by the great hospitality I received in the US. I know how dearly people there long for peace and freedom and justice in Ireland. We must not be deflected from that task. Some people in the US may be understandably nervous at the situation in Ireland. So am I. But this is a time for cool heads and steady nerves.

President Bill Clinton is maintaining an even-handed and balanced approach to all parties seeking a peace settlement in Ireland. Others in the US may be tempted to saddle him with responsibility for the breakdown in the peace process. They may wish to make this an election issue or to point it up as a failure. This would be reprehensible.

The worst failure of all is the refusal to talk. Breakdowns in other peace processes caused leaders to redouble their efforts. That is why they succeeded. That is how this one will succeed.

Every commitment given by me has been honored by me. I make no apologies to anyone for the path we have taken. Sinn Féin's peace strategy remains as the central plank of our party policy. Peace in Ireland remains my priority.

So, where do we go from here? We have learned the hard way that no war does not mean peace, and that cessations cannot be taken for granted. Peace means dialogue, inclusive and in good faith. A new process must be rooted in clear, unambiguous public assurances that all-party talks will begin by a specified date, and that they will proceed with urgency, upon an inclusive agenda, and without any preconditions whatsoever.

Last week I wrote to John Major urging him to take up the challenge. His answer to me was a perfunctory one. This afternoon (Monday), at Sinn Féin's initiative, Martin McGuinness led a delegation to meet British officials. Tonight I am writing to Mr. Major again.

For the last number of weeks I have engaged in a wide range of contacts and discussions with allies in the search for peace in our country. This includes a wide range of political, labor and business leaders in the US. Between us all we must make real peace negotiations in Ireland an issue now in Irish America.

It is over two years since I first set foot on US soil. For the two years since then John Major and the Unionist leaders have refused to talk. They must be persuaded to start talking now. We need more than an interlude between wars. We want justice. The peace process can be put together again. It has to be. Peace, a real and lasting peace, is the prize. Irish America must keep its eye on the prize.

Inside Our Meeting
With the IRA

Gerry Adams and John Hume met with the IRA on February 28, 1996. The same day, the Taoiseach and British Prime Minister met at Downing Street in London where they issued a Joint Communiqué announcing all-party talks for June 10.

JOHN HUME AND I met almost immediately after the end of the IRA cessation on February 9. In the course of our deliberations we pledged ourselves to do our utmost to restore the peace process and to increase our efforts to talk to everyone who could help to bring this about. We decided at that time, as part of our wider initiative to seek a meeting with the IRA leadership. Early last week we were told that representatives of the leadership of the IRA would meet with us on Wednesday, February 28. By coincidence, as we met that day, Taoiseach John Bruton and British Prime Minister John Major were meeting in London. In fact, in the course of our meeting we heard news reports of the joint communiqué issued from Downing Street.

John Hume and I had prepared ourselves well for our engagement. So apparently had the people we met. Our discussions lasted just over two hours. The IRA was represented by a fairly large group and everyone at the meeting spoke, though their contribution was led mainly by two people.

John Hume and I spelt out our view of the current situation and of the need to restore the peace process. Mr. Hume was at his most focused and persuasive. I consider it to have been a very good meeting. There was always the possibility that it could have gone off on a tangent. Instead, there was a detailed and frank exchange of views. Although our discussion wasn't structured formally it became a review as well as a look forward.

There were negative and positive aspects to this. The IRA people put their position in straightforward terms by outlining their view of the agreements and commitments made in the run-up to the cessation. These made up the alternative strategy for change which convinced them to call the cessation. One IRA volunteer actually gave a detailed breakdown which went back as far as the time of

Peter Brooke's tenure as British minister in charge of the North. He elaborated on how Republicans had attempted to create a positive climate, including an IRA decision to accept a British government request for a two-week ceasefire in May 1993, and how the British reneged on this. From then until August 1994 we were taken through the various twists and turns of the evolving situation.

It was made clear that the cessation was a very difficult step to achieve. It was also made clear that this was a leadership-led initiative. There was deep cynicism and skepticism throughout Republican ranks about the British demands for ceasefires as a precondition to dialogue. The Army Council's cessation decision was within its authority, but it came about only because the leadership placed its credibility on the line.

John Hume and I knew this, of course. We had helped to shape the consensus which underpinned a political and diplomatic alternative. The package which I worked out with Mr. Hume, the Irish government and key elements of Irish-American opinion aimed at reaching agreement among all sections of our people to deal with the causes of conflict. This sought to encompass new agreements on constitutional change and political arrangements and structures which would be acceptable to all the people of the island. It sought to bring about democratic rights, to remove issues of inequality and injustice in the North, and achieve the total demilitarization of the situation involving the removal of the apparatus of war and the release of prisoners.

The IRA decided upon its cessation on the basis of the understanding that a determined approach would be brought to bear on these matters by the breadth of Irish national political opinion, and on the basis of the public commitment by both governments that negotiations would commence within a specified period of three months and without preconditions, vetoes or any attempt to predetermine the outcome.

What then had ended that cessation, we asked. The consistent bad faith of the British government and the placing of new preconditions were seen as evidence that the British were waging war by other means and that they were seeking to fracture Irish Republicanism and to split the IRA. The open provocation of the punitive attitude to Irish prisoners alongside the release of the British paratrooper Lee Clegg and the attitude of the RUC on the ground were all irritants. However, it was the absence of real negotiations which crucially undermined the cessation because this undermined one of the two key elements which had led to the cessation in the first place.

There was also criticism of the Irish government's role. John Bruton responded, it was said, more to the British agenda and made no significant attempt to advance an Irish agenda in Ireland, in Britain or internationally. He seemed more content to manage the situation than to build upon it. Mr. Bruton's call for the IRA to make a gesture on arms last March, his refusal to meet John Hume and me in October, his support for the Unionist election proposal and its inclusion in the joint communiqué in November, and his public rejection of any Nationalist consensus approach, undermined significantly the second element on which the cessation was based.

Once this basis was removed through the breaking of the consensus and the reneging on negotiations by the British the collapse of the peace process became inevitable.

The IRA representatives were very aware of the positive gains of the period. They mentioned especially and in favorable terms the Irish-American role. They made it clear that while the cessation was ended they were prepared to restore it, but in the absence of a viable alternative their commitment was to continue their campaign.

One or two of their representatives spelt out graphically their commitment. "We sued for peace, the British wanted war. If that's what they want, we will give them another twenty-five years of war.

"We were always skeptical about the British. Despite this the discipline of our cessation is probably unequaled in any other conflict situation. But if it takes time for the British to address the needs of conflict resolution, then the Irish government has to take up the slack.

"There will be no surrender of IRA weapons under any circumstances, and to anyone. Disarmament of all the armed groups is only viable as part of a negotiated settlement, and nobody knows that better than the British. We will accept no preconditions whatsoever.

"We are prepared to proactively embrace a real resolution of this conflict. We pursue armed struggle because of conditions in the Six

Counties and the British claim to sovereignty in Ireland. We know the conflict has to be ended, but this requires a real peace settlement. In that context we can live with the pursuance of Republican objectives through unarmed political or social struggle.

"I have given most of my life to the struggle. I want to see it ended. I know the effects of armed struggle. If there is an alternative I'm all for it.

"The Brits should know by now that we are serious. When we say we want to make peace they shouldn't mess."

About twenty minutes before the end of our meeting, there was a brief adjournment. After this there was some consideration as to whether our meeting should be kept private. However, because it emerged that the IRA wanted John Hume and me to pursue our commitment to the peace process, we would have to tell others of our meeting.

This meant it was bound to be public. It was agreed, therefore, that the three parties to the meeting would issue our own statements about it. John Hume and I were given a commitment that the IRA leadership would reflect on the case we had put to them. They also told us that they would explore any viable alternative strategy to bring about justice, and that they would embrace a real effort to end the conflict through inclusive negotiations without preconditions. Broad commitments were not good enough. These had already been given and broken. A new deal was required.

So there it was. A candid and clear commitment on the one hand to pursue Republican objectives through armed struggle, and an equally candid and clear commitment to play a responsible role in building a real peace settlement or embracing a viable alternative to armed strategy.

The distrust of the leadership of the IRA for the British Prime Minister and the lack of confidence in the Taoiseach must be bridged by specific and unambiguous assurances. That's what John Hume and I are trying to do. It should not be left to the two of us.

The Latest Political (and Musical) Trends

Gerry Adams attended the International Fund for Ireland dinner in Washington March 14, 1996 at which Taoiseach John Bruton made an impassioned plea to the IRA to restore its ceasefire. On March 21, the British government, picking up on a germ from Paragraph Fifty-five of the Mitchell Report, issued a "Framework for a broadly acceptable elective process leading to all-party negotiations." The paper scheduled elections in the Six Counties for May 30, the results of which would lead to entry to a Northern Ireland Forum, set up to "promote dialogue and mutual understanding" and without legislative, executive or administrative powers.

SINCE I RETURNED to Ireland after St. Patrick's Day I haven't had a minute to myself. It has been almost as frenetic as my latest trip to the US. I would like to extend warm thanks to all those who received me so warmly in Washington, DC, New York and Scranton. It was a great visit. My only regret was that I arrived late for *Riverdance* at Radio City Music Hall, and that I had to leave early to catch the plane back home. As a consolation I got the *Riverdance* CD on board, and since I returned I have also taken possession of the new Eileen Ivers CD, *Wild Blue*. Eileen is probably the most exciting musician in North America today. And maybe in Ireland as well.

Back here there has been little chance to play music. While the main focus of my work has been to restore the peace process with all the to-ing and fro-ing which that involves, there has also been the question of two by-elections which marked today with our candidates doubling their votes; one in Donegal, the other in Dublin. There was also the Sinn Féin Árd Fheis on the weekend after Paddy's Day. And mad cow disease! Which caused a huge identity crisis for Unionist farmers who decided sensibly that their cows were "Irish and not at all associated with the blight which affects only British cows."

Now Easter is looming. Indeed, by the time you read this, Easter will be over. You may be interested to know that we are blessed with good weather at this time, and that primroses are blooming and whin bushes are showing their first hint of yellow.

By the way, all the above is brought to you because I have this theory that if I was living in North America I would want to know about the weather and music and all other such tittle-tattle as well as – or maybe instead of – the serious political stuff.

So how does old Ireland stand? Maybe I should give you some sort of progress report on the efforts to restore the peace process.

One critical lesson of the last three years is that if the peace process is to be re-established the British government must give clear, specific and unambiguous assurances that the negotiations required for a peace settlement will be inclusive, with no item on the agenda allowed to become an insurmountable obstacle to progress, and all to be conducted within an agreed time-frame. There must be no further preconditions. None of those engaged in the negotiating process can have a veto. And there can be no attempt to predetermine the outcome, nor to preclude any outcome, to the negotiations.

In short, we need a new approach by the British government which is positive and in good faith, an approach which enables, facilitates and encourages agreement among all the Irish people. If the mistrust of generations, deepened by eighteen months of bad faith, is to be overcome, the Irish government, supported by international opinion, must guarantee that the British are no longer allowed to abuse and manipulate any reconstructed peace process for their own selfish political interests. Without clear and firm guidance at government level there is no prospect of resolving these problems. A proper structure and process of negotiations must be created and used in the most constructive manner.

Nothing can be agreed until everything is agreed and all relevant issues must be addressed in a full and comprehensive fashion so that there is at least the possibility that change will be the outcome of these deliberations. For example, there can be no exclusively internal or partitionist settlement. There must be substantial and significant change on constitutional and political matters, and while this presents huge difficulties for the Unionists, there must be a serious effort to reach agreement on this matter.

Parity of esteem and equality of treatment will have to be dealt with; the imbalance in the unemployment ratio; equality in economic development; greater and more equally shared prosperity; empowerment and inclusion of deprived and marginalized communities. Parity of esteem for the Irish language and culture is also required.

The whole issue of demilitarization needs to be resolved. This includes prisoners, disarmament, policing and the administration of justice and an end to repressive legislation.

The negotiating process must endeavor to reach a new agreement which can earn the allegiance of all the Irish people by accommodating diversity and providing for national reconciliation. For peace to be achieved everyone involved must be committed to reaching agreement. It is essential, therefore, that both governments shape the negotiating process in a way to ensure that all parties are present on an equal basis and that no party has an undemocratic advantage.

For its part the Irish government has said that meaningful negotiations will commence on June 10. Unfortunately, the Irish government has up to now been unable to hold the British government to commitments given, has been unable to ensure an even-handed approach, and has been unable to prevent the imposition by the British of a Unionist agenda. In fact, the Irish government has at key points exhibited a damaging disunity of purpose and approach. For example, while the Tánaiste Dick Spring was articulating a rational and coherent opposition to an elective process, in keeping with the views of Nationalists in the North, his colleague in government, Proinsias De Rossa, was declaring his public support for this Unionist proposal, while the Taoiseach John Bruton signed up to the Joint Communiqué which included the Unionist proposal.

Such inconsistencies have had a debilitating effect on the ability of the Irish government to counter-balance the clear Unionist bias of the British government. If there is to be confidence that British bad faith will not again be allowed to subvert the search for agreement and peace, the Irish government must demonstrate that it is able to act as an effective counter to the British government, and that it speaks effectively with one voice.

I am convinced that it is still not too late to create a peaceful atmosphere in which real all-party negotiations can take place and succeed. But British Prime Minister John Major must honor the commitment given and then broken, he must stop using the rhetoric of peace and take concrete steps which can make it happen.

The British proposals for an elective process and an elected body are a perversion of democracy. This may not be clearly understood in the US. Nonetheless, this is the reality. There is no confidence in Nationalist Ireland that the objective of a negotiated settlement is served in any way by Mr. Major's proposition.

We cannot have peace in Ireland unless the British government wants peace also. The resistance of the British government to political change and to negotiations as the means to political change remains the single biggest obstacle in the way of peace. This is an obstacle we have yet to surmount so that an effective political process, capable of resolving the causes of conflict, can at last be created.

Having said all of this, I remain firmly convinced that we will find a way to restore the peace process. It will not be easy, but that is the commitment with which I and Sinn Féin face into the future. This is the eightieth anniversary of the 1916 Rising. The least that Irish Republicans and Nationalists, and our friends in the US, can do is to maximize our endeavors to conclude that unfinished business.

Canvassing for Change

Sinn Féin announced in May 1996 that they would sign up to the Mitchell Report and principles, in proper all-party talks. Gerry Adams forecast that the election to the Northern Ireland Forum would renew his party's electoral mandate for all-party talks in June. But, with the precondition remaining of the necessity for an IRA ceasefire first, would Sinn Féin be allowed entry to the talks on a democratic basis?

THE BEST THING about electioneering, and the only good thing about these particular elections, is that I get to go walking. This week I have walked in Derry and Down, in Mourne country and along the Ards peninsula, crossing Strangford by ferry. I have wandered through Carrickmore and Crossmaglen, under the shadow of Slieve Gullion, the magic mountain, and then off up towards Slieve Gallion, in and out of Cookstown, Omagh, Strabane, and Magherafelt. Fermanagh was lushly green all along the wee lakes, and the big ones, too, around Enniskillen town. The rain pelted down on us, and the sun took the dampness out of our clothes in great steaming clouds.

I met Ian Paisley in Newtownbutler. In Newry I just missed John Hume. By today, as I return to Belfast, having canvassed fourteen of the eighteen constituencies, my nose is sunburned, and I am fitter than I was when I started. That is about the only definite thing that can be said so far about the search for peace in Ireland.

John Major was moved to say in a recent article in the *Irish Times* that after the elections the route to all-party talks will be direct and automatic. I have written to Mr. Major since then to assure him that I will be pleased to meet him half way in easing the situation for everyone so that there can be real talks involving all the parties. He has yet to respond. In the meantime, Patrick Mayhew has refused to agree on an agenda or any procedural matters with the Tánaiste, Dick Spring. Last week a marathon talks session by both men and their officials came to naught. They are to meet again this week, but no one is holding their breath for a positive conclusion. And all the time the June 10 date, on which talks are scheduled to begin, looms nearer.

A date for all-party talks was first announced on the eve of President Bill Clinton's visit to Ireland. Then it was to be the end of February. That seems a lifetime ago now. It is actually over six months. And the London government has yet to move to implement any of the processes that it signed up to in a raft of framework documents, ground-rule papers, and other agreements with Dublin.

Last week I tried to create some space for everyone when I announced that Sinn Féin would sign up to the Mitchell Report and principles, in proper all-party talks along with every other party. My view is that if the British government with its record of conflict in our country, or the Unionists with their involvement, and the Loyalists with their record can sign up to the Mitchell Report and principles, so can Irish Republicans.

Was this initiative welcomed by the Unionists or Downing Street? Sadly no. In fact, David Trimble is becoming increasingly articulate and adept at saying no. As he and Ian Paisley vie for the leadership of Unionism, their language is becoming more and more negative. While some of the rest of us are trying to lead our people forward towards the millennium, they appear to be rushing headlong back to 1912.

For all this messing about, one thing is certain: we will have a peace settlement. That is the clear message from the doorsteps. People here want change. And there is going to be change. Mr. Major cannot dodge his responsibilities forever. Mr. Trimble and Mr. Paisley cannot fool their followers forever. I cannot say when the real talks will start. They should have commenced some long time ago.

But commence they will! I face the uncertainty of the immediate future buoyed up by that certainty. And by the other certainty that those talks will usher in a new era for all the people of this small island. In the mean time we have an election to fight. Sinn Féin will renew its electoral mandate, and receive a negotiating mandate from its Irish Republican section of the electorate in the Six Counties. Those in high places who preach and pontificate about the primacy of the ballot box would not dare ignore the results of this week's poll. Or would they?

Unionists Must Not Derail Talks

International media gathered to see Sinn Féin being refused
entry to the "all-party talks" on Monday June 10, 1996.

MAKING PEACE IS a difficult business. That much at least is clear. The search for peace in Ireland these last few years has been circuitous and convoluted. For every step forward it seems that we all have to take half a step backward.

So it was on Monday, at the commencement of what were supposed to be all-party talks. These have now been renamed "multiparty" talks in a vain attempt to disguise the fact that the two governments have denied Sinn Féin the right accorded to us by the electorate to participate. Before the elections, British Prime Minister John Major told everyone that they would provide a "clear, direct and automatic" route into all-party talks. For everyone, that is, except Sinn Féin.

We all know how these talks have been delayed for so long by British government stalling and Unionist intransigence. During the election campaign I made it clear that if Sinn Féin did not receive a mandate it would not expect to be at Monday's talks. But it did receive that mandate and has the right and authority to be there. So on Monday the Sinn Féin peace negotiators, elected to represent 15.5 percent of the people in the North, went to Stormont where the negotiations were to be launched by the two governments. We were locked out. The story of our going there and of the media circus which greeted us must wait for another day. Suffice it to say that the international media understood clearly what was happening.

The to-ing and fro-ing between our delegation and an unfortunate British official took up most of the day's media coverage. When we were left outside after the talks had started inside another story began to emerge. The Unionists had united in an attempt to gain control of the proceedings. Their first target was former Senator George Mitchell. The Unionists refused to accept him as chairperson and he was forced to sit in a side room listening to the proceedings which were piped to him as a spectator. The Unionist leaders subjected the senator to hours of petty abuse and harassment.

They also objected to the agenda. These objections came despite the Unionists' refusal to engage in the earlier agenda-setting discussions which made up one track of the twin-track approach established on the eve of President Clinton's visit to Ireland last November. All the other parties, including Sinn Féin, did engage in this track. The Unionists limited their involvement in this twin-track process to the decommissioning track and since the publication of the Mitchell Report they have been selectively using this report to frustrate the process. At that time they loudly sang the praises of Senator Mitchell. Now they sing a different tune.

Of course, all of this is entirely predictable. It has little to do with Senator Mitchell or with the agenda or even the issue of decommissioning. It has everything to do with control, with Unionist leaders who cling to the notion that they must dominate. In a none-too-subtle form of intimidation and bullying, the two governments were forced to abandon the live broadcast of the opening plenary session for fear of a Unionist stunt.

Now, at the time of writing, Ian Paisley is threatening a walkout and David Trimble, who is trying to out-Paisley Paisley, says he will only accept Senator Mitchell if his brief is changed. Mr. Major has said no. Mr. Bruton has said no, and the two governments say, as co-sponsors of the talks, that they have the right to appoint the chairperson and to decide his terms of reference. Meanwhile, Senator Mitchell is confined to his room, and as the second day draws to a close it is impossible to predict how this will be worked out.

Will the Unionists have their way? Will the governments stand by their position? Is there a compromise?

Most people here in Ireland are not surprised by all of this. Unionist domination is based on their unwillingness to embrace change. In the past the Unionists have been fortified by the British government policy. They will only contemplate coming into modern times when the government is prepared to stand up to them. Not in a belligerent way, but in order to uphold common sense and democratic practice. Everyone is watching to see how the present stand-off plays out.

It is important that none of this is allowed to divert or take the focus off the search for peace. It may delay the process. That is unfortunate, but that has been the character of this process and will unfortunately be so until the ice is broken.

Despite Sinn Féin's exclusion, which is equivalent to excluding fifteen senators from the US senate, despite the Unionists' refusal to engage properly and the considerable cynicism among Irish Republicans and Nationalists about London's commitment, and despite all the other variables in the situation, I remain convinced that there will be a peace settlement. This will grow from a process of honest dialogue and real negotiations. Sinn Féin will be a part of that collective effort. Monday could have been the auspicious beginning of that necessary next phase of the search for peace. Many people feel cheated that Sinn Féin, and more importantly, those whom we represent were locked out. Others are annoyed at the Unionists.

Despite all of this, however, we must persevere. No one said it was going to be easy. Making peace is a difficult business.

How Would the British Treat Another IRA Ceasefire?

Despite the Manchester bombing on June 15, 1996, the IRA stated to RTE on June 19 that they were "still prepared to enhance the democratic peace process." However, a key question for Republicans was – would the British government treat another IRA cessation as it did the first?

MAKING PEACE IS very difficult. That phrase is now almost hackneyed, but it is true nonetheless. Everyone has their own version of what peace is. Understandably enough, many want peace on their own terms. Some may not even want peace at all, although of course they cannot say this publicly. So they pay lip service to the ideal.

It is important to keep all of this within context. If it was easy to make peace then there would not be a conflict, or it would have been resolved a long time ago. It is also probably in the nature of any effort to bring peace about that there will be down periods and periods of confusion and despondency.

All of this is very obvious even to a casual observer of the Anglo-Irish situation. As John Major said, the IRA cessation, now regrettably over, was the best opportunity for peace in seventy-five years. You will recall the great expectation, hope and optimism which marked the beginning of that initiative. You probably experienced the frustration as that opportunity was slowly but relentlessly frittered away because of British policy. And you will have watched in bewilderment as the peace process collapsed.

In the wake of all this, the naysayers and the begrudgers have returned to their depressing choruses. Little wonder that some of you may feel overwhelmed by it all. Who could blame anyone, and especially those who stuck their necks out against the old ways of exclusion and marginalization, if they feel that all is now lost?

But it isn't lost! As least not yet. The opportunity to make peace may be battered and bruised but it hasn't gone away, you know. And it won't go away until and unless we give up on it. And I for one have no intention whatsoever of doing that. Now is the time to be resilient. Now is the time to dig deep!

Of course, there are risks. Making peace is a risky business. But those who are clamoring loudest here in Ireland and in Britain that the old agenda should be resurrected, or those who are following that old agenda once again, are the ones who have yet to take any real risks for peace.

So where stands the peace process now? How is old Ireland and how does she stand?

The peace process needs to be put back on the rails again. Instead of a peace process, the potential of our situation has been reduced to a little charade up at Stormont. Everyone knows that at best this is an incomplete process because Sinn Féin is locked out. Everyone knows that even if it goes better or even if it goes at all, that it cannot bring about a solution because it is incomplete. Everyone knows that we are witness to yet another round of parrying between the parties in attendance. No one has any real expectation of success from the Stormont talks because everyone knows that real peace demands real talks. Everyone knows that a legitimate outcome – a lasting peace – will only grow out of a legitimate process. That is what must be constructed. No problem can be solved by ignoring it.

Meaningful talks – honest dialogue – must tackle the causes of the conflict. They must be framed around the needs of the people of Ireland, Nationalist and Unionist, and led by the two governments. Any effort to present the British government as an honest broker, the neutral mediator, has been exposed. Mr. Major cannot sit on his hands and pretend that he has done enough. None of us can. None of us have done enough.

Events of recent weeks, including recent IRA operations, present difficulties. But these can be overcome if there is a political will to tackle the issues which are at the root of all of this. The IRA has said that it is prepared to enhance a democratic peace process. British government policy is critical to any effort to restore the peace process. The British government has said that it wants a democratic peace process. Surely this gap can be narrowed.

For the eighteen months of the IRA cessation there were no armed actions. There were also no negotiations. Instead, there were new preconditions. There was bad faith.

As far as Sinn Féin is concerned, we should be part of the talks process. We have a right to be there. We have fulfilled every requirement. We put no preconditions and we accept no preconditions. But the British government says that there cannot be real all-party talks unless there is another IRA cessation. From my contact with the IRA it appears to me that the question that John Major must answer is: would he treat another IRA cessation the same as the last one? This is the nub – the core – of the current difficulties facing those who are endeavoring to restore the peace process. The IRA leadership, once bitten, appear to be twice shy.

As I said above, the opportunity for making peace hasn't gone away. The gap between the IRA leadership and the British government must be narrowed. It is obvious that they distrust each other. It is obvious that each, from their opposite perspectives, feel that they have good reason for distrusting each other. If this wasn't the case we wouldn't have a conflict and we wouldn't need to restore the peace process. But we do. And this core issue of British policy must be the focus of all of our endeavors.

Drumcree
Mark Two

Violent clashes occurred in Portadown on July 10 when the RUC reversed their decision to ban the Garvaghy Road Orange march. The following evening, the Nationalist Lower Ormeau Road was placed under curfew for twenty-six hours to allow an Orange parade pass on the morning of the Twelfth. Riots ensued throughout the North.

A WEEK, AS the cliché tells us, is a long time in politics. Events over the last week here in the Six Counties have been traumatic. For Nationalists, their worst fears have been realized by the capitulation of the British government to the campaign of mass intimidation, murder, violence and threats of violence orchestrated by the political leaderships of Unionism.

However, instead of collapsing under the weight of the cave-in by the British government, Nationalist Ireland is united in its anger, especially among young people. To cope with this situation, Sinn Féin mounted a round-the-clock operation throughout the North. In some areas we merely monitored the situation. In others we provided a backup to the local people who were providing shelter for evicted families. In the main, our efforts were aimed at keeping the situation calm. This was difficult, especially in Belfast, but by and large most people responded to our call for restraint. It is to their credit that they did so because the early part of the week here was marked by forced evictions of Catholic families, the burning of Catholic churches and schools, and nightly incursions by Loyalist gangs into Catholic areas.

The ports were closed, as were the airports. RUC patrols colluded with masked Loyalists at road blockades. No one was able to move except Orangemen, who were allowed free access to the rallying point at Drumcree where David Trimble had called for them to "muster."

On Thursday, Mr. Trimble gave the British government a deadline. The Orange parade had to go down the Garvaghy Road by July 11. The government collapsed. The RUC were unleashed on the Nationalists of Garvaghy Road. The television images of RUC men beating men, women and children back off the Garvaghy Road sent a tremor through Ireland.

The following day the Lower Ormeau area was placed under a military curfew. I went there myself at the request of the local residents group. I had spent the few days before that in other flashpoint areas. Before going to the Ormeau Road, I helped to disperse a large group of Nationalists just outside the curfewed area, in the Markets.

On my way to the Ormeau, I phoned the RUC and asked to speak to a senior officer about the deteriorating situation. After an hour on the phone I got no further than a constable. Eventually I told him that I would be going into the Ormeau area at the request of local residents. He told me that I could meet a senior officer at the first road-block.

I did. He barred me from going any further. He surrounded me with about a dozen RUC men, and refused to give me his name, authorization, reason or the legislation under which he denied me freedom of movement. Some elements of the foreign media who gathered saw the contrast with the RUC attitude to the Unionist leaders.

I spent almost four hours at the road-block. It was a surreal setting. I have been detained at British Army and RUC road-blocks for longer periods, but never on the Eleventh night. Enveloped in a crush of media heavies, I conducted a series of interviews until the media pack were forcibly moved back at the behest of my senior officer. Behind me a huge Loyalist bonfire was set alight.

In front of me, one hundred yards up the road, another RUC cordon kept back a group of Ormeau Road Nationalists who had heard of my plight. We stood one hundred yards apart, separated in our mutual solidarity. Later a fireworks display lit up the Loyalist night sky. The RUC men ducked at the sound of the fireworks. A group of visiting TDs called to see me. Some drunks sang raucous rebel songs. The RUC changed shifts. In between times it rained. Every ten minutes I asked the senior RUC officer to permit me to proceed. All the while I was dying for a pee.

Sometime after 1:00 in the morning, I was allowed to go on my way, and I joined Gerard Rice, a local community leader, and the beleaguered Lower Ormeau residents behind the British Army and the RUC ring of steel. I stayed that night in the area. Everyone was hemmed in. Men, women and children had been prevented even from going to local shops. I intervened when a local woman was prevented from crossing a street to visit her mother. Even under the draconian laws of this place, the RUC were clearly behaving illegally.

Later I watched, hemmed in once again, an RUC riot squad as an unwanted Orange parade was escorted through the area despite the dignified and peaceful protestations of the local people. I felt a sense of sadness as I peered beyond the riot shields and the helmets of the RUC men who pressed against me, as I watched the bowler-hatted, soberly-suited, be-sashed brethren marching in time to the "Sash" and flanked by a heavily-armed RUC escort as they plodded down a deserted road past a bemused muddle of international media.

That was at 8:30 on the morning of the Twelfth. At 7:00 that evening the areas were still under curfew. It lasted for a full twenty-six hours.

By this time Nationalist areas of the North had erupted with a vengeance. One man was killed by the British Army in Derry. Another generation of our children learned how to riot. Hundreds of them are wounded, some very seriously, mostly by plastic bullets. Many of the wounds were head- or chest-high. Again, the illegal use of a deadly weapon.

All week my office plagued the RUC to establish how many of these bullets were fired. Tonight, Tuesday, our suspicions were realized. Six thousand plastic bullets were fired. Of these, 339 were fired during the Unionist revolt. The remainder – twenty times as many – were fired at Nationalists. Orange law and Orange order.

Then, most gratuitously for the British government and the Unionist leaderships, at a time when they were in the dock for their behavior, there was a bomb explosion at the Killyhevlin Hotel in Co. Fermanagh. The IRA denied involvement. I myself, like many others, am skeptical and suspicious about who the authors may have been. One thing is for sure – the only ones who could have benefited from this attack were the British government and the Unionists.

All of this, including revelations on a BBC *Panorama* program of David Trimble's involvement with a prominent Loyalist paramilitary figure during the Drumcree stand-off while he refused to talk to the residents of Garvaghy Road, has had many profound implications.

The Unionists went back to Stormont today for talks. Sinn Féin was locked out. David Trimble and Ian Paisley and the Loyalist parties can flout the Mitchell Principles and still be welcomed back by the British government as if nothing had happened just last week. It is little wonder that Nationalists remain outraged. It is little wonder that the Catholic Cardinal expresses a sense, in unprecedented terms, of "betrayal," and that John Bruton has railed against British policy in a clear and forthright way.

Despite all this, of course, we must persevere. But the lessons of the past week have to be learned. If we are to successfully rebuild a peace process which has any hope of achieving a real peace settlement, then I believe that there must be a wholesale review of the events of the recent past by all the parties involved, and particularly by the two governments. There must be a new, coherent and viable way forward.

The breakaway Republican group known as the Continuity Army Council later admitted responsibility for the Killyhevlin Hotel bombing of July 14, 1996.

Negotiation or Confrontation?

The twenty-fifth anniversary of internment in the North passed off peacefully. In Derry the same weekend, the Unionist Apprentice Boys agreed in last-minute talks to postpone their march on the section of the city walls overlooking the Nationalist Bogside.

THE FOCUS OF most political comment in Ireland this last month or so has been on marches, and particularly on Orange marches. These are, of course, but a symptom of the wider political problem. Last weekend saw this problem represented in stand-offs between Orange marchers and small Catholic communities throughout Counties Antrim, Derry, Armagh and Fermanagh. The media attention was on Derry City. There the Bogside Residents' Association led the fight against triumphalist sectarian incursions into Nationalist areas. They sought accommodation and opposed domination.

It was touch and go but talks between the Apprentice Boys and the Bogside Residents' Association and the leadership of the SDLP and Sinn Féin in Derry averted a clash. The talks themselves were a considerable breakthrough. The problem of contentious parades has not been resolved and indeed it appears that we may still have a long way to go before the Loyalist institutions accept that they must seek the consent of the host communities for their marches. But the Bogside Residents' Association was flexible in its negotiations and in voluntarily re-routing one of its protests and in canceling another.

After the high drama of Derry the Apprentice Boys made their way homewards across the North. En route about a thousand of them diverted their buses to the small and entirely Nationalist village of Dunloy. Here they laid siege to the small village but were thwarted by hundreds of local Nationalists. There was trouble, too, in Bellaghy, where the RUC was particularly brutal in clearing away Nationalist protesters.

Another Loyalist institution, the Royal Black Preceptory, returned to Bellaghy on Sunday. Its members were confronted by the local Nationalist population and after an overnight stand-off negotiations again produced a peaceful conclusion to what was also at times a tense situation.

The residents' groups in all of these areas should be commended. They brought a calming influence and played a constructive and positive leadership role. Thanks also should go to the observers from international agencies, from local human rights and peace groups and from political parties in the Twenty-Six Counties.

The Orange marching season is not over. There are a number of other marches this month, including Royal Black Perceptory demonstrations on August 31.

The days of Loyalist institutions marching over people's rights are numbered. Most of the Orange parades are tolerated benignly by Nationalists but resentment – going back over decades – about the triumphalist coat-trailing nature of some of these demonstrations was brought to the surface by the Garvaghy Road cave-in and the curfew on the Lower Ormeau Road.

Garvaghy Road was a march too far. And if the Loyalist institutions were looking for someone to blame for their dilemma then they should look no further than David Trimble and Ian Paisley. There is no reason for a crisis over Orange marches. The lesson of this month is that dialogue can work. If the events of this past week are not to be repeated then negotiations should begin now. In all of this of course the main responsibility lies with the British government. Its pretense that the problem here is one of security is the crux of one of our main difficulties. Because a security problem requires a security response. Thus the marches are dealt with in this way instead of as part of a proactive political program which seeks to resolve all pertinent matters by way of dialogue.

Last weekend saw an entirely peaceful and disciplined twenty-fifth anniversary of internment. Against the background of the tension created by the Orange marches here in Belfast, all Nationalist areas celebrated their survival in week-long festivals. Here in West Belfast, Féile an Phobail hosted the ninth People's Festival. Internment, of course, is now recognized as the total failure of British policy. It is yet another example of them reaching for a security response. It is also telling testimony of the failure of this strategy.

As I concluded this piece, I received news that British secret agent and UDA boss Brian Nelson was secretly released from prison in Britain six months ago. His release, before having served even half his sentence, is as much a part of the dirty war Britain has fought in Ireland over twenty-five years as was Nelson's role as a British agent involved in collusion between Loyalist death squads and British crown forces which led to the murder of scores of Catholics.

Brian Nelson was a key player in all of this. Then British attorney general, Patrick Mayhew engaged in another form of collusion when he struck a sordid deal to protect Nelson from more serious charges and from the likely publication of evidence exposing British dirty tricks. The release of Brian Nelson does not close the door on collusion. On the contrary, I am confident that this issue will return to haunt the British government.

British Changing of Rules Could Lead to Collapse

Despite the efforts of John Hume and Gerry Adams in presenting new proposals for building peace, there was disappointment in the lack of response from the British government, which continued to alter its demands with regard to Sinn Féin's full participation in the peace process. That party held a national conference on conflict resolution in Athboy, Co. Meath on November 23, 1996.

THIS COLUMN IS usually produced on a word processor. Word processors are great yokes. If you know how to work them, which I do, some of the time. Other times I'm driven to distraction. Tonight, while trying to create a new document in my *Irish Voice* folder, I unintentionally went into an old one. The opening paragraph began: "The British government are still refusing to create the conditions for real talks and a process of honest dialogue. . ." That was Easter or thereabouts last year. The more things change, the more they remain the same. Or do they?

It is difficult for me to spell out the detail of exactly what is happening at this time but it is now a matter of public record that, since the collapse of the peace process in February, John Hume and I have been working to reconstruct the opportunity created in 1994.

So what is happening now? Some six weeks or so ago Hume/Adams Mark Two, as some sections of the media here are describing it, was presented to John Major. At this time we are still waiting for a definite reply. In the meantime there has been a lot of speculation and much media briefing but so far no clarity from London. The essence of the propositions presented to the British government are also in the public arena. They are:

- That the decommissioning issue be removed as a precondition, that it be a matter with all others for negotiation, and that it will not become a block in the negotiations;
- That a realistic time-frame be established by the two governments, and be proposed by them for the conduct of the negotiations;

- That the British government give a commitment to implement confidence-building measures. These could range through emergency legislation, prisoners, the Irish language, discrimination, the RUC and other related democratic rights or equality issues;
- That Sinn Féin entry into talks be on the same basis as all the other parties.

Many of these are already subject to agreements by the two governments. At this time, there is little confidence among Nationalists that London or the Unionists are really interested in a negotiated settlement. Apart from the events of the summer – and there was a reminder of all this last Sunday when hundreds of Orangemen laid siege once again to the small Nationalist village of Dunloy, as they have done with some Catholic churches in North Antrim for the last few months – there are continued and worrying stories about the ill-treatment of Irish prisoners in England. It is obvious that this is most unhelpful at any time. It is particularly so at this time.

The media here are alive with rumors. While most of the better-informed or more independently-minded journalists take a measured view of what is happening, I'm sure the general public is bemused by some of the headlines. The people of Athboy, Co. Meath certainly were last Saturday. Athboy was the venue for a Sinn Féin conference. Athboy is a quiet, prosperous little town, typically Irish in its long-one-street friendliness. The entrance of Old Darnley Lodge Hotel was surrounded by a posse of press people. They were watched by quiet men on tractors and weary countrywomen burdened down by shopping, as they ambushed passing Sinn Féin delegates making their way into the hotel.

The conference was a low-key affair. No more or less than a stock-taking exercise for the Sinn Féin activists in attendance. These are held regularly at different levels within the party on different issues. Because Saturday's event was a national affair and about conflict resolution, it may have been expected to get some media attention. Because it was held at this time, it dominated the headlines here over the weekend. Sinn Féin have no complaints about that, of course. To be sure, to be sure! But some hacks have a view that it was a re-run of the Letterkenny conference of 1994. It most certainly was not. Some even thought it was deliberately held in John Bruton's constituency. I wasn't even aware of this until the media told me.

One more serious aspect of the media reports, especially after Mr. Major received the Hume/Adams propositions, is the suggestion that if there was a renewed IRA cessation, Sinn Féin would have to go through some further period of decontamination. The Unionists were openly lobbying for this, and Downing Street actively briefed on the need for Sinn Féin to fulfill other criteria. This flies in the face of what John Hume and I have been doing. We were working at all times on the basis that, as outlined by the two governments in their February 28 communiqué, what is required is an unequivocal restoration of the 1994 cessation. I had verified this on a number of occasions in recent months. If the British now seek to change the goal-posts once again, it will wreck the months of painstakingly patient rebuilding of the initiative that Mr. Hume and I have sought to create along with others. Mr. Major must know this. It is of particular concern to me that these new and additional preconditions were only voiced after Downing Street received our proposals.

John Major has taken considerable time to respond. Six weeks is a very long time in politics. If and when he does respond, there is the real worry that his response will be aimed more at Tory public opinion than concerned with dealing with the real issues. Some people here fear that it will be a minimalist and ambiguous response. Mr. Major must respond adequately, in the spirit of what is required, and in good faith. That's the only way to do business.

Another Unnecessary Death

On February 12, 1997, a twenty-three-year-old British soldier was killed in Bessbrook, Co. Armagh.

ANOTHER PERSON, A British soldier, has been killed here. It was a killing waiting to happen.

The British Army and the RUC have been on full alert for some time now. These forces have never been on a ceasefire, although the British Army was less visible in some areas during the IRA cessation. South Armagh was not one of these areas. But even there raids and road-blocks and searches have increased over the last few months. The soldier who died was named Steven Restorick.

Young soldiers like him have stopped me regularly all my adult life. I, like most Nationalists or Republicans, have a general rule which we stick to when we are stopped by the British Army or the RUC. It they take it easy, we take it easy also. Generally speaking, we endure the indignity of being accosted in our homes or on the roads of our own country by a heavily armed foreign army. But we are polite. Sometimes we even smile or joke or wave cheerfully. Anything for an easy life.

I have often thought that that is why some people, in the old days, perfected tugging the forelock. The Irish have generally become expert at doing this without being subservient. In fact, we brought this "top o' the morning to you sur" subversion to an art form. We smiled at the landlord when we met him on the road as we went off to poach "his" game. His sport. Our food.

We did the same with "the polis." And the "sojers."

A version of this happens nowadays in the North. Sometimes it isn't so Somerville and Ross-ish. Sometimes it can get very ugly indeed. Sometimes the troops are hyped-up and aggressive. Sometimes they are petty and vindictive. Especially with young people. Sometimes they kill people. At other times they are bored or distracted. Or in good form and cheerful.

It must have been very ugly that night last week when Bombardier Steven Restorick was killed. A local woman who was herself slightly wounded in the attack which killed the soldier has described graphically the moment of this death. His death, like all the other deaths, diminishes all of us.

Yes, he was a soldier. Yes, he was heavily armed and well-trained. But he did not need to die. Not in Ireland. Not at the age of twenty-three.

Why did it happen? Steven Restorick is the latest victim of the long war on this island. His death is an indictment of those who refuse to talk peace. It is tragic proof of the failure of our efforts to end the war here. Steven Restorick paid with his life for the short-sightedness and stupidity of British policy.

My heart goes out to the parents and family of Steven Restorick. His death is a tragedy not just for them, though they are the bereaved, but for the rest of us also. It did not have to happen. The organization behind the killing has, of course, to face up to its responsibilities. But so too have the rest of us.

Days before the shooting at Bessbrook I wrote to John Major asking him to authorize his officials to meet with Sinn Féin representatives in an effort to find a way to establish real talks. On Saturday Patrick Mayhew said that there would be no talks at this time between his officials and Sinn Féin. He did not say how he hoped to bring about peace without a process of inclusive talks. Many people here suspect that Patrick Mayhew's commitment to peace in Ireland is to *Pax Britannica.*

In the same interview Mr. Mayhew dismissed calls for an apology for Bloody Sunday. Earlier last week he met with relatives of the victims of Bloody Sunday at a meeting arranged by John Hume to put new evidence before the British minister. In his arrogant dismissal of the families' appeal Patrick Mayhew cited the internationally discredited Widgery Report.

But despite all of this, we have to continue with the effort to make sense of it all and to find an avenue out of these difficulties and into a peace settlement.

Last week's visit to Belfast by the men and women of the US Congressional Committee on International Relations was a positive contribution in an otherwise bleak week. Their call for Sinn Féin's immediate inclusion in all-party talks is the only sensible way to move towards peace with justice in Ireland. The delegation, which included tried and trusted allies of peace and democracy in Ireland, invited all the parties to meet with them. Their open-door policy is at odds with the British no-talks stance. But it is the only way forward.

Coming as it does on the heels of hearings in Washington by the Congressional Ad Hoc Committee for Irish Affairs to discuss the plight of the seven Irish-American deportees and their families, and the support for Róisín McAliskey, the congressional visit serves to highlight the critical role Irish America has to play in rebuilding the peace process.

The question of peace in Ireland is a life and death issue for some of us. Despite all the difficulties I remain convinced that an opportunity still exists to inject a new momentum into the situation. A new initiative is still possible. I am not giving up. Sinn Féin will not give up either. The people of our small island have a right to peace. A permanent peace. With justice for all our people. Free from the arrogance of British ministers. Free of deaths of young British soldiers.

Sinn Fein Has
Election Fever

Sinn Féin prepared to contest elections to the British parliament at Westminster, the Irish parliament in Dublin, and local elections in the North.

B RITISH PRIME MINISTER John Major has called a general election. At last!
Election day is on May 1. There are also local government elections here in the North on May 21. Elections for Leinster House, the Irish Parliament, are expected before June. Depending upon who is talking, dates for this include April 14, May 5, mid-June and a myriad other days in between. Truth to tell, no one really knows except of course for the Taoiseach, John Bruton, and his partners in government. So we will have three elections in as many months. And Sinn Féin is contesting all three.

For a small party like ours that is a mighty undertaking. In fact, it would be a mighty undertaking for any party. In any event, we are the only ones. Ourselves, alone? The other parties are organized on partitionist lines and Sinn Féin is the only political party which is substantially organized nationally. Which means we get to fight more elections than anyone else.

The main focus here is understandably on the May 1 contest. Most people who have supported the peace process see this election as presenting a new opportunity to rebuild that process. There is a hope that a new, stable government in London will be able to focus on Ireland.

There is also an expectation that Labour Party leader Tony Blair will lead that government. Old Labour's record on Ireland is not a good one. But I share the hope that the new administration will have a majority, and while undoubtedly there will be a concentration on domestic issues, no new British government can afford to ignore the issue of Ireland. So for this reason more than any other, the elections are seen as hugely important.

This is reflected also in the recent interventions from the US. I am thinking especially of the very important speech by Senator Edward Kennedy. His call for London to set a date for Sinn Féin's entry into talks if there is an IRA cessation was rejected by British Minister Michael Ancram. Mr. Ancram knows that without such a date Sinn Féin's ability to influence the IRA is nil. He also knows the key issues which the London government needs to resolve if we are to make a creditable argument that an inclusive and meaningful process of negotiation is on offer.

The issues are:

- The removal of preconditions to and in negotiations;
- A definitive time-frame for the negotiations;
- Confidence-building measures;
- Sinn Féin's entry into talks.

In many ways, these matters are also at the nub of the election campaigns here. The electorate will be making its judgment on how the parties handled the peace process.

There are eighteen seats in the North. Four of these are held by the SDLP, the rest by the UUP, DUP and UK Unionists. There is actually the potential for non-Unionists to hold seven of these seats – the extra ones are in Fermanagh/South Tyrone, Mid-Ulster and West Tyrone, with the possibility of an eighth one in North Belfast. It needs an electoral pact between the SDLP and Sinn Féin to achieve this. And the SDLP have ruled out any such pact.

I am a supporter of such an electoral deal. It would change the face of electoral politics here forever. There appears to be little chance of the SDLP changing their mind. They are badly divided on the issue and they have set two preconditions – that the IRA halt its campaign and that Sinn Féin drop our abstentionist policy. These are clearly aimed at distracting attention from the way the SDLP stance thwarts the potential to maximize Nationalist representation. Because whatever about the first precondition – and Sinn Féin voters should not be saddled with the responsibility for the IRA – even if the party wanted to change abstentionism, and we don't, it would take a two-thirds majority of our party to vote in this change.

In the absence of such a pact, Sinn Féin is contesting sixteen seats. The main media focus is on West Belfast where, contrary to popular opinion, we have an uphill battle, and West Tyrone and Mid-Ulster.

There is an added interest in Mid-Ulster because Bernadette McAliskey surprised everyone this week by announcing the candidacy of her daughter, Róisín. Róisín is a remand prisoner in Britain, where she was taken from her home in Tyrone to await the processing of an extradition request from Germany. She is also eight months pregnant. She should not be in prison at all. She could easily be given bail. Instead, Róisín is held in solitary. She is subjected to strip searches and to a range of petty prison punishments.

This type of punitive regime is the norm for Irish prisoners in Britain, whether they are on remand like Róisín or sentenced prisoners. Of the sentenced prisoners, those held in the Special Secure Units are subject to the worst conditions. The case of Paddy Kelly has received a lot of publicity. Paddy has been diagnosed as suffering from cancer but he is refused hospital treatment.

The announcement by Bernadette McAliskey of the electoral intervention was followed by another one on Sunday night announcing the withdrawal of her daughter's name in order not to further split the Nationalist vote. It was a welcome development.

Sinn Féin hopes to consolidate our vote of last May. This may be difficult, but I have traveled extensively throughout the North over the last few months and there is no doubt that the Sinn Féin election machine is gearing itself up for a mighty effort. So while I have learned never to count the votes before they are cast, I am cautiously optimistic.

The building of a peace settlement should not have to wait until after the election, and neither should short-term electoral considerations be allowed to divert us from that task. Be assured that is Sinn Féin's view. Be assured also that while John Hume and I are in opposite camps trying to do our respective best for our parties, we continue to work away.

After a lengthy international campaign, Paddy Kelly was at last transferred to Portlaoise Jail in Ireland, where he could be close to his family. He died in June 1997.

What's In a Name?

Being stopped at British-staffed checkpoints is a fact of life for Nationalists in Northern Ireland.

" 'ALLO MR. ADAMS. 'Ow you doin'? We won't keep you long. Jest gotta check yoor identity."

That was last week. Outside Banbridge in Co. Down. On the dual carriageway. The same British soldier has stopped us on an average of once a week for the last few months. This time it would take about a half an hour or so before he let us go.

The soldier is behaving illegally. Funny thing is, while our car is detained at the road-block not another vehicle is stopped. Security forces? My arse!

Marooned in our own little Checkpoint Charlie, to pass the time I phone around media newsrooms on the mobile phone. Eventually I get put through to Eamonn Dunphy on Radio Ireland. Eamonn and I chat away about my predicament. Halfway through our interview the RUC arrive at the road-block and Radio Ireland's listeners are treated to the RUC's version of zero tolerance policing.

"Well, Mr. Adams, I know who you are so you are free to go . . . but I need to check out the driver's identity."

I smile benignly at him in gratitude at his good humor and in appreciation of his sense of fun. A friend of mine had a similar experience once on his way to Derry.

"Where are you going?" asked a peeler at a road-block outside Dungiven.

"To Derry," my friend replied as you do on these occasions, when that is where you are going.

"Are you sure?" the peeler responded.

"Sure I'm sure."

"It wudn't be Londonderry?"

"Definitely not! I'm going to Derry."

"Okay sir. If you just wait here awhile, we won't keep you long."

Fifteen minutes passed. My friend sat quietly in his car on the side of the road. Eventually the RUC man came back to him.

"Where did you say you were going, sir?" he smiled.

"Derry," my friend replied staunchly.

"Not Londonderry?"

"No! I'm going to Derry."

"That's okay sir. I'll try not to keep you much longer."

Another twenty minutes passed. My friend fumed quietly and subversively until the peeler arrived back again.

"Well sir. . . still not going to Londonderry?"

"I've been here a long time. I'm late for my appointments. I've changed my mind."

"Good," said the peeler.

"Aye," said my friend. "I'm too late for Derry. I'm going to Strabane instead."

Jimmy Barr from the Falls Road had a similarly satisfying encounter with the forces of law and order. Jimmy was up a ladder minding his own business in his own street when this English accent reached up to him in a bellow.

"You, moite. Give me yoor noime!"

"My noime?" Jimmy queried.

"Your name," the accent corrected itself menacingly. "Now!"

"What do you want my name for?" asked Jimmy.

"I am authorized, under the Northern Ireland Emergency Provisions, to take your name."

"Who says?" Jimmy continued, perched confidently on his ladder, high above everything.

"I f——n' say," thundered the Brit. "Give me your bleedin' noime."

"I will not," Jimmy said firmly.

At that an officer arrived. The squaddie explained the situation to him. The officer peered up the ladder towards Jimmy.

"Why, sir," he asked. "Why won't you give your name to this soldier?"

"Because," said Jimmy, "he has a name of his own and if I give him my name then he will have two names and I'll have none."

Ah, the sweet logic of it all.

I have had similar name-dropping experiences with the British Army and the RUC. For almost two decades I never gave them my proper name. For some of this time I was on the run. That is, I was avoiding the danger of being interned.

Internment is a neat little British device for imprisoning Irish dissidents without the nuisance of trials or silly things like that. Even when there was less danger of being interned I tried to avoid being stopped by British patrols. I still do. If I was unlucky enough to get stopped I always gave a bum name.

This had more than the predictable effects on family life. When our Gearóid was very young, occasionally we would be stopped together when I was leaving him to school. He was about five or so. Once I had him on my shoulders and he listened intently as I advised the offending British soldier that I was his Uncle Richard – Gearóid's Uncle Richard, that is.

But most of the time I would be stopped on my own. By this time I was appearing every so often in the British media. Although I was usually quite successful at avoiding Brits, after a few years I began to think that I was fooling no one by giving them a false name when I was stopped. I figured out that they were noting my movements and so on and pretending they believed me when I gave a bum name. But every so often I also heard of someone who knew someone who looked like me and they kept getting beaten up by British patrols. Despite this disconcerting news, I resolved that I would give my proper name the next time I was stopped.

This was a mighty step for me. To take ownership of my own name was also to reclaim my own space. At first, as I mulled over my decision, I was quite excited and apprehensive. Then I came to like the idea very much. I started to look forward to being myself again after almost a lifetime of being somebody else.

I wasn't stopped for a good while after that. Then one day outside Newry a British Army patrol waved down our car. A young soldier motioned me to roll down the car window.

"Wot's your name sir?" he asked.

I looked him straight in the eyes.

"Gerry Adams," I said.

"Spell that please," he continued, without even blinking.

"I'm not obliged to do that," I responded.

"Okay," he said testily. "That's G-A-R-Y . . . roight? A-N-D-R-E-W-S . . . Gary Andrews, right?"

"Roight," I sighed.

"You English?" he asked in a friendlier tone.

"Nope," I said.

He was obviously disappointed.

"Go on," he said, waving us on our way.

"Thanks," I said.

Elated Nationalists Hope for Fresh Start

In the British elections Labour won a landslide victory, while Gerry Adams won back his West Belfast seat, and Martin McGuinness was elected MP for Mid-Ulster.

S INN FÉIN IS now the third largest party in the Six Counties, which is a very good thing indeed. We only missed West Tyrone by a short head. The Rev. Ian Paisley's DUP is now in fourth place. And it could have been even better. The Nationalist turnout was the largest ever since partition, and despite all the focus on Sinn Féin's gains, the SDLP got its best results yet. Think how much better the overall result would have been if the SDLP had agreed to an electoral pact with us? That is something we will have to return to in the time ahead.

For now, the most important thing is to ensure that the electoral rivalry between the SDLP and Sinn Féin does not deflect us from the more important task of rebuilding a credible peace process. And there now appears to be a real opportunity to do just this. That is certainly the hope here after the elections and, as the dust settles down, people are looking to the new British Prime Minister Tony Blair's massive majority as the assurance that he can now do whatever is needed to sort things out here.

That is, if he wants to, and I certainly hope that he does. Political will is what is required, and there can be no doubt if the will is there that this new London government can play a historically unprecedented role in creating and sustaining a lasting peace settlement in Ireland. So we must suspend concerns about previous British Labour administrations and their record in Ireland, and go forward on the basis that there is everything to play for in the challenging task of working out our future.

Sinn Féin is certainly ready to deal with the new government. In my view there should be no delay. A continued vacuum leaves everybody hostage to fortune, and that should be avoided at all costs. Of course, there has to be time for the new administration to settle in, but that should not become a distraction in itself. The new British Secretary for the North, Dr. Mo Mowlam, is well briefed on all the pertinent matters. She knows what has to be done and I wish her well in her endeavors.

I think the election of Tony Blair will help British national morale. And that is important. Especially if that morale is based on a reality of changed times, and more caring, progressive and positive policies. Certainly the televisual images of the young and happy Blair family at 10 Downing Street are in marked contrast to the faded and jaded optics of eighteen years of Toryism.

I wish Mr. Blair well also. He is the British Prime Minister who will lead his people into the new millennium. More importantly, from the Irish standpoint, he can also be the Prime Minister who lays the foundation for a peaceful and just millennium for the people of our island as well as his own.

Labour's majority at Westminster has certainly loosened the Unionists' death grip on that establishment, and that is a good thing. My own often stated notion is that it was Mr. Major's own Unionism – of the British variety (which Unionism he himself confirmed often during his premiership) – which underpinned his attitude to Ireland, as well as the Tory Party's dependency on the UUP that gave David Trimble's party considerable leverage. Those days are over.

And within Unionism itself, Mr. Trimble no longer should be fearful of the likely negative reactions of entrenched fundamentalists like Rev. Ian Paisley. As leader of the largest Unionist party, David Trimble needs to grasp this new opportunity to lead his section of our people forward. We all have to be creative and forward-looking.

The Taoiseach, John Bruton, also has a special responsibility. He meets Mr. Blair this week and it is crucial that he is focused on the big picture which the Irish national interest involves. And some time soon Mr. Blair will be meeting President Bill Clinton, so the Irish-American role remains an important one. The President's statement of congratulations to Mr. Blair and the way he tied his concern for the Irish peace process into those comments is very encouraging.

So all in all, as I pen these lines, it is with a certain sense of satisfaction. It is hugely gratifying for me as I met the people during the election campaign to have been at the receiving end of so much support and goodwill and love here in my own place in this part of

Belfast. That's the best pay-back of all. It is a humbling as well as an uplifting experience. To once again be the MP for West Belfast is also satisfying. But it is a daunting responsibility also. To have so many people depending on me is a little scary. Because this time it is different. And it is all those people who vote for me and people like me who help to make that difference.

Last Friday on the day of the election count they invaded Belfast City Hall and spilled over outside into the city center. Young men in denims and sweatshirts, young women, babies in prams, besuited senior citizens in their Sunday best, blue-rinsed grandmothers, a sprinkling of yuppies here and there, schoolchildren, young and old united in delight, men and women alike in places Fenians rarely get to go. Especially Fenians with attitude. Fenians singing. Fenians drinking champagne. Or wasting it by spraying froth everywhere. Even the peelers relaxed.

The mood was infectious as we poured up Royal Avenue in the bright sunshine. Especially when Cruncher started singing *Something Inside So Strong*, and we all joined in the chorus. By the time we got to the Falls Road there were thousands of us. Singing and chanting and clapping each other on the back, and hugging and kissing and punching the air. And singing, singing, singing.

And Justice For All?

Sinn Féin, fresh from their success in the May UK election, were confident of further prospects in the Irish general election on Friday, June 6.

IRELAND IS BASKING in a heat wave. I have not been in the office for what appears to be a very long time now, and I am really enjoying going out and about trying to get a few extra votes in the Irish general election, and picking up a tan in the process.

Sinn Féin is standing fifteen candidates in fourteen constituencies. We could stand more, but our strategy group which deals with these matters decided that it is better to concentrate on selected areas where we have the potential for growth. I agree.

This year it seems to me that I have been fighting elections for a very long time indeed. It is exhausting work, and, as I write, I am as banjaxed as I ever hope to be. But there are two consolations. Firstly, we are doing very well so far, thank you very much. Sinn Féin returns in the local government elections in the North have cheered us all up. Our success has also annoyed all sorts of other people. But that has only served to cheer us up even more. And secondly, in this heat wave the countryside is beautiful. Every part of it.

I awoke the other morning in a house outside Clones. We had arrived after dark to spend the night after a hard day's canvassing in nearby Cavan. The room I slept in had huge windows, so as I bedded down I kept the curtains open.

Hours later the sound of the dawn arising drew me from my slumbers. Outside the meadows were bathed in mist, and I sat up in bed and watched the most beautiful sunrise I have ever seen. Then a while later, as the rest of the island slept, we drove from Monaghan up through Tyrone and into Donegal. It's little wonder the English wanted the place. Apart from anything else, I can understand how the beauty of our place must have drawn them. By now, I have been in almost every village, and every pub in every village in Co. Cavan. That's where we are hoping for a break through. Not in the pubs, though it's hard to avoid them, but in the Cavan/Monaghan constituency.

Caoimhghín Ó Caoláin is a hardworking councilor in Monaghan with a good base of support and a consistent record of leadership work in the search for a peace settlement. Cavan/Monaghan is the constituency which elected hunger striker Ciaran Doherty in 1981, so there is a strong Republican base here. And no matter what anyone tells you, the North is an issue in this election. There is also a lot of anger at the establishment throughout the Twenty-Six Counties, at the way it has been handling its own affairs within the state.

We are hoping to provide a democratic outlet for this genuine and justifiable anger. And not only in Cavan/Monaghan. Wherever we are standing Sinn Féin will do well. From Kerry, where Martin Ferris is polling strongly, to Dublin and Sligo and all the places in between.

The cause of the anger is more obvious in the inner city areas where there is no beautiful countryside to camouflage the deprivation and discrimination which is actively subverting the very lives of large sections of our people, many becoming prey to drug addiction and/or drug-related crime. At a Mass for the dead in Dublin central, eighty-two names of the victims of this scourge were read out. I met a young woman who is on treatment, and who had buried six members of her family, including her parents. It is a national disgrace that there is no coherent strategy to eradicate this problem which threatens to pollute the most valuable of our resources – our children.

There is also anger at the corruption in politics here. While many members of the Dáil are hardworking, well-intentioned individuals, there is no doubt that graft has become a political way of life for others. Recent revelations about the cover-ups and scams, the cozy cartels and back-handers, have done little to build public confidence. No doubt, despite it all, people will vote for the same old parties, and this will remain the case until a viable and relevant alternative is built, but there is another danger. The danger of cynicism and materialism.

In my view our people are a caring people who want a decent life for themselves and their neighbors. They have never been as conservative as they are painted, but we are a colonized nation, and that has its effects on all of us. Ireland is a changing place, and there is a great need to make sure that the changes are for the better. That's also what this week's poll is about – change.

Real or imaginary? We will all know soon enough. This election will have profound effects on all of us. The next Irish government will probably go into the next century. It will certainly have to pick up the pieces of the peace process and move speedily to re-establish this on a solid foundation. And if it has any sense of justice it should certainly try to ensure that the benefits of the so-called Celtic Tiger are spread more evenly to all sections of our people. And maybe, just for once, to the advantage of those who need these benefits the most.

The Times They Are A-Changing?

Alban Maginness was welcomed as the first Catholic Lord Mayor of Belfast on June 28, 1997.

SATURDAY NIGHT I was at the Lord Mayor's installation dinner at Belfast City Hall. No big deal, says you. Fair enough! But on Saturday we were installing the first ever Catholic mayor in this city, an SDLP man, Alban Maginness. He was elected as first citizen by the thirteen Sinn Féin councilors, his own party, the Alliance party and one Unionist councilor, so it was a wee bit of history in the making.

The ending of Unionist domination in the City Hall is no mean thing, as any Belfast exile will explain to the rest of you. So Sunday night in the City Hall was a nice night for all involved. The Unionists stayed away, which is a pity. A wee bit of social intercourse would have gone a long way. They said their absence was caused by my presence, which doesn't help my paranoia, and by the absence of a royal toast – a toast to the English Queen. I don't know if we could have compromised with them in any way which would have changed their minds but no one could have objected to the toast on the night anyway. It was to Belfast and all its citizens.

"I'll drink to that," said I. And I did.

Last week, Martin McGuinness and I accompanied Caoimhghín Ó Caoláin into Leinster House, the Irish Parliament in Dublin. Caoimhghín is the first Sinn Féin TD in seventy-five years to take up his seat in that assembly. That too was a bit of history. The last time Sinn Féin was there was during the treaty debates. We lost that one.

Martin McGuinness and I watched the election of Bertie Ahern as Taoiseach and it was with considerable pride and satisfaction that we listened to Caoimhghín making his debut speech, as he explained that he would be voting for Bertie for the top post. Some may think that was the natural thing for Sinn Féin to do and maybe it was, but our support for Mr. Ahern is solely on the basis of his party's record in the search for peace.

There are many issues in the program for government which

Sinn Féin does not agree with. There is a need for a strategy to eliminate poverty and to alleviate the unfair tax burden which weighs down on low-paid and blue collar workers. There is also a need for a coherent strategy on the North, which requires substance and sustainability. All of this will present great challenges for the new Dublin government. I wish them well.

As well as all the historic dinners and grand entrances, last week also saw the publication by the British government of the decommissioning paper agreed by it and the Irish government and the *aide memoire* sent to Sinn Féin.

I welcome the efforts being made by Tony Blair to address the issues which have blocked the reconstruction of the peace process. I accept that he is not responsible for the legacy of distrust and suspicion among Republicans which was created by the behavior of the previous British government.

Nor indeed is he responsible for the difficulties currently facing everyone concerned to find a way of off-loading this legacy. However, he is responsible for implementing a policy to overcome the problem. More than anything else this is a question of political will. The way to peace follows the will to achieve it. The will is derived from a desire to end the strife.

Sinn Féin has already acknowledged that the attitude of the present British government and its approach to the issues we have raised is an advance on that of John Major's government. It is important to recall, however, that these issues are not Sinn Féin preconditions. These are obstacles erected by a British government to prevent the commencement of all-party inclusive talks because that was a British strategy at that time. They can be resolved only by a British government which has a different strategy.

The style of this Blair-led British government is different. But what of its strategy? Anyone wanting to get a sense of the difficulties which have to be overcome as we try to thread a way forward has to understand the damage caused by the way the last British government used the issue of decommissioning, in collusion with the Unionists, as an obstacle to the talks themselves and to prevent these talks moving to the core issues.

That is why clarity is so important. The document on decommissioning presented in Westminster represents the position of the two governments at this time. Both have said that the aim of their proposals is to address the decommissioning issue without blocking the negotiations. This is welcome.

But my attention is consistently drawn to press briefings by British officials and comments by Tony Blair in Westminster, which say something entirely different.

The potential for the decommissioning issue to be raised further up the road to prevent movement in the negotiations is still a grave and justifiable concern for some. Given the history of how it has been used for this precise purpose, there needs to be a clear understanding of how Mr. Blair intends to employ his government's proposals to prevent further blockage. Given his stated desire to have inclusive talks; given the evidence that he may be prepared to embrace a different strategy from his predecessor and given the urgency with which he has applied himself to these matters, surely he understands how important this is.

I have also a serious concern that in Mr. Blair's Westminster speech, in the two governments' proposals and in the *aide memoire*, there are no more than passing references to the rights of Nationalists. The equality agenda, which is given some attention in previous British government and Irish government documents, is not spelled out. This also needs some urgent attention.

There is the question of prisoners, acknowledged in every conflict situation the world over as a key consideration in conflict resolution. There are Republican prisoners now entering their twenty-second year in prison in England. There are prisoners in England who have not seen their families for three years because of punitive visiting restrictions. There must be confidence that all of these matters are not just treated aspirationally but with firm intent. The release of all political prisoners must be part of an overall settlement; in the meantime, prisoners and their families have to be treated with dignity.

In asking that the British government takes a programatic approach to these matters, and gives clear expression to this as part of the need to build confidence in its commitment, I have been accused of upping the ante. This is not the case. The British government has had decades to deal with equality issues. It has failed – or refused to do so. Why should anyone believe that it will do so now? It is probable that some of these measures will only be implemented in the course of a real and evolving peace process.

But even if such has to be the case, there is no reason why the commitments to do so cannot be clearly and unequivocally stated. And if this helps to rebuild the peace process, as it surely will, is this not a compelling reason for it to be done?

And finally, I switched on the wireless this very second. It is just before 5 p.m. Irish time, and, as I have just discovered, almost midnight Chinese time. By a fluke I am tuned into a live radio broadcast from Hong Kong. What a jolly fine broadcast it is. British rule in Hong Kong will end any second now, and, if I can manage it, at exactly the same time as this column. Times certainly are a-changing.

Drumcree
Mark Three

New Secretary of State Mo Mowlam and RUC Chief Constable Ronnie Flanagan announced in the early hours of Sunday, June 6 that they had decided to allow the Orange parade to march down the Garvaghy Road.

I MAGINE, IF YOU would, the map of Ireland. Imagine a car speeding from the south-west, in and out of towns and villages, through a beautiful dawn, along new stretches of motorway and pot-holed back roads rushing towards the north-east. That was me.

Last Saturday night, I was down in Tralee in north Kerry at a function for Martin Ferris's election workers. I left the event at one o'clock on Sunday morning, the 6th. I wanted to be back in Belfast before the Orange march started at Drumcree. I made it before the march but not before the RUC and the British Army attacked the people of the Garvaghy Road.

Readers who are unfamiliar with the workings of colonialism or of how unjust societies function may be confused into thinking that this place is a muddled mess of ethnic conflict and sectarian division between two intransigent groups. That certainly was the view expressed by the British Secretary of State, as she sought to explain why an Orange march was forced down the Garvaghy Road last Sunday morning. It was, she declared, the fault of two intransigent groups. She had done her best.

The people of the Garvaghy Road cannot be described as an intransigent group. They were not planning to march into an area where they were not wanted. All they asked was that the Orangemen should speak to them, sit down with them and give them their place. The Orangemen refused. David Trimble, the local MP, refused to talk to his own constituents. The onus was then clearly on the British government to stand up for the residents.

Do you remember the two governments signing up to a Framework Document which set out a whole process to introduce equality in employment, on economic issues, on democratic issues, on the issues of language and culture, and so on and so on? These matters should have been legislated for and implemented a long time ago.

Two intransigent groups?

There is no comparison between a secret, anti-Catholic organization and people in a neighborhood who were organizing peaceably and within the law. What was unlawful about the peace camp on the roadside at Garvaghy? What was the legal basis on which the RUC attacked those people?

We are still waiting for answers to these questions and many more, but the publication of a leaked British government report on Monday night which shows that London had made plans over two weeks ago to force last weekend's Orange march through the Nationalist Garvaghy Road does clarify matters.

This revelation shattered claims by the British Secretary of State that she was engaged in a genuine attempt to find an accommodation, or that up to the morning of the march no decision had been taken on what to do. It also exposed as a lie the claims by the boss of the RUC, Ronnie Flanagan, that the decision to force the march through was taken to protect Nationalists against a Loyalist backlash. There is no mention of this concern in the leaked British report.

There is a real sense among Nationalists that all of this is evidence that the British were involved in a planned betrayal of the residents of the Garvaghy Road. As an Irish Republican, I am not surprised that the British government behaves in this way. Those who are surprised nurture an innocent if not naïve hope that with this new government, things were going to be different. It doesn't work like that. Expediency rules British policy in Ireland. I learned that many moons ago. That is not to say that I did not hope for better things. Of course I did, but I think it was inevitable that Unionism had to test this new British government.

Unionist influence is very negative. It's about "not an inch." It's about stopping change. It's about slowing change down. And Unionism is also very much, in my view, on the defensive. The vision of Unionism isn't about a new Ireland or a new society. It is about the old order.

Unfortunately for the rest of us, the influence of Unionism isn't restricted to the Orange lodges. It has its champions in the RUC. And if you look at the leaked British document, you find that it's the same officials and advisers from the old regime. The same people who advised this same decision last year, and the year before; the same people who advised the last government to hold up the peace process – all the same people.

I made this point when Tony Blair made his first keynote speech as British Prime Minister in Belfast a few weeks ago. I pointed out to those who were dismayed by the pro-union and pro-Unionist content of his script that the scriptwriters were from the old school, that it was the old advisers and officials. And that he would have to stand up to them if he wanted to have some positive movement forward.

Either Tony Blair as the British Prime Minister runs this place on a political agenda, or the people who want war and conflict and a security agenda run it. Last weekend's decision and the way it was implemented shows once again that it is the security/military and intelligence people who are in charge.

The crux of this problem is that British secretaries of state come to this part of Ireland to defend British interests. British policy, which lies at the heart of this conflict, is based on the union, and the union is founded on the Unionist veto. So British policy is primarily concerned with defending the status quo. That much at least is clear. But what signal does it send to those of us who are trying to rebuild a new peace process? How does Tony Blair hope to build on this basis? He needs to tell us and everyone else.

I am asked where does all of this leave Irish Republicans? How could Sinn Féin trust Mo Mowlam? We don't need to. It's ourselves and our allies we need to trust. Patrick Mayhew was the last British Secretary of State here. He told lies. He put papers into the library of the British Parliament which the media exposed as lies. Did that stop us talking to Patrick Mayhew? Of course not. Because we have a vested interest in peace.

So we will not be deflected by the stance of the new British government. Of course it has made our task more difficult, but we must face up to those who pursue this strategy. And we must face up to them intelligently, coherently, giving calm, reflective leadership to the people we seek to lead.

There's a saying in Irish which loosely translates: "Beware the horns of the bull, the hooves of the horse and the smile of the Englishman." Or woman.

I'm an Irish Republican. I think the people of our island can do a much better job of running this place than any English politician. I have no doubt about that because whatever we do we will do in the broad interest of the people of this island. And I believe that many people here are increasingly coming around to the Republican view that the British government is not a neutral referee but a government which has vested interests and policies to advance those interests.

The challenge for those in the US who want peace in Ireland must be to seek a change in British policy away from security measures and into politics. Away from the easy rhetoric of peace and into the reality of peacemaking.

The democratic imperative is now on the Irish government to state the case for equality of treatment. It needs to apply itself to seeking international support for the rights of people in this part of Ireland to equality. It has to uphold the legitimacy of Irish unity as a policy objective and to outline a vision of generosity to the Unionists.

And the onus is also on Tony Blair if he wants to do business with Sinn Féin, if he wants to be part of the movement towards peace, if he wants to be different from his predecessors to prove that he will accept that all citizens are equal, that Irish Nationalists have equal political and civil rights. In this instance, that should mean the British government defending the right of Nationalists on the Lower Ormeau Road by refusing to allow a march by the Orange Order to pass through that area this weekend. Last weekend's mess should not be compounded by a replay this weekend.

An Equality Ethos
Is Required

Against the background of events on the Garvaghy Road which led to rioting throughout the North, the Orange Order called off the July 12th parade scheduled for Belfast's Lower Ormeau Road.

E VEN DURING THE trauma of the past four weeks Sinn Féin has been pro-actively engaged with all of the other players who have a willingness to rebuild a new peace process.

The British government damaged itself badly in the eyes of many who expected better of it when the Orange march was forced down the Garvaghy Road on July 6. It was the anger and the disciplined mass mobilizations of Nationalists which prevented it from doing the same thing on the Ormeau Road and on other contentious march routes on the 12th and which led to the Orange Order's postponement of marches.

While acknowledging the significance of this development – it was after all the first time since the order was founded that such a step was taken – it is crucial that we understand the dynamic which led to this new departure so that the respite created can be built upon.

The watchword in all of this must be equality. The harsh reality, graphically illustrated by the events on the Garvaghy Road, is that Nationalists living in the Six Counties are not equal citizens under British law or in the eyes of the institutions of this statelet. The "Nationalist nightmare" which we were told ended in 1985 after the Anglo-Irish Agreement, remains largely unchanged after almost three decades of direct British rule. Nationalists in the North still live in a society in which the cancer of inequality and injustice pervades all aspects of daily life, and in which basic human, political and civil rights are denied.

The northern state was founded on discrimination, inequality and intolerance. It was and is not a democratic entity. Twenty-five years ago the British government took direct responsibility for the Six Counties. Since then there have been many fine words uttered but little of practical value to tackle inequality. In reality the antidiscrimination laws which were passed in the 1970s and again in 1989 have been deeply flawed and have made little impact in challenging discrimination and inequality.

In its recent report the Standing Advisory Commission on Human Rights reaffirmed that Catholics are over twice as likely to be unemployed as Protestants. And it found that the main British government policies specifically aimed at tackling inequality – Targeting Social Need (TSN) and Policy Appraisal and Fair Treatment (PAFT) – "left a lot to be desired in their effectiveness. Indeed research indicated that few government departments and public bodies have pursued these policies in a pro-active way . . . it is disappointing to find that it (TSN) has not been taken seriously in Government Departments and agencies . . . PAFT too was introduced in 1994 as a major government initiative to build issues of equity and equality into policy formation and the implementation of public services. The research for this review revealed very patchy but largely ineffective implementation."

It is now perfectly clear that, as currently constituted, the PAFT guidelines represent another attempt, like the Fair Employment laws, to head-off external criticism rather than a genuine attempt to initiate fundamental change. It appears to Nationalists and Republicans that the myriad laws and agreements promising equality for all citizens have actually had no real effect. What is required to achieve real and measurable change towards equality, and what has been absent on the part of the British government to date, is the political will to do what is right and implement what is required.

Equality should be at the heart of government decision making in London. It isn't. Successive British governments have lacked the political will to tackle these matters and their policies are primarily concerned with defending the status quo. No one should be surprised by this. As an Irish Republican who has watched expediency consistently dictate British policy I am not surprised by the failure of the British government to defend Nationalist rights. A refusal to bring in change – a minimalist approach – dominates the mindset within the corridors of power at Stormont and Westminster.

The minimalist approach must be confronted and changed. Equality cannot be simply an illusion. It must be a fact. We need a whole-hearted commitment to ensuring equality in decision making and delivery of services. This is a central component of any democratic process. There must be full accountability for equality measures; transparent and testable procedures governing their implementation; genuine and full participation to ensure that citizens feel their concerns are taken into account and reflected in decisions which affect them; goals and timetables for its implementation, and regular review and assessment of progress and impact.

To achieve that we need:

- equality in employment opportunities;
- equality in economic investment into areas of high unemployment;
- equality for the Irish language and culture;
- equality in the provision of resources for education;
- equality for political representatives.

We need:

- to tackle the difficult issue of cultural symbols, of flags and emblems;
- an end to repressive legislation;
- a new unarmed policing service under democratic control;
- speedy progress on the issue of political prisoners, their conditions, transfer and release.

These and much more are matters for the British government. Matters of policy – not for negotiation. These are rights, civil and political rights, to which every citizen in every democratic state should be entitled. They are enshrined in international law, they have been advocated by international courts and human rights forums and organizations worldwide. The report of the International Body chaired by Senator Mitchell recognizes the need for action on these issues.

Even within the Framework Document there are many references to continuing inequalities and the need for them to be addressed. Reference is made to "secure and satisfactory political, social and cultural rights and freedom from discrimination for all citizens, on parity of esteem, and on just and equal treatment for the identity, ethos and aspirations of both communities." These are laudable aspirations but they must be taken beyond aspiration. The responsibility for that rests primarily with the British government.

It must propose and implement a culture of rights to bring about equality for all citizens. The British government must propose and ultimately implement policies which will make equality and parity of esteem a reality.

There is a responsibility on the British Prime Minister, who claims to have placed human rights at the top of his international agenda, to place it at the top of his Irish policy. If Tony Blair wants to demonstrate his good faith he will have to prove that he accepts that Irish Nationalists have equal political and civil rights and that his government will respect those rights.

There is also a democratic imperative on the Irish government to assert the right of Irish citizens living in the North to equality of treatment. It must seek international support, through the European Union, the United Nations, the other forums and bodies it holds membership of and through the diplomatic relationships it shares with other nations.

If a durable settlement is to be reached there must be a constructive context within which to resolve the conflict. Experience of the management of peace process elsewhere, most significantly in South Africa, has demonstrated the importance of creating such a context in ensuring a successful resolution of conflict. That context is a shared responsibility and can only be created by creating a level playing pitch in which the rights and the equality of all are guaranteed.

The imperative now must be to intensify the work of building a meaningful and credible negotiations process. Sinn Féin will not be deflected from this task. There is a common responsibility on all of us, but especially the two governments, to remove the obstacles which still stand in the way of real peace talks.

This will not be easy. The road ahead will be difficult, dangerous and risky for all of us but we can succeed. Crucial to that success is a willingness to sit down and engage in good faith in a process of honest dialogue. During these talks Sinn Féin will press for maximum constitutional change, for an end to the union, for the political, economic and democratic transformation of this island. We will encourage the Irish government and others to pursue a strategy for Irish unity. And inside and outside of the negotiations, we will press for equality. Now.

Another Chance

On July 20, 1997, the IRA began "the unequivocal restoration of the ceasefire of August 1994."

TODAY IS A beautiful Belfast summer day, thank God. I should be out in the rare Irish sun relaxing on this simmering Sunday. Instead I have spent today doing interviews and now I am slaving before a hot word processor. Such is life. Today, you see, is the day the IRA cessation commenced. At noon.

You would think everybody would be happy. Or relieved. You would be wrong. Most of us are. In fact I think the vast majority of us are. I certainly am. But sections of the British establishment are begrudging, and the leaders of Unionism are behaving as if they do not want a cessation at all.

Today is the first day of a new era for the people of Ireland.

I hope.

The first day of a new beginning for us all – if there is a political will to make it so.

The British government has a huge amount of distance to cover to prove their democratic credentials to Nationalist Ireland. The recent brutality on the Garvaghy Road as the RUC hacked their way through the residents is proof that this new British government is susceptible to the old agendas and the old methods. The mass mobilizations to prevent this being repeated on the Ormeau Road forced Mr. Blair to make a choice and the Orange Order to make a welcome postponement of four of their parades.

Last year there were 2,405 Loyalist marches. This puts their decision in context. Nonetheless, I recognize the significance of the Orange Order's decision and I commend it. I also commend the great discipline of ordinary Nationalists in the face of great provocation and a vicious Loyalist killing campaign which left an eighteen-year-old Catholic girl, Bernadette Martin, shot to death this week as she slept.

This was the background and sometimes the foreground against which the protracted effort to restore a new peace process was played out. As I have said a number of times, usually in the immediate wake of a serious incident, the Sinn Féin leadership has never faltered or allowed anything to deflect us from the task of creating the conditions for real negotiations. At all times we continued our pro-active contact with all the main players, whether in London, Dublin, or the USA.

Now that the cessation has been restored, I am asked what single item helped to bring this about. There was no single item. The election of new governments in London and Dublin certainly helped, but this weekend's announcement was the cumulation of work which I and others in the Sinn Féin leadership started directly after the collapse of the last process.

Our focus was on two main elements. The need to remove the obstacles which John Major had placed on the path into all-party talks, and the need for commitments to genuine negotiations and to an equality agenda. Firstly, given that the commitments by the last British government to inclusive negotiations were reneged on after the IRA cessation of August 1994, what was needed were assurances that inclusive and meaningful negotiations would be in place. The process of obtaining detail and clarity on these issues was painstaking but essential and they were provided in a series of documents from London and a number of telephone calls. Secondly, there was a need to establish a continuing commitment by the Irish government, the SDLP and Irish-American opinion to credible negotiations, to issues of equality and to demilitarization. These are the two pillars on which this new phase is built.

I have made it clear over the eighteen months since the collapse of the 1994 cessation that I would only approach the IRA to restore its cessation if I was confident that the Army's response would be positive. But when Martin McGuinness and I provided a detailed report and assessment to the IRA we could not be entirely sure what the outcome would be. If we had not got the response we desired nothing would have been heard of our initiative. We would have gone back to the rest of the Sinn Féin leadership and returned quietly to the task of threading a way forward. And we would have continued to do this until we succeeded.

Fortunately that was not necessary. The IRA announcement came without delay. It is a momentous decision. It gives all of us a chance, another chance. Because most people know how the previous chance was squandered, it is little wonder that the hope in everyone's heart is tempered with a sense of reality.

That is why people must take ownership of this new possibility. It should not be left to governments or political parties. Where the people lead the politicians will follow. There is an onus on church leaders, trade unions, the business sector, editorial writers and opinion makers of every kind to argue for talks. Real talks! Honest dialogue.

The Unionist leaders need to decommission their negative mindsets. Sinn Féin has engaged in a long-term project with Unionists. Those who we are in touch with want dialogue. Their leaders should declare ceasefires in their minds. They need to find new language, a new vision. They need to have the courage of their convictions. I could find lots of reasons for not talking to the British or the Unionists. But I want a democratic peace settlement. And talking is the only way to achieve this.

There is an awesome responsibility on the Dublin government and in particular on the London government, to bring this about. There is also a historic challenge to Unionist leaders because any political settlement must involve fundamental and thorough political and constitutional change. Unionist domination is finished. Forever. This generation of Irish Nationalists will not put up with the injustices heaped upon our parents and our grandparents.

As an Irish Republican party, Sinn Féin will be guided by our aim of a united Ireland. We will be seeking an end to British rule in Ireland and we will be asserting the constitutional rights of Nationalists. We will be encouraging the Irish government and others to do likewise. And we will be pressing for a speedy demilitarization of the entire situation, including the release of all those who are imprisoned as a result of the conflict.

Am I optimistic? I am a realist. These are difficult and dangerous but challenging times. Making peace is not easy. But I have learned that sometimes the optimism of the will must overcome the pessimism of the intellect. That is how we got to this point.

So this can be the beginning of the end to conflict in our country. If the political will exists to make it happen.

Postscript

O N WEDNESDAY AUGUST 6, a Sinn Féin delegation which included Sinn Féin President Gerry Adams MP, the Party's Chief Negotiator Martin McGuinness MP, General Secretary Lucilita Breathnach, Árd Chomhairle member Martin Ferris, and Caoimhghín Ó Caoláin TD, met a British delegation led by Secretary of State Marjorie Mowlam MP and including Paul Murphy MP, Political Development Minister.

They held intense discussions for over two hours. The Sinn Féin contribution was based on the following paper.

PEACE IN IRELAND – AN AGENDA FOR CHANGE

Introduction

Sinn Féin welcomes these discussions. Dialogue is the only way to resolve peacefully the many differences between us. We look forward to a positive engagement which we hope will move the peace process forward. Sinn Féin enters these discussions on the basis of our electoral mandate. This is a matter of democratic rights and not a privilege to be given or withheld. We welcome your recognition of this.

It is, of course, a matter of regret that the negative approach adopted by the previous British government delayed the search for an agreed and lasting peace settlement for a period of at least three years.

The great challenge which remains is to remove the causes of conflict by making real progress towards a lasting peace settlement. Progress requires meaningful negotiations – a frank and genuine dialogue and a good faith engagement on all sides. We believe the process of negotiations should be as transparent as possible so as to build public confidence in the process itself and to create a sense of public ownership.

Irish Republicans want peace. Peace demands democracy, equality and justice. We want an end to conflict; an end to division; to poverty and inequality. We want an Ireland free and independent.

Sinn Féin enters negotiations as an Irish Republican party seeking to promote the broad Nationalist objective of an end to British rule in Ireland. Partition is wrong. It is a failure of the past which must be put right.

The British state in Ireland – the six county statelet – is the product of British policy. British policy has underpinned the climate for conflict and has prevented substantive change. The British government must accept its responsibility for this and, therefore, its responsibility for resolving the conflict. Historically, British rule in Ireland has sustained a culture of discrimination, inequality and intolerance. The injustices which have resulted need to be speedily and effectively addressed. Peace requires that these be resolved.

In our view the issue of sovereignty, the claim of the British government to sovereignty in Ireland, is a key matter which must be addressed in negotiations. So too is the achievement through dialogue among the Irish people of an agreed Ireland. The objective political and historical evidence shows that political independence, a united Ireland, offers the best guarantee of equality and the most durable basis for peace and stability. An internal six county arrangement cannot work. There has to be fundamental constitutional and political change. The status quo is unworkable.

It is our view that the overwhelming majority of people throughout Ireland and Britain wish to see all parties participating in a meaningful and inclusive negotiations process. Sinn Féin wants to see the Unionist parties at the negotiating table in September. We want Unionists there because peace in Ireland and a genuine peace settlement is best and most speedily achieved by Unionists playing a full and active part in bringing that about. We urge the leaders of Unionism to open their minds to the possibilities created by the new situation we are in. We are asking them to negotiate with us. Sinn Féin is not threatening the Unionists' heritage or identity.

Unionists are an intrinsic part of Ireland. This is your home. Republicans don't want you to leave it nor do we wish to dominate you. You have a right and a responsibility with the rest of the Irish people to shape our shared future. We acknowledge our responsibility, as part of a reciprocal process, to try to convince Unionists of our good intentions with regard to their future on this island. In a situation of deep division such as exists here, all of us have to suspend the distrust we harbor regarding the intentions of others.

Let us listen to each other. Sinn Féin is prepared to do that. We urge others to do the same.

We have a vision of a new future of which we can all be proud, a pluralist society based on tolerance, fairness and equality, in which we all lose our fear of difference and cherish diversity. Let us all give the future a chance.

Sinn Féin's peace strategy is about bringing an end to all conflict, of setting behind us the divisions and inequalities which still haunt our country. We want to move forward into a new inclusive future.

Notwithstanding the many obvious political differences between us, I am sure you will agree that dialogue offers us all the best hope of doing that. We will, therefore, approach these discussions and the wider negotiations process in a constructive, responsible and determined manner.

1. We hope this dialogue will help create a healing process which removes the causes of conflict and addresses its consequences. Everyone shares the responsibility to bring about a real and lasting peace in Ireland. Republicans have demonstrated the will to face up to our responsibility in this. This is evident in the initiatives we have taken, both unilaterally and with others in Ireland, to advance the search for peace. The courageous initiative taken by the leadership of the Irish Republican Army, on July 20, in restoring its cessation of August 31, 1994, is most significant. We now have the opportunity to achieve a political settlement.

2. Our long-standing position has been one of willingness to enter into dialogue with a view to removing the causes of conflict. Democratic, political and practical imperatives clearly require the involvement of all political views if a democratic resolution is to be sought and achieved.

3. Inclusive and all embracing peace talks led by the two governments should, in our view, address three broad areas:
   (a) Political and constitutional change;
   (b) An equality agenda;
   (c) Demilitarization.

   3.1. Equality of treatment is an essential ingredient of any process of democratic negotiations. Sinn Féin endorses an approach, where all parties are subject to the same rules and procedures in an effective process of negotiations which aims to remove the causes of conflict.

3.2. The political climate in which these talks occur could be significantly improved if the British government acted positively and speedily to demilitarize the situation. An end to British Army/RUC operations and the speedy release of all political prisoners, for example, would generate confidence in and greatly assist the peace process.

3.3. The British government should also outline a programatic approach on issues of equality. Parity of esteem and equality of treatment must be realized. The imbalance in the unemployment ratio needs to be redressed and effective provision for equality of opportunity in employment realized. Equality in economic development and greater and more equally shared prosperity are required. The Irish language and culture need equality of treatment. In other words there needs to be equality in all sectors of society – in social, economic, cultural, justice, democratic and national rights issues.

3.4. These issues do not require negotiation. They are issues of basic civil and human rights. The British government should act on these issues immediately to demonstrate a real interest in building confidence in its approach to the search for a lasting peace.

4. The route to peace in Ireland is to be found in the restoration to the Irish people as a whole of our right to national self-determination. National self-determination is universally accepted to mean a nation's right to exercise the political freedom to determine its own social, economic and cultural development without external influence or impediment and without partial or total disruption of the national unity or territorial integrity. Agreement on how that right is to be exercised is a matter for the Irish people alone to determine.

5. British sovereignty over the Six Counties, as with all of Ireland before partition, is self-evidently the root cause of division, political instability and conflict.

6. Consequently, and with due regard for the real difficulties involved, our objective is to bring about a change of British government policy in regard to this and an end to British jurisdiction on this island. This should, of course, be accomplished in the shortest possible time consistent with obtaining maximum consent to the process.

7. We believe that the wish of the majority of the people of Ireland is for Irish unity. We believe that an adherence to democratic principles makes Irish unity inevitable. The emerging political and economic imperatives both within Ireland and within the broader context of greater European political union support the logic of Irish unity. Since its creation in 1921, the six-county statelet has been in constant crisis. Its survival has always been dependent on division, repressive legislation, coercion and discrimination. Its existence lies at the heart of the present conflict and divisions, both in Ireland, and between Britain and Ireland. The conflict is a political problem not a security problem. It requires a political solution.

8. It is our view therefore that the British government should play a crucial and constructive role in persuading Unionists to reach a democratic agreement on the issue of Irish national reunification with the rest of the people of this island and to encourage, facilitate and enable such agreement.

9. No one can have a veto over the negotiations or over their outcome. If they are to be successful, inclusive negotiations must address all relevant issues without vetoes, without pre-conditions and without any attempt to pre-determine the outcome.

10. We recognize that the concerns of the Unionist population about their position in an Irish national democracy must be addressed and resolved in a concrete way, including legislation for all measures agreed in the course of a process of negotiations. This process of national reconciliation must secure the political, religious and democratic rights of the Northern Unionist population. That is not only the democratic norm but a practical necessity if we are to advance the cause of peace in Ireland.

11. The most urgent issue facing the people of Ireland and Britain is the need for a genuine peace process which sets democratic equality, justice and political stability as its objectives and, has as its means, dialogue and all-embracing negotiations in the context of democratic principles. We are convinced that if the political will exists then we can finally move away from conflict through the achievement of a democratic political settlement. The potentially historic opportunity which currently exists should be enthusiastically grasped by all sides.

August 6, 1997

Chronology

1993

May IRA two-week ceasefire

June President Mary Robinson visits cultural celebration in a school in West Belfast and shakes hands with Gerry Adams

August 8 First Nationalist rally outside Belfast City Hall since partition in 1921

September 25 Hume/Adams joint statement

October 23 IRA bomb fish shop on the Shankill Road, killing ten and injuring fifty-eight people. By the end of the month, Protestant gunmen had retaliated by killing twelve people, seven of them in a bar in Greysteel, Co. Derry

October 29 Joint communiqué in Brussels by British and Irish governments repudiating the Hume/Adams peace initiative

December 15 British/Irish joint declaration

1994

January 31 Gerry Adams visits New York for the first time on a special forty-eight-hour visa

February Annual Sinn Féin Árd Fheis meets in Tallaght, Co. Dublin

March IRA mortar-bomb Heathrow Airport in London

April 14 Theresa Clinton shot in her home by Loyalists

June 18 Six Catholics killed in a public house in Loughinisland, Co. Down

June 24 Sinn Féin peace commission report published

July 24 Sinn Féin national delegate conference in Letterkenny, Co. Donegal

August 7 Kathleen O'Hagan, seven months pregnant, shot in front of her five children

August 28 Hume/Adams joint peace statement; followed by a statement by Taoiseach Albert Reynolds

August 31 IRA ceasefire

September British Prime Minister John Major visits Belfast

October Gerry Adams tours cities in US and Canada

October 13 Loyalist ceasefire

October 28 Forum for Peace and Reconciliation begins in Dublin Castle

November 10 Postal worker Frank Kerr killed during a robbery; RUC blame IRA

November 16 Irish Labour party withdraw from Albert Reynolds' government

December 5 Fianna Fáil and Labour negotiations broken off. John Bruton of Fine Gael becomes Taoiseach in a coalition government with Labour and Democratic Left

December 8 Gerry Adams' first visit to White House, to meet National Security Advisor Tony Lake

December 9 Martin McGuinness leads Sinn Féin delegation to Stormont to meet British officials

December 13–14 Economic conference in Belfast hosted by John Major

Chronology

1995

February 22 Launch of Framework Document for Agreement by British and Irish governments

March Friends of Sinn Féin office opened in Washington; fund-raising ban lifted

March 1 In Washington, Dick Spring warns that waiting for an IRA surrender or decommissioning is a "formula for disaster"

March 16 Gerry Adams attends House Speaker's annual lunch for St. Patrick's Day at the White House; President Clinton and Gerry Adams shake hands

March 17 St. Patrick's Day celebrations in the White House

April 24 British end ban on ministerial contact with Sinn Féin

May Sinn Féin three-week fund-raising tour in US. On May 9, 400 guests attend a $1,000 a plate dinner at the New York Plaza. By June 30, almost $900,000 collected

May 24 Gerry Adams first meets Sir Patrick Mayhew in Washington

May 25–27 Economic investment conference on Ireland hosted by President Clinton in Washington's Sheraton Hotel

June Sinn Féin delegation visits South Africa and meet Nelson Mandela and African National Congress leadership

July Private Lee Clegg, jailed for the murder of a Belfast teenage girl, released after serving two years of his sentence

July 18 Gerry Adams and Martin McGuinness meet Sir Patrick Mayhew and Michael Ancram in Derry

July High tension and demonstrations during the marching season, particularly at the Ormeau Road in Belfast, at Drumcree, and at the Garvaghy Road in Portadown where a crowd of Orangemen led by David Trimble and Ian Paisley hemmed in the Nationalist community for three days

August 12 Apprentice Boys allowed to march in Derry for 25th anniversary of the Battle of the Bogside, despite strong Nationalist protest

September 11 Gerry Adams visits US. Discussions with Tony Lake and Vice-President Al Gore

November Gerry Adams visits US. Meetings in New York and Washington outlining crisis in peace process

November 28 Downing Street Joint Communiqué by British and Irish governments launching a "twin-track" approach and outlining all-party talks by the end of February 1996. They propose an International Body to investigate de-commissioning

November 30 President Clinton visits Northern Ireland

December 18 Sinn Féin make submission to Mitchell Body at Dublin Castle

1996

January 22 Mitchell Report published

January Gerry Adams visits US. Meetings in Washington, and travels to Pittsburgh

February British Army agent Brian Nelson released from prison after serving four years of a ten-year sentence

February 9 Breakdown of IRA ceasefire: Canary Wharf bombed killing two and injuring over a hundred people

February 24 Public peace marches in Dublin and Belfast, and other centers

February 26 Martin McGuinness leads delegation to meet British officials

February 28 IRA meet John Hume and Gerry Adams; John Bruton and John Major meet in London and announce all-party talks for June 10

March Gerry Adams visits US. March 14, attends International Fund for Ireland dinner

March 21 Procedures and date for Northern Ireland elections announced, and plans for Northern Ireland Forum

May Sinn Féin agree to the Mitchell Report and its six principles

May 30 Elections for political party representatives to Northern Ireland Forum; Sinn Féin win 15.47% of the total poll

June 7 Garda Jerry McCabe killed in Adare, Co. Limerick during a robbery by the IRA

June 10 Multi-party talks begin, excluding Sinn Féin. Senator George Mitchell is finally accepted as chairman on June 12

June 15 Arndale shopping center in Manchester bombed by IRA

July Marching season. July 11, RUC reverse their decision to ban the Garvaghy Road Orange march in Portadown. July 12, Lower Ormeau Road in Belfast under curfew for twenty-six hours.

July 14 Killyhevlin Hotel bombed in Enniskillen; later, the Continuity Army Council (CAC) admit responsibility for the attack

August Last-minute negotiations dissuade Apprentice Boys from annual march on Derry's city walls.

October John Hume and Gerry Adams present further peace proposals to British government

1997

February 12 Killing of British soldier Bombardier Steven Restorick

May 1 British general election; Labour party sweeps to power. Gerry Adams wins back his seat in West Belfast and Martin McGuinness wins a seat in Mid-Ulster

May 21 Local government elections in Northern Ireland

June New Labour Prime Minister Tony Blair visits Belfast

June British government publishes decommissioning policy document agreed with Irish government

June 6 Republic of Ireland elections; Sinn Féin's Caoimhghín Ó Caoláin wins a seat in Cavan/Monaghan constituency

June 16 Two RUC officers shot dead in Belfast

June 28 Alban Maginness installed as the first Catholic Belfast Lord Mayor

July Marching season. July 6, high tension at Garvaghy Road where Orange march forced down despite strong Nationalist protest. Four other Orange marches called off

July 20 Restoration of IRA ceasefire

August 6 Gerry Adams and Mo Mowlam meet at Stormont Castle in Belfast

September 2 Gerry Adams meets with US National Security Advisor Sandy Berger at the White House

September 15 Date set for all-party talks

Biographies

Bertie Ahern Taoiseach 1997– . Leader of Fianna Fáil party 1994–

Michael Ancram Former British Minister for Northern Ireland

Tony Blair British Prime Minister, 1997– . Leader of British Labour party 1994–

John Bruton Leader of Fine Gael party 1990– . Taoiseach 1994–1997

Ray Burke Irish Minister for Foreign Affairs 1997–

William Craig Minister of Home Affairs in Stormont government of Northern Ireland 1963–4, Minister of Health and Local Government 1964, Minister of Development 1965, and Minister of Home Affairs again in 1966–68. Established the Ulster Vanguard Party in 1972 with strong support from paramilitaries

Proinsias De Rossa Leader of Democratic Left 1992– . In coalition government with Fine Gael and Labour 1994–97. Former member of the Workers' Party

Mary Harney Tánaiste in coalition government with Fianna Fáil 1997– . Leader of the Progressive Democrats party 1993–

Michael D. Higgins Former minister of Arts, Culture, and the Gaeltacht. Member of the Irish Labour party

John Major Former British Conservative Prime Minister 1990–97. Signed 1993 Downing Street Declaration

Sir Patrick Mayhew Former Secretary for Northern Ireland 1992–97. Former British Attorney General

James Molyneaux Former leader of the Ulster Unionist Party 1979–95

Dr. (Marjorie) Mo Mowlam British Secretary of State for Northern Ireland 1997–

Brian Nelson British Army agent, placed by British Army into the UDA as director of intelligence

Dr. Conor Cruise O'Brien Former member of Irish Labour party and Minister of Posts and Telegraphs 1973–77. In 1976, he amended Section 31 of the Irish Broadcasting Act, restricting the freedom of the media. Senator 1977–79. Writer, scholar and broadcaster. Stood with UK Unionist Party in Northern Ireland Forum elections in June 1996

Rev. Ian Paisley Set up the Free Presbyterian Church in 1951. Founder and leader of the Democratic Unionist Party 1971– . MP for North Antrim since 1970.

Albert Reynolds Former Taoiseach and leader of the Fianna Fáil party 1992–94. Signed 1993 Downing Street Declaration. Instrumental in ceasefire negotiations with John Hume and Gerry Adams.

Bobby Sands (1954–81) Republican prisoner in Long Kesh. Went on hunger strike for political status. Died after 66 days. Elected as MP during the strike.

Dick Spring Leader of Irish Labour party. Former Tánaiste and former Minister for Foreign Affairs. In coalition government with Fine Gael 1981–2 and 1982–87, with Fianna Fáil 1993–94 and with Fine Gael and Democratic Left 1994–97

Margaret Thatcher British Conservative Prime Minister 1979–90. Signed the Anglo-Irish Agreement in 1985 with Garret Fitzgerald, then Taoiseach and leader of Fine Gael

David Trimble Leader of Ulster Unionist Party 1995– . Encouraged idea of a new Northern Assembly

Glossary

Alliance Party Moderate, reformist, Unionist party in Northern Ireland, set up in 1970, led by John Alderdice

Amhrán na bhFian "The Soldier's Song." The Irish national anthem

Anglo-Irish Agreement Document agreed to by the Fine Gael/Labour coalition in Dublin and Margaret Thatcher's Conservative government in London in 1985. It stipulates that there shall be no change in the constitutional position of Northern Ireland for so long as the majority wishes to remain as part of the United Kingdom

Árd Chomhairle National Executive

Árd Fheis National Conference

Árd Runaí General Secretary

Articles Two and Three of the Irish Constitution These two provisions of the Irish Constitution, dating from 1937, describe the national territory as constituting the island of Ireland, and are often cited by Unionists as the major hurdle to their co-operation with the Dublin government in any talks concerning the future of the Six Counties

Bloody Sunday January 30, 1972. Fourteen people attending a demonstration in Derry against internment were killed by British soldiers

B-Specials Controversial Unionist state militia first formed in 1920 as a back up force for the police. Disbanded and reformed as the Ulster Defence Regiment (UDR) in 1970. This in turn was disbanded and replaced by the Royal Irish Regiment (RIR) in July 1992

Continuity Army Council (CAC) Small break-away Republican group

Conservative Party (Tory Party) Britain's main right of center political party. Allied with the Unionist parties in Northern Ireland

Craic Fun

Dáil Eireann Irish Parliament

Democratic Unionist Party (DUP) Right-wing Unionist party, formed in 1971, led by Rev. Ian Paisley

Democratic Left Irish political party, led by Proinsias De Rossa

Downing Street Declaration Statement issued December 15, 1993 by the British and Irish governments. Set out principles around which the two governments would seek a settlement for Northern Ireland

Fianna Fáil Founded in 1926 by Eamon De Valera; the largest of the Irish political parties, led by Bertie Ahern

Fine Gael Formed in 1933, the second largest political party in the Irish Republic, led by John Bruton

Fleadh ceoil Irish traditional music festival

Forum for Peace and Reconciliation A consultative body set up in Dublin Castle on October 28, 1994 by then Taoiseach Albert Reynolds. Its remit was to consult on and examine ways in which a lasting peace, stability and reconciliation could be established by agreement among all the people of Ireland. Its final report was published February 2, 1996.

Framework Document Published on February 22, 1995 by the British and Irish governments, it outlines the parameters as agreed between the Dublin and London governments for a talks process

GAA Gaelic Athletic Association

Gaeilgeoir(í) Irish speaker(s)

Gaeltacht Irish speaking area

GPO General Post Office, in Dublin, occupied by the revolutionary forces as a focal point of the Easter 1916 Rising

Government of Ireland Act Act of the English Parliament that claims British jurisdiction in Ireland

H-Blocks Maze Prison, so called because the floor plan is shaped like the letter H with four prison wings and a connecting administrative building

Hume/Adams Initiative A political initiative undertaken in talks between John Hume and Gerry Adams, after an initial contact in January 1988. It led to a joint statement in September 1993, outlining the right of national self-determination, the importance of earning the allegiance of the different traditions on the island, and placing the responsibility of framing all-party talks on the Irish and British governments

Internment The imprisonment of dissidents without trial in Northern Ireland. Used in 1922, 1939, 1956 and 1971–5, internment has been applied principally against Republicans

Irish Republican Army (IRA) Title given to original Irish Nationalist militant group which fought the British after the establishment of the first Dáil in 1919. Divided into the Official IRA and the Provisional IRA (Provos) in 1969.

Joint Declaration See "Downing Street Declaration"

Labour Party (Ireland) Third largest political party in the Republic of Ireland, founded in 1912, currently led by Dick Spring

Labour Party (UK) Britain's main left of center political party, led by Tony Blair

Loyalism Belief in loyalty to the British Union. Unionists who use violence to achieve their ends are often described as Loyalists, although not all those who would call themselves Loyalists support political violence

Member of Parliament (MP) Elected political representative of UK parliament which meets at Westminster in London

Nationalism Belief in establishing a united nation encompassing all of Ireland

Orange Order (Orangemen) Name taken from the victory of Protestant William of Orange over Catholic King James II. A powerful secret sectarian order of Protestants characterized by ritualistic pageantry and supremacist celebrations.

Progressive Democrats Political party in the Republic, formed by a break-away from Fianna Fáil in 1985 by Desmond O'Malley, led by Mary Harney

Republicanism Political ideology born out of the French and American revolutions. Believes in the right of Irish people as a whole to determine the future of Ireland. Seeks a democratic, non-sectarian, pluralist society – a thirty-two county Irish Republic

Radio Telifís Éireann (RTE) Irish radio and television network

Royal Irish Regiment (RIR) See "B-Specials"

Royal Ulster Constabulary (RUC) Paramilitary state police force in Northern Ireland; rejected by most Nationalists

Social Democratic and Labour Party (SDLP) Nationalist and second largest party in Northern Ireland, founded in 1970, and led by John Hume

Seisiún Music session

Sinn Féin "We Ourselves" or more commonly translated as "Ourselves Alone." Irish Republican party founded in 1905, and led by Gerry Adams. The only party substantially organized throughout the thirty-two counties of Ireland

Six Counties Six of the nine counties which make up the province of Ulster. The six counties (Antrim, Armagh, Derry, Down, Fermanagh, Tyrone) are under British jurisdiction

Stormont Seat of the Unionist government and parliament from 1932 to 1972, when direct rule from Westminster was re-established

Tánaiste Irish Deputy Prime Minister

Taoiseach Irish Prime Minister

Teachta Dála (TD) Elected member of Irish parliament (Dáil)

Thirty-Two Counties The Republic of Ireland and Northern Ireland - a united Ireland

Tiocfaidh ár lá "Our day will come." Popular Republican slogan

Twelfth of July Commemoration of the Battle of the Boyne every year by the Orange Order, part of the "marching season." More than parades and pageants, this is a time when Unionist fervor is at its height and clashes occur regularly with Catholics when the loyal orders seek to march through Catholic areas

Twenty-Six Counties The Republic of Ireland

Ulster This should correspond to the ancient nine-county Irish province of Ulster. However, when the State was being set up, the Unionists rejected the nine-county unit because it contained too many Catholics, and settled for the six counties which they could control. The term is now commonly, but erroneously, used by Unionists to refer to the Six Counties

Ulster Defence Association (UDA) Founded in 1971, the major Loyalist paramilitary group, now outlawed

Ulster Defence Regiment (UDR) See "B-Specials"

Ulster Unionist Party (UUP) Largest Unionist party, led by David Trimble, also known as the Official Unionist Party

Ulster Volunteer Force (UVF) Originally formed in 1912 to oppose Home Rule, it is now a banned Loyalist paramilitary group

Unionism Belief in maintaining the 1800 Act of Union with Britain

Widgery Report A controversial judicial inquiry undertaken by the British Lord Chief Justice, Lord Widgery into the events surrounding the fourteen civilian murders on Bloody Sunday by British soldiers. Published in April 1972, the report has been criticized and discredited by hundreds of eyewitness accounts and by relatives of the deceased who seek a new inquiry.

Index

Index

279

Index